editorial advisory group

Maria Brenton, *University College, Cardiff*; Phillida Buckle, *Victoria University, Wellington, New Zealand*; Leonore Davidoff, *University of Essex*; Janet Finch, *University of Lancaster*; Jalna Hanmer, *University of Bradford*; Beverley Kingston, *University of New South Wales, Australia*; Hilary Land, *University of Bristol*; Diana Leonard, *University of London Institute of Education*; Susan Lonsdale, *Polytechnic of the South Bank*; Jean O'Barr, *Duke University, North Carolina, USA*; Arlene Tigar McLaren, *Simon Fraser University, British Columbia, Canada*; Jill Roe, *Macquarie University, Australia*; Pat Thane, *Goldsmiths' College, University of London*; Jane Thompson, *University of Southampton*; Clare Ungerson, *University of Kent at Canterbury*; Judy Walkowitz, *Rutgers University, New Jersey, USA*.

The 1970s and 1980s have seen an explosion of publishing by, about and for women. This new list is designed to make a particular contribution to this process by commissioning and publishing books which consolidate and advance feminist research and debate in key areas in a form suitable for students, academics and researchers but also accessible to a broader general readership.

As far as possible books will adopt an international perspective incorporating comparative material from a range of countries where this is illuminating. Above all they will be interdisciplinary, aiming to put women's studies and feminist discussion firmly on the agenda in subject-areas as disparate as law, physical education, art and social policy.

WOMEN IN SOCIETY
A Feminist List edited by
Jo Campling

Passbook Number F.47927

Women and Mau Mau in Kenya

Muthoni Likimani

with an introductory essay by Jean O'Barr

MACMILLAN

First published 1985

Published by
Higher and Further Education Division
MACMILLAN PUBLISHERS LTD
Houndmills, Basingstoke, Hampshire RG21 2XS
and London
Companies and representatives
throughout the world

Printed in Great Britain, at the
University Press, Oxford

British Library Cataloguing in Publication Data
Likimani, Muthoni
Passbook number F.47927: women and Mau Mau in
Kenya.—(WIS)
1. Mau Mau   2. Women revolutionists—Kenya
I. Title   II. Series
322.4'2'096762   DT433.S77
ISBN 0–333–37944–6
ISBN 0–333–37945–4 Pbk

*Dedicated to women freedom fighters
and to my children, Sopiato, Soila,
and Jane, and to my grandchildren*

Muthoni Likimani

Muthoni Likimani

Contents

Acknowledgements

I would like to acknowledge the help of the following individuals. Jean O'Barr of Duke University, Durham, North Carolina, struggled to locate me in Kenya and took an interest in my work. Jo Campling worked hard with Jean O'Barr to see that the manuscript would be published by Macmillan. Above all, Arthur Hazlewood of Oxford University has consistently followed the development of this book, giving his encouragement and advice.

My former housemaid, Alice Wanjiru, was an active member of the Mau Mau movement who transported food to the fighters. She gave me an inside view of women's position during the Mau Mau struggle. Ndegwa Wanjiru, a messenger in the Ministry of Health who was a Mau Mau organiser, suffered greatly during this period. His wife died as a result of being tortured by the colonialists when she refused to disclose where the Mau Mau – including her husband – were hiding. My sister, Naomi Mwangi, who was a teacher on the slopes of the Aberdare Mountains at this time, witnessed the suffering, torturing, and death of Kenyans. She was locked in a barbed wire enclosure and went through an interrogation. She has shared with me an intimate knowledge of what it meant to suffer.

Acknowledgement must also go to my children, Sopiato Likimani and Soila Tessema, for their assistance in my writings.

Finally, I wish to thank my secretary, Jane Muliande, who has tirelessly typed the entire manuscript.

Nairobi, Kenya   MUTHONI LIKIMANI
22 September 1984

Introductory Essay

Jean O'Barr

Around the world, the voices of women past and present, are being heard as their experiences, expressions and expectations are recorded. Muthoni Likimani's description of the impact of the Mau Mau Revolt[1] in Kenya in the 1950s on women's daily lives takes us with the African women of that country through the ordeals they faced, as they sought to provide for their families while yet aiding their communities in the political struggle. Likimani's seven accounts, based on her own observations as well as those of family and friends, present a broader vision of women's roles in Kenya's nationalist movement than any we have had before. For we see here from the women themselves the critical roles they played in the successful nationalist struggle and that they had reasons of their own for joining the movement. An analysis of those motivations and aspirations helps to explain not only the relationships among some women and Mau Mau, but the political positions women have assumed in independent Kenya.

Women's relationship to Mau Mau can be appreciated fully only if we understand the context in which the revolt occurred, particularly the situation of African women in the colonial period. To that end, the pages that follow provide background on Kenya in the post-World War II era and on how the process of colonialisation affected African women in Kenya.

At first mention, Kenya seems familiar to American and European audiences. Historically, a large number of Europeans, primarily British nationals, migrated to Kenya in the early part of the twentieth century, creating ties of kith-and-kin that still keep Kenyan affairs in the forefront of international consciousness.

1

Currently, Kenya has the largest international tourist industry on the continent. Many Europeans and Americans with no knowledge of African affairs seek out her beaches, her national parks and wildlife, and her spectacular mountains for their holidays.

To those with special interests, Kenya is even more familiar. Movie buffs readily recall the many natural history films and documentaries set in the Kenya landscape as well as the Tarzan sites at Nyahururu, the town previously known as Thomson's Falls. The European literature of Kenya – *An African Notebook, Born Free, The Flame Trees of Thika, Out of Africa,* and *Uhuru* to name just five – has topped the international fiction lists for decades. When missionary societies discuss Africa, it is often Kenya, due to the extensive amount of church activity there by many denominations. Leakey's discovery of fossil remains of the earliest hominids in East Africa and his associations with Kenya and *National Geographic* magazine have kept the area on the current events map. Finally, the international concern with wildlife conservation continues to give Kenya prominence in popular as well as academic circles. If Kenya receives a familiar and accepting nod when mentioned, the words 'Mau Mau' evoke a strong but much less positive response. For many Westerners the words Mau Mau encode that which is un-known and unknowable in Africa – the dark and less desirable side of a people.

The initial and widespread negative reaction to these events some twenty-five years ago has been replaced over time by an apprecia-tion of how Mau Mau relates to the historic quest of a people seeking political and cultural freedom. The historiography of Mau Mau in recent years has established the complex and intriguing questions raised by such a series of political, economic and cultural events. As the story of Mau Mau has been written, interpreted and re-analysed, one element has been largely missing – the contribu-tion of women to the struggle. The story of the women freedom fighters has yet to be written. With the publication here of Liki-mani's accounts, we now have available a first-hand account by a woman of women's responses to this nationalist struggle.

1. Kenya and Mau Mau

Mau Mau refers to the events beginning in the late 1940s and ending with independence in 1963. The chronology in Table 1 sets out the main dates and events in Kenyan political history as they relate to Mau Mau. The colonial government's arrest of Kenyatta and other African leaders in 1952 is considered the beginning of the state of emergency in the colony. The development of fighting units, based in the Mt Kenya and Aberdare forests in the central part of the country, and the colonial attempt to eliminate them are considered the active phase of the revolt, lasting until 1960. The revolt's lack of military success was followed by significant economic and political concessions, concessions which in turn led the way to independence by 1963.

Recounting the events of Mau Mau as a series of military dates belies its importance. The infusion of European plantation agriculture, commerce and mission activity into Kenya prior to World War II, paralleled by the establishment of colonial government which relied on transplanted versions of British political structures, created the set of circumstances in which Kenyans began demanding control of themselves, their economy and their future. Their demands did not form a unitary agenda, articulated and co-ordinated by a single leader. Urban peoples formed associations demanding educational improvements, increased wages, reforms in land holding and crop policies and a general removal of economic discrimination against Africans. Rural peoples sought reforms as well, less frequently in formal organisations than in groups which stressed ethnic solidarity and an awareness of the loss of traditional strengths. Increasing land alienation, economic frustrations, urban poverty, lack of influence over the course of events and a continual demeaning of African pride, all combined to set in motion the many sets of activities which merged into the nationalist movement.

Mau Mau was a revolt by African peasants against the economic, political, and cultural conditions in which they lived. The Kikuyu people, Kenya's largest ethnic group and the one most adversely affected by European economic activity throughout the century, formed the majority of Mau Mau participants; a few members of other neighbouring ethnic groups also participated. During the revolt, people engaged in four primary sets of activities. People demonstrated their allegiance to members of their ethnic groups and their opposition to colonial authority; this demonstration took the form of oaths and rituals, signifying solidarity of purpose. People resisted the economic and political institutions placed over them by attacking and destroying the most immediate manifestations of those institutions, for example, colonial farms and police

Table 1

Significant dates in Kenyan history relating to Mau Mau[2]

1880s	The beginnings of colonialisation, first by the Imperial British East Africa Company and then the Foreign Office.
1890s	The building of railways, mission activity, and European settlement.
WW I	East Africa one of few war areas outside Europe. The influenza epidemic takes many lives in East Africa.
1920s	Kenya changes from 'Protectorate' to 'Colony' status under a settler government. Political associations of Africans organised in the capital city of Nairobi to resist the European attempts to cut African wages, to seek improvements in education, and to remove the colour barrier. In the rural areas protest focuses on land alienation and the conditions of agricultural labour.
1930s	The growth of African associational activity centred on land issues and the extension of political consciousness to a colony-wide constituency, including a strike in Mombasa in 1939 and squatters' strikes through the decade.
1940s	Mass political movements seeking African majority rule grow in Africa as a whole; in Kenya, the *Kenya African Union* meets constitutional resistance, led by the settler community, and battles regional differences.
1946	First official evidence of oath of unity as an instrument of political mobilisation.
1948	First official report referring to Mau Mau.
1952	African leaders, including Jomo Kenyatta, arrested and state of emergency declared on 21 October in response to what the colonial government interpreted as an outbreak of crime and violence and what later interpreters understand to have been the growing expression of long standing political, economic, and cultural grievances, particularly among the Kikuyu and related ethnic groups.
1952–56	The active phase of the Mau Mau Emergency in which nationalist activities spread through the African population and the government employed military and police forces against the Mau Mau and their supporters, assisted by loyalist militia called Homeguards.

1957–60 Military activity ceased and rehabilitation programmes for detainees carried out. The Emergency officially ended in 1960 with the publication that year of the official government report on Mau Mau by F. C. Corfield *Historical Survey of the Origins and Growth of Mau Mau* (Cmnd. 1030).

1960–63 Intense political and constitutional activity as Kenyan leaders established political relationship among themselves and negotiated for the transfer to majority rule with the British authorities and the local white settler and Asian communities, realising many of the ambitions first voiced in the Mau Mau movement. Jomo Kenyatta elected President of Kenya.

---

stations. People promoted their evolving sense of consensus by forming organisations, usually based on indigenous ones in form, and by recognising leaders who could articulate their goals. And finally, people reacted to the military attacks on them not only by counter-attacks, but by creating support networks in as many places and with as many people as possible.

Seen from the government's point of view, Mau Mau was an outbreak of violence on the part of Africans who lacked the wherewithall to succeed in life on European terms. From this perspective, Mau Mau was a series of governmental orders aimed at control – declaring an emergency; regulating the population by curfews, travel restrictions, individual registrations; ferreting out the agitators; figuring out how to enunciate improved policies of colonial rule which would not break down and thus fail.

Mau Mau activity eventually subsided, and the government put forward the interpretation that they had been militarily successful in eliminating terrorism. Yet the very actions of the colonial government in the few years from the end of the Emergency to independence belie their interpretation. Those years saw a negotiated transfer of power from colonialist to nationalist which acknowledges the very points Mau Mau symbolised. In this sense, though participants in Mau Mau may not have known the precise form of what they sought, they created a large part of the circumstances which allowed others to articulate and achieve a precise set of goals.

There is yet no direct answer to the question 'just what was Mau

Mau?' It was many things to the many actors in the situation. Here, Likimani illuminates what it was to one set of actors, African women who have heretofore been invisible in previous answers.

2. Previous Treatments of Women in Mau Mau

What part then did Kenyan women have in that series of events known as Mau Mau? The accounts that follow provide for the first time a view of what women faced and accomplished during the revolt. Before the publication of this work, the treatment of women's predicament in Mau Mau has been shadowy. In social science analysis, in the firsthand accounts, and in Kenyan fiction, women emerge only as nameless supporting characters in a play dominated by men. The extensive social science literature on Kenya's nationalist movement fails to confront the issue of women's participation either as freedom fighters joining the men in the forests or as supporters in the local communities working clandes-tinely to keep the fighters supplied with information, food, and firearms. The firsthand accounts of involvement in Mau Mau, all written by men, acknowledge women's presence but do not explore women's roles beyond those of sexual partners and couriers. Again, these women are left nameless. The literary treatments of Mau Mau as a political and cultural reaction to colonialism feature women characters but only chronicled through a man's eyes and for what they could do for their men or for what they symbolized to their men. The longings and fears of the women characters are left unexplored. The view of women in all three sources – social science analyses, life histories and fiction – is a limited one when set beside Likimani's materials. A brief review of what each set of sources had said about women will help us to appreciate more keenly the contribution which Likimani's work makes and will document more fully what yet needs to be known about the women's point of view.

Before proceeding, a *caveat* is in order. It concerns the use of the terms *African women, Kenyan women, Kikuyu women*. Clearly, there are enormous differences among and between all three categories. Treating African women as a single entity obscures significant variation found among them and contributes to continu-al misunderstandings of women and their positions. The same thing needs to be said about Kenyan women, for Kenya contains many ethnic groups. Likewise, new research on Kenyan nationalism points to the diversity that existed within the ethnic group, the Kikuyu, most directly involved in Mau Mau and cautions against over-generalising. Despite the problems of treating diversity as if it were similarity, one must nonetheless employ common terms in order to draw out patterns. Thus in the pages that follow, the reader should be aware that the collective terms are employed cautiously and that differences among women of different groups and status are described when possible.

2.1 *Women in social science interpretations*

From the hindsight of 1985 and the emergent concern in contemporary scholarship with women as social actors, the lack of attention to the part women played in Mau Mau seems extraordinary. Tracing the historiography of Mau Mau from the first official interpretations to the more recently recorded firsthand accounts and social science treatments, the inescapable conclusion is that discussions of women are limited and peripheral at best.

Furley reviewed the main writings on Mau Mau for the 1971 Conference of the Historical Association of Kenya. The conference theme, *Politics and Nationalism in Colonial Kenya*, encouraged him to point out the serious gaps in information for this period and the lack of a comprehensive perspective on the Mau Mau organisation itself. He noted the need for studies of its relationship to the various segments of the Kikuyu community as well as other ethnic groups, and of its interplay with the nationalist movement in Kenya and with politics after independence. The first reports and documents on the events of Mau Mau were prepared by the colonial government: 'The aim was to exonerate themselves as much as possible from the guilt of having created the political, social and economic frustrations for Kenyan Africans which in turn created the conditions for Mau Mau, and also to play down the political aims of the movement' (Furley, 1972, p. 105). The missionary accounts published soon after Mau Mau viewed the revolt as an anti-Christian outbreak which could be 'cured' only by a combination of spiritual renewal and improved social and economic conditions. Settler memoirs followed, justifying the British actions and denying that African involvement had any purpose other than a reversion to an earlier and more primitive state of affairs.

The next set of writings about Mau Mau came from historians, political scientists and sociologists who attempted in the mid-1960s to rethink all the material before then and put forward explanations linked to broader questions of how and why. Two secondary sources on Mau Mau from this time are now considered standard works: Rosberg and Nottingham (1966) and Barnett and Njama (1966). These works suggest in Furley's words that 'whatever the Mau Mau rising was, it was certainly not a simple historical event, for which there is an easy explanation' (Furley, 1972, p. 105).

Ngugi wa Thiong'o, writing in 1972 (p. 26), summarised this position eloquently:

The conflicts in the land of Kenya, at their most marked in the relationship between the African and European, have operated on three planes: political, economic, and cultural. The white settler came early in the century and he immediately controlled the heart of the economy by appropriating the best part of the land to himself. Alienation of land, after all, was then the declared British colonial policy for the region which later became Kenya. The settler was told that this would be a white man's country, and he was able to use his political power to consolidate his economic position. He forced black men into labour gangs, working for him in the 'White Highland.' He rationalized this exploitation of African land and labour by claiming he was civilizing a primitive people. The government and the missionary aided the settler in this belief: after all, the three were an integral product or representative of the same social force: capitalism. That the African was a child was a basic premise: if the African wanted a share in the government, he was told that he had yet to grow. He had to acquire the ways and style of life of the white man – through the slow process of watching and imitating from a distance. The white settler, then, effectively exploited differences in culture to keep the reins of political and economic power out of the black man's hands.

It will therefore be seen that in the Kenyan scene of the last sixty years you cannot separate economics and culture from politics. The three are interwoven. A cultural assertion was an integral part of the political and economic struggle.

Only in terms of all these different and yet closely interrelated planes of conflict can the Mau Mau revolution of 1952 be understood. To single out one of them especially the cultural, and work it into an elaborate explanation of this great political revolt is a gross oversimplification.

Despite the eloquence of Ngugi's words or the new sophistication of recent social science analysis, no one has begun to come to terms with the position of women in Kenyan society during Mau Mau. Throughout these treatments of Mau Mau, women remain a few scattered footnotes. They appear as participants in protest movements prior to Mau Mau (Rosberg and Nottingham, 1966: pp. 51–2, 55); as co-conspirators with their husbands (Rosberg and Nottingham, 1966: p. 338); as problems for the men trying to run the forest camps (Barnett and Njama, 1966: pp. 221–2, 226–7). Nowhere though are they given direct and serious treatment as actors with purposes of their own.

2.2 *Women in life histories*

In the years since Mau Mau, many firsthand accounts of the nationalist movement have appeared. These accounts share two features: they are written by men, and they fail to account for the contributions women made to the revolt. The authors often claim women played important roles in Mau Mau, but do not document what those roles were, how they might have compared to the traditional roles women played, how the roles of women during the Emergency differed from those of men or how women's activities during Mau Mau linked with those following the revolt. Moreover, women are a nameless population in these firsthand accounts except when mentioned as wives. Perhaps to justify this failure to comprehend women's role in Mau Mau, we must remember that these accounts, like Likimani's narratives, are drawn from personal experience and can at best only describe a portion of the human landscape of Mau Mau. It is still a legitimate question though as to why men have kept blinders on their memories when it comes to women active in Mau Mau.

Reading a sample of male-authored accounts provides an outline of how men saw women's place in the nationalist struggle[3]. Both women and men were members of Mau Mau, and both sexes took the oaths, although some claim women's oaths were less fearsome and binding (Kinyatti, p. 103; Mathu, pp. 10, 41–2; Wachanga; p. 13). Several accounts chronicle the fact that men and women suffered equally as fighters – women as well as men were tortured to obtain confessions (Kabiro, p. 46); the government authorities searched for women as well as men with the intent to kill (Gikoyo, p. 104); occasionally women were among the corpses delivered to the camps (Muchai, p. 40).

The Land and Freedom Army sought out women to act as spies and as couriers for food and armaments because they were less closely watched (Kinyatti, p. 103; Mathu, p. 51; Wamweya, p. 68). They frequently hid warriors in their huts for long periods of time (Itote, 1979, pp. 194–7). According to these sources, women were also valued as seducers of the enemy. In *We Fought for Freedom* women were used as bait to trap traitors and other enemies (Gikoyo, p. 41). In *Swords of Kirinyaga* the homeguard recruited women left on the reserves as warriors and guards – the Hika Hika; women loyal to Mau Mau were known as the Wangu group (Wachanga, p. 93).

Once in the forest, or under direct supervision of the elite, the women's role had several traditional aspects – they were responsible for cooking, water hauling, knitting sweaters (Gikoyo, pp. 60, 91–2). Warriors were, however, forbidden to engage in sexual contact, for fear it would weaken them (Gikoyo, p. 64; Wachanga, p. 37). Women's roles might then seem even more restricted to that of servant rather than spouse or lover; how strictly the ban on sexual intercourse was maintained is unknown. If captured, women faced the same tortures as men, although sexual assualts and abuse are also recorded. In the detention camps, colonial officials had little concern for women's special conditions, such as pregnancy, and there are reports of women giving birth unattended in the exercise yards (Muchai, p. 40).

While men are generally mentioned by name and position, women are most frequently referred to as simply 'a girl'. Women are rarely mentioned in positions of leadership. In Gikoyo's *We Fought for Freedom* one woman is mentioned as a great female leader, but the fact that the writer married her may explain her visibility in his book.

The stories in this volume move a long way toward recording the history of these anonymous women. Although, we are still without a picture of women in the forests, Likimani's narratives delve deeply and convincingly into the day-to-day lives of women bereft of normal family and community supports as they struggled to secure both a life for their families and their nation.

2.3   *Women in Ngugi's fiction*

In addition to the life histories, biographies and autobiographies written by men of their Mau Mau experiences, the early fiction of Kenya's leading writer, Ngugi wa Thiong'o, provides insight into the ideas and actions attributed to women during the Emergency. Ngugi's first three novels and one of his plays often refer to the women's presence in the nationalist struggle.[4] Ngugi's portrayal of women provides another insight into the conventional male view of women in Mau Mau. By examining Ngugi's female characters, and comparing his fictional women to those that Likimani puts before her reader, we have a third basis for understanding the importance of her contribution. Although Ngugi's and Likimani's works share many features, Likimani's ability to write from a woman's point of view contributes a better understanding of women's participation than heretofore available.

Ngugi's first novel, *Weep Not Child*, assumes that women are part of the community but never looks at the community through their eyes. The main character is a male and the women are seen by him as mothers promoting their sons (pp. 3–4), and being rewarded by their sons' achievements (p. 18); as wives controlling the unruly behaviour of husbands (p. 7); and as non-political actors excused by the authorities from involvement in nationalist activities (p. 114).

The River Between, Ngugi's second novel set during the Emergency, casts women primarily as potential wives. Muthoni, who chooses to be circumcised, and her sister, who does not, represent the two sides in a cultural transformation. The central male character is caught between them. A woman's decision to accept or reject the traditional symbol of female adulthood – circumcision – is discussed only for its effect on the man who will choose her as a wife. The author does not define as a question of a woman's control over her body, her sexuality or her sense of self. It has meaning only if it reflects the choices that confront the male character. Ngugi's discussion of women in his second novel parallels that of his earlier work. Women are important only as they relate to men, and through men to the community at large; women are not seen as individuals, social beings with aspirations of their own; they are transformed into symbols of the struggle of two cultures.

With *A Grain of Wheat*, women assume a more central place in Ngugi's fiction. He recounts numerous instances of women's political activity: women's participation in protests is described (pp. 17, 18), as is their life as detainees in the camps (p. 20) or as couriers and fighters (pp. 23, 156–7, 204). Nonetheless, the women usually remain as nameless political participants (p. 12), and when women are discussed as political leaders, that leadership is treated as an oddity (p. 14). Women also continue to symbolise the agony of change and its resulting loneliness (pp. 7–8). Ngugi describes women's participation as emerging from their maternal attributes or as being based on their sexual prowess. In an episode (p. 23) where one woman's courage, skill and responsibility as a courier are chronicled, in her daring escape from the homeguard, Ngugi attributes her cunning to an ability to embarrass the men by comparing herself to their mothers. The account reinforces the assumption that all women are mothers, that women's social power stems exclusively from their motherhood. It denies the imaginative power and skills that women bring to the social role of mother.

In an episode where a woman fighter dies from a beating inflicted by the homeguard (p. 156), the beating was both sexually and politically motivated because the woman had once refused the homeguard's sexual advances. Ngugi's focus on the homeguard's sexual hostility has an unfortunate consequence for an understanding of women as political actors. While sexual assaults were undoubted and tragic occurrences for the women involved in Mau Mau, the sexual imagery has a literary power which overwhelms the imagery of the women's willingness to struggle and suffer for her political convictions; sexual imagery has a transcendant quality that minimises personal choices and characteristics.

A Grain of Wheat contains an account (pp. 161–72) of Emergency times by Mumbi, a woman who is the novel's central character. She tells of her long wait for her husband who is in detention, of her struggles to feed and protect her family, of her forced labour days, of her confrontation with authorities. Her retelling of the time parallels the fuller accounts that Likimani provides. As in the earlier episode, the woman is sexually assaulted by a man and bears his child. Her violation coming at the end of the Emergency symbolically eliminates her personal and political contributions to the struggle, denying her a social status other than that based on sexuality and maternity. Again, the woman is transformed into a symbol for Ngugi's vision of a transformed Kenyan society.

The play *The Trial of Dedan Kimathi* demonstrates women's roles during the Emergency as fighters and as leaders. Yet these portrayals of women as participants present a constant double standard. Women lead men to heroic action (pp. 51–3), urging them on to prove themselves as men. Women, however, are not expected to prove their bravery. Women fighters are always identified as 'women' while men are referred to as 'terrorists' or 'guerillas' (p. 73). The implication is that women can have no identity other than that of 'woman' and 'mother'. Ngugi portrays men as fighting for their land and the women and children they left behind, the motivation of women fighters is not addressed in the play. Throughout the action, the dialogue confirms the presence of women yet it keeps them nameless and without motive. Thus, their involvement is minimized if not denied. Likimani's accounts, in contrast, allow us to examine in some detail the activities and the motivations of the women who populate namelessly the life histories and the fiction of Kenya's men.

3. The Position of African Women in Kenya

Men's accounts of women's participation in Mau Mau is only one part of the context for reading and appreciating Likimani's accounts. A second part is the position of African women in Kenya at a time of the revolt. Just as a full analysis of the origins, development and consequences of Mau Mau and its relationship to nationalism are beyond the scope of this introductory essay, so too is a review of all that has been learned about African women in the last three decades of research and writing. Nonetheless, setting the stage for Likimani's accounts requires looking at three sets of questions.

1. What economic and political activities were characteristic of Kenyan women and how did the imposition of colonial structures alter them?
2. What is the relationship between women's activities and positions on the one hand and the effects of wars, revolutions, protests and nationalist movements on the other?
3. What is the contribution of the Kenyan material to an understanding of women's participation in nationalist movements and their positions in the new nations?

3.1 *Colonialism and the economic and political activities of Kenyan women*

Descriptions of the economic and political activities of African women in Kenya come from at least three written sources[5]. The earliest accounts are the observations of the nineteenth-century travellers and explorers. Women's lives were not their primary subject; information about women can only be gleaned from casual references enmeshed in descriptions of other events and ideas. In their journals, reports, and books, these men emphasized how the women they saw differed from European women. Thus, travellers and explorers' brief accounts highlight women's work, as farmers, as traders and as physical labourers generally. Slightly better material may be derived from the accounts of European missionaries.

Second and historically later sources of information on Kenyan women are the ethnographies of the colonial period. Again, ethnographers were generally men, talking through male interpreters to male informants, about men's affairs. Rarely did an ethnography look specifically at women. Rather, it addressed a 'general' cycle of life assuming that women either acted just like men or were not sufficiently important to justify separate treatment. In these ethnographic observations, women are seen as lacking any significant influence. African women continue to be noticed as hard workers. Their lives are described as closely controlled by and for family, kin and community needs. African women are described as the media of exchange and reproduction, used by men to create and maintain public order and men's place in it. The private sphere of women is not investigated nor is its crucial relationship to the maintenance of public order considered. Ethnographers discussed women, but only as they were to be pitied or praised for their hard labour or as they served men's interests. In short, ethnographers did not consider women as social actors who had a world view of their own nor as a group of people who exercised any indirect or direct influence over men or each other.

Beginning in the 1960s, and motivated by the popular debates on women's positions in Western countries and the beginnings of feminist scholarship there, scholars began to look directly at African women. What they saw challenged the conventional wisdom, and African women, now with access to education and advanced employment in public and private sectors, have joined in this reassessment (see Essay 8). For this third group of observers, African women were much more than passive pieces of property manipulated by men. The work of these scholars and activists established two important and interrelated ideas. One was that African women did indeed have social aspirations of their own that they pursued – and continue to purse – in addition to and apart from men's. To do this, African women utilised their own economic, political and cultural institutions whose very existence was often unknown to outside observers. The failure to see these differences came from a failure to look. The second idea was that while the harmful effects of colonialism were now well-documented, a gender-based analysis showed that the effects had been even more detrimental for women. Colonialism not only destroyed any indigenous female social institutions, but imposed new institutions favouring men over women.

The idea that African women in precolonial times controlled more power and resources than they did in the colonial period is argued on two grounds. First, investigations document women's varied influences on social life. Second, the new scholarship describes how colonialism both devalued women's influence and restricted their access to new opportunities that developed in the contemporary situation. The argument is not put forward that men and women enjoyed equality or symmetry of power in the past. Rather, it appears that the amount of control women had over their lives was greater then than it was under colonialism and the loss of autonomy was disproportionately greater for women than for men.

The details of the division of labour between women and men varies with ethnic group, region, agricultural season, and historical period, and deny simple summarisation[6]. Nonetheless, a general pattern characterises the position of women in small scale subsistence societies and is usefully outlined as a basis for reading *Passbook Number F.47927*. African women in precolonial times had central economic responsibilities. In most subsistence agricultural societies, women were the producers, processors, preservers and protectors of the food supply. The organisation of the farm was a joint endeavour, with women and men contributing to the decision-making process. Each had special expertise and hence control over specified crops, pieces of land, parts of the season, etc. Both sexes were generally involved in clearing and preparing plots. Planting and weeding were usually women's work. Harvesting again called on everyone's skills. After harvest, women processed the grains, saw to their preservation throughout the year, protected the storage against spoilage and theft, and retained seeds for the next cycle.

In societies where animal husbandry played a dominant role, women also had major positions in the production cycle. They owned some of the animals directly. Women usually did the daily milking, nursed sick animals, supervised parts of the butchering process and preserved the meat and by-products like skins and fat.

Beyond the primary economic activities of agriculture and animal husbandry, Kenyan African women kept kitchen fowl, traded to a limited extent, had responsibility for many aspects of building and maintenance of dwellings and yards, made or procured clothing and household utensils. Hauling water, collecting firewood and cutting grasses to feed animals kept in the house and yard were strenuous female chores. Thus, by her very role as an economic mainstay, the Kenyan African woman controlled resources and gained power on a day-to-day basis that defies the simplistic notion that because women were often not official political or religious leaders, they were not forces to be reckoned with by society at large.

This brief description of the Kenyan women's economic roles lays the foundation for the interpretation that East African societies can best be seen as one in which we can identify multiple and complementary spheres of activity. African women had their own spheres of activity in which they were not necessarily subject to male authority. The idea of relatively autonomous spheres is a difficult one for Westerners to grasp because the growth of the state and its enhancement of patriarchal institutions make such a system unimaginable. Yet the African material suggests that alternatives have existed in which women and men co-operate as equals in more spheres than has been the experience in the West. That women were ultimately subject to male clan and religious authority does not deny the vitality of their religious, economic, age group, and neighbourhood associations.

Marriage too was a central organising principle for Kenyan women. Each woman was expected to marry and to bear and raise as many children as she could provide for. Women viewed themselves as members of families first, defining themselves as empowered rather than limited by their membership in the family group. Much like the nineteenth century American feminists who saw themselves as representatives of their families, African women in pre-colonial Kenya did not debate whether marriage and mother-hood should be the norm for them. Within marriage, they carried out the full range of human responsibilities. They did not see marriage as eliminating social participation; they saw it as the avenue into it. Through marriage they took on economic, political and cultural roles with determination. Again, the twentieth century Western idealisation of the monogamous marriage that protects women from the stressful activities of social life and assigns them a set of psychological responsibilities to provide a relief from the 'real' world is alien to the experience of Kenyan women.

Thus, African women's productive and reproductive contribu-tions to their societies translated into control over many facets of life – domestically and politically – in their communities, as they made links to their past.

Colonial rule had profound consequences for African women, consequences only now being studied. The idea that women and their activities were largely invisible to the colonial authorities has been argued above. The result of invisibility was neglect. In at least four areas – the introduction of scientific agriculture, the establish-ment of Western education, the creation of new political and religious authority, and the control over access to the market economy – colonial policy had a differing impact on women as opposed to men. A review of the major changes in these four areas contributes to an understanding of the circumstances women faced during Mau Mau.

The introduction of cash crops, instruction in use of terracing, fertilisers, soil conservation, animal disease control and modern breeding techniques, the establishment of co-operatives – to name only a few programmes – were all aimed at man-the-farmer. This is not to say that women did not occasionally attend training program-mes or benefit from information trickling down from men. They did. They were not however the chief beneficiaries of these im-provements because they were seen as farmer's helpers, not far-mers, in the colonial world view. This colonial vision had repercus-sions for women. By stressing the development of cash crops and plantation agriculture rather than the improvement of subsistence farming, colonial policy set in motion the conditions which underly today's chronic food shortages in the third world. Colonial labour policy in plantation agriculture focused on the recruitment of men,

leaving women as dependants. Moreover emphasis on a monocul-
ture to the exclusion of home production eroded both women's
traditional control over resources and the ability to withstand the
price fluctuations and droughts which affected the principal crop,
often a non-food commodity. As the market and wage economy
became dominant over the traditional economy, men had more
resources with which to deal than did women. Yet, overall, local
communities became more dependent on social and economic
forces beyond their control.

The provision of Western-style education, likewise was gender
biased. In shortest terms, men got more education than women and
the kind of education they received was different from that which
women received. The combination of a colonial education policy
favouring men and a strengthening of those indigenous values that
stressed the greater importance of male achievement meant that
fewer and fewer women advanced past each educational level.
Thus, if only two out of every five primary school students were
female during the colonial period, only two out of ten secondary
school students were female, and an estimated one out of ten
university students was female. In addition, colonial education was
predominantly single sex, with the formal curriculum as well as
informal ties being sex specific. Women learned domestic service,
while men studied skills necessary for office work. Women were not
seen as future leaders; rather, they were trained as wives. The fact
that many spoke out against such assumptions by choosing alternative careers reflects the strength and vitality of African women.

The history of colonial administration and missionary Christiani-
ty in Kenya is replete with the assumption that women do not matter
in civic and religious domains. That women made good political
supporters and voters was acknowledged; that church attendance
and good works depended on women was understood. But the
colonial mind did not entertain the idea that women could emerge
from the bottom of the pyramid and lead, so they were neither
asked nor trained. And in Kenya – as opposed to West Africa where
women had held many high political offices in indigenous states –
this colonial assumption met little resistance. African societies in
Kenya gave females informal influence and power rather than
formal authority. Colonial structures, not appreciating the sub-
tleties of that informal power, imposed new formal structures where
women were simply absent.

The growth of urban centres and plantation agriculture represent another area where the result of colonial policy was the neglect of women. Men were recruited to both these outposts of the world economy for wage labour. Given the high value Kenyans place on land, women were left as guardians of the *shamba* or farm. Certainly women migrated to cities and worked as wage labourers, but by and large they did so at much lower rates than men. Colonial laws and policies acted to restrict women's access to the cities and plantations. Cities and European farms became places of male employment and male wages, where females and families came second.

The results of these changes for women reverberated at the end of the colonial period and have only now begun to be analysed. First and foremost women were economically marginalised. The decline of the vitality of subsistence agriculture combined with the growth of the market economy. Women simply controlled fewer and fewer economic resources with which to play social roles. Unlike men who were trained for new social roles, albeit limited ones, in colonial times, women were not provided with the education or training needed for influence in the colonial and national regimes. Without training in new areas and with a decreasingly viable indigenous community, women's organisations did not emerge. Often, groups of women mobilised in Kenya for specific purposes, but a general social movement that analysed women's position relative to that of men and claimed redress did not emerge.

In Likimani's stories we meet Kenyan women who must labour against the colonial regime and the social inequalities it had perpetuated not simply to enhance their own positions but to salvage their communities. Yet their efforts preserved a society in which they were destined to play a diminished role.

3.2 *Passbook Number F.47927*

Passbook Number F.47927 is an account of how women were involved in Mau Mau, other than as freedom fighters. It is written by a Kenyan woman who lived in Nairobi at the time and uses her own passbook number for its title. The accounts are woven from many sources. The majority of characters and situations stem from Likimani's observations of family and friends during the years of the emergency. Some episodes undoubtedly come from her own experiences. The author takes what she saw and heard, transforming it into full descriptions of what it was like to be caught up in a massive political struggle. The accounts are set in a country caught up in the turmoil of revolution; it is this revolution that marks the boundaries of Likimani's world. The geography and life of normal times have little bearing on a world turned upside down. Likimani's accounts are the only firsthand ones by a woman of women's reactions to that struggle. For this reason they are an invaluable record of African women and social movements.

Each of the following accounts tells a self-contained story. Some are set primarily in Nairobi, while others describe life in the rural areas, both in the central mountain region where Mau Mau activity was most intense and on the coast far removed from the fighting. Several describe the transfer of people and supplies between the rural areas and the capital. All emphasise the close ties that existed within communities and the way in which people relied on their fellow citizens for information, support and protection. The residential areas of Nairobi, the white farms in the highlands, the African settlements, the detention camps and the squatter communities are all portrayed. Ordinary people populate the stories; only two narratives feature Kenyans who are members of the newly educated elite.

The stories illustrate the difficulties Kenyan people faced during the nationalist revolution: passbook requirements in Nairobi; strictly enforced curfews; arduous forced communal labour; feeding, supplying, hiding, and often joining the weary freedom fighters; the search for husbands and wives and families separated by arrest, employment, or arbitrary government regulations; constant fear of arrest, raids, and violence by the colonial authorities and homeguards; the inhuman treatment of those held in detention; and the general fear of constant arbitrary imprisonment and mistreatment.

The first two accounts in Likimani's book look at the initial stages of Mau Mau when the passbook system was set up and communal labour projects introduced. *Passbook Number F.47927* describes the beginning of the state of emergency when the passbook system was announced and enforced. The account floods the reader with images of the colonial period that one prefers to forget: the cold aloofness of the colonial officials contrasted with the bewildered African population of Nairobi faced with complying with little-understood regulations. The demands for registration came on top of the increased restrictions on movement; people lost precious days of work having to wait in long lines to register and then endured a process of degradation as officials challenged and badgered them. The first account describes the effect of the pass-book regulations on Nairobi's women. The regulations divided women into two categories: wives and prostitutes. Only those in the first category could obtain a passbook, the others must be repat-riated to their ancestral villages even if they had been born and raised in Nairobi. The story relates one woman's attempt to remain in Nairobi, forced to pretend to be married so as to fit the colonial definition of a proper woman. The second account, *Forced Com-munal Labour,* narrates the burdens of day-to-day road building activities for women under the forced communal labour policy. The story centres on the struggle of the women of the community to keep together, to aid each other in work, gardening, childcare, in those daily tasks for which the burden of communal labour had left little time.

The next three stories examine how women carried on their family lives during Mau Mau. *Kariokor Location* chronicles the story of a woman caught in the terrors of a night-time raid by the homeguard and colonial officials while she is giving birth to a son. Around the plight of this woman other women emerge to help; first a hospital nurse who allows her to escape before she can be detained, and then the women of another location who hide and care for her, and see to it that the children the woman was forced to leave behind are also sheltered and fed. In these two stories as well as the remaining ones, the reader senses the tension in every situation: women are confronted with challenges to their lives and loyalties. Women thought to be loyalists become nationalist sup-porters and act to help other women and men despite the hazards of their tasks.

Komerera – Lie Low returns to the theme of the colonial definition of woman-as-wife and examines the meaning of travel restrictions for women. Women were permitted to travel from their villages to the cities only when their husbands' employer and location officials had prepared documents and sent them to local officials. For wives who did not know their husbands' whereabouts this meant that they were forced to stay in their villages not knowing what happened to their spouses. In this chapter, three women travel secretly from their village to Nairobi to search out their husbands and experience firsthand the restraints of a system that failed to acknowledge women's independence. Once in Nairobi, two of the women are forced to 'lie down,' that is, pretend to be a man's wife since they could not find their own and needed to be wives to obtain the all important passbook.

The fifth narrative covers the theme most familiar in accounts of Kenya during Mau Mau. It lauds women's contributions to the Mau Mau effort by hiding and assisting the freedom fighters. In *Unforgotten Flames* a woman comes upon freedom fighters as she farms her small riverside plot. She hides them in her mother-in-law's house until they successfully attack the homeguard post, burning it to the ground. The woman's assumption that she had the wherewithall to hide the fighters overcomes her personal concern for safety. The reader is left with a vivid impression of Kenyan women's strong sense of self and political priorities.

The last four stories are set outside the traditional rural areas – three in detention camps and one in Mombasa. In these four accounts the characters are active participants in the social changes that were intensified during the state of emergency. *Squatter's Tragedy* explores the difficulties rural people confronted when relocated to detention camps and protected villages. *The Interrogation Camp* depicts the humiliation and arbitrariness of the process of deciding among friends and enemies of the colonial regime. *Vanishing Camp* examines the life of a Kikuyu nurse and her decision to use her official position to help Mau Mau leaders escape the harsh treatment of the detention camp. The final chapter, *Hero's Welcome*, is the story of a young man's return from school in England, and his transformation into a Mau Mau supporter. The women of his community had raised the funds to send him abroad and they are there at the Nairobi airport to celebrate his homecoming. Their sacrifices and strength of personality lead the young man to his support of Mau Mau.

The women in Muthoni Likimani's short stories are developed and complex characters. As the difficulties of colonial rule and struggles for independence in Kenya are described from women's points of view, the importance of women in Kenya's struggle come to life for the reader. It is the women who had the hazardous task of providing Mau Mau with food and supplies, and it was the women who provided hiding places for the Mau Mau. The survival of families during forced communal labour and early curfew can be attributed to the incredible feats of women. They organised them-selves, both as groups and as individuals, in order to finish all the necessary chores in the little time they had. In these respects women are portrayed as clever, inventive, tough, brave, careful, alert, responsible – in short, leaders who could and did assume responsi-bility for community life. They are not depicted as women who live and die for men but as people who value above all the love and well-being of their families, the soil they live on, and the country for which they are fighting. Together, the women put aside personal differences and pull themselves and their families through the difficult birth of their nation.

3.3 *Women and Nationalism*

Did the nationalist movement empower Kenyan women? Or did it reinforce old assumptions about women, and not contribute to their participation in contemporary life? A debate has been growing among feminist scholars in the West about the influence of wars, revolutions, and nationalist movements on women. To date, many observers have claimed that situations of dramatic political change are watersheds – times resulting in tremendous gains for women. Now, others, who research women's involvement both during and after national crises, are suggesting this is not necessarily so.

The earlier view assumed that dramatic events open new oppor-tunities for women and may alter the balance of power between women and men. Both logic and data appeared to support the watershed view. The assumption was that in times of national emergency, gender conventions may go by the wayside as societies utilise all of their labour resources, i.e., including women. Case study data from the Russian Revolution, for example, emphasise the relatively large numbers of women who were politically promi-nent. Observers point out that women remain in the party hierarchy today, giving the Soviet Union high rankings when tallies are made of women in political life. In a similar vein, it is often argued that the economic mobilisation of large numbers of American and Euro-pean women during World War II launched patterns of labour force participation that opened access to other role changes in the follow-ing decades. Similar ideas are applied to African women, suggesting that women's participation in nationalist movements and revolu-tions has heralded the start of new opportunities for them.

African women participated in the nationalist revolutions in diverse ways. The various kinds of nationalist movements, as well as the period in which they occurred, provided the contexts within which women acted. The earliest, relatively non-violent and non-Marxist revolutions of West Africa (in Nigeria, Ghana, Sierra Leone, or former French West Africa, for example) were followed by similar movements in East and Central Africa. A second set of nationalist movements occurred in the entrenched 'settler' economies of Kenya, Algeria, and Zimbabwe, where violent struggle was necessary. A later wave of more self-consciously socialist and Marxist-Leninist movements led to intense fighting in Guinea-Bissau, Angola and Mozambique. Finally, there remains South Africa, where nationalist activity continues in the face of strong repression.

In Nigeria, where the nationalist movement was less violent and centred on electoral struggles, organisations of market women were key supporters of the political parties during the elections. Market women's support became the leading factor in a party's control of an area. The women themselves were active in endorsing and financing candidates, extracting promises, and generally participating in the political process[7]. However, they limited their politicking to demands related to market activities and continually underestimated their own more general political strength. Thus, as time went on, the political clout which they had once exercised, almost inadvertently, tended to decline. In other West African cases, such as Sierra Leone, women did institutionalise their participation both during and after the nationalist period.[8]

In Guinea, in former French West Africa, the nationalist movement assumed a more socialist ideology and had a greater commitment to political roles for women. Here women played a direct role in the rise to power of Sekou Toure, the principal nationalist leader, and they maintained that power thereafter. Toure appealed early to women as active participants. They responded with active involvement – they gave money, they provided communication links among the revolutionaries, and their leadership participated in policy formation. After independence, women stayed in the party and in power.[9] In comparison to other regimes of that period, Guinean women exercised political power extensively as a result of recognising and building on the support they had given the winner, and as a result of his eagerness to use them. Like the leaders of nationalist movements in Angola and Mozambique, Toure worked from a dual base *vis-à-vis* women. On the one hand, he had an ideological basis for his socialism which demanded the equal participation of women. His view of the body politic required equal involvement of all citizens, male and female. On the other hand, he was an astute judge of his limited resources and well aware of his need to mobilise all of them. Guinean women, by tradition and through modern market involvement, were key resources, and he reached out to them.

In Algeria, a former French settler colony in North Africa, the nationalist movement became an armed struggle against the colonisers. Women's activities were extensive and varied, but eventually self-defeating. Garbed in traditional clothing, Algerian women became the primary means of transmitting food, weapons and information. They were able to traverse the cities unknown to the French authorities, providing the links necessary to the rebels' success. Some became involved in policy-making. Accounts of the period describe how difficult Algerian men found it to listen to the advice of women but how the demands of the revolution forced them to lay aside gender stereotypes and incorporate women as fellow comrades. The French too saw a political role for Algerian women; for them the political role was a modern one. In their propaganda, they appealed to Algerian women to stick with France as the primary means to reduce their oppression and to take advantage of a new life style. Some Algerian women supported the French, seeing alliance as a means to a new equality.

With the achievement of independence, Algerian nationalists rejected that which had been French, including the proposed political roles for women, and stressed the return to an indigenous state. The fact that women had taken enormous individual political risks to bring about the revolution was pushed aside in the fervour to restore legitimacy. Male leaders, both Algerian and French, had perceived that as a practical matter they needed female support and participation in order to win. In the intensity of the revolution, the constraints for appropriate gender role behaviour in both cultural traditions went by the board, creating new opportunities for women. Once independence was achieved, and the crisis past, women were edged out, and were not rewarded with the power they had earned. Algerian women, active in the revolution, had not the organisational base afterwards to use for capitalising on their revolutionary work, when the political agenda later shifted with independence.[10]

A survey of women's participation in the African nationalist movements would be incomplete without mention of the experience of South African women, black and white, in the protracted struggle of that country. The nature of South African politics makes it difficult to compile a full picture of how women have aided the yet unfinished anti-colonial struggle. Historical accounts demonstrate how white women's roles were interrelated with national politics during the Anglo-Boer War.[11] The Black Sash, since 1963 a multi-racial, liberal organisation of women opposed to apartheid laws, stand as an important example of how South African women have found ways to resist the dominant political culture.[12]

The link between apartheid policies and the intersection of gender, race, and class in the South African cultural system is described in *For Their Triumphs and for Their Tears*.[13] Bernstein demonstrates how the sex-gender system of white South Africa is fundamental to apartheid, through policies that systematically manipulate black family life and the place of women in society. In South Africa, as elsewhere, women were active in the political movements, in this case the African National Congress in the post-second World War period. The highly repressive state reaction to activism and the separate path taken by South Africa since the 1960s mean that our knowledge of women's participation in resistance is limited. Nonetheless, it appears that women, black and white, individually and collectively, have resisted the intolerable situations, usually by finding ways around the constraints, sometimes by initiating protest, often by joining with men in opposing repressive conditions. One area in which black women continue to be active is in labour organisation.[14]

Arguments against a 'watershed' theory are developing as more and more information on women's involvement in national emergencies comes to light. For example, while wars open new opportunities in which women can demonstrate their capabilities, skills and power, policy-makers often concentrate on the themes of women's traditional attributes and the need for women in particular to be self-sacrificing. Such an emphasis promotes ideas about gender differences while in fact the reality contradicts such an ideology. Furthermore, this emphasis rewards women's 'traditional' behaviour and ignores the innovative ways in which women organise during crises and cope with new demands through creating new structures. Another critique of the idea that crises work to women's benefit emerges from the debate over how long-lasting or full-ranging the changes actually are. While not minimising the importance of what women do during wars and revolutions, it is necessary to ask whether women in post-crisis situations continue to have the same opportunities. Is women's initiative rewarded after-wards as it was during the crisis? Does women's leadership con-tinue? Are the gains achieved during the war or revolution main-tained?

Berkin and Lovett[15] have proposed a framework for the analysis of material on women, war and revolution. They begin their study of diverse cases by suggesting that wars and revolutions do not neces-sarily imply any status progress or role differentiation for women other than their immediate economic mobilisation. Drawing on case studies of the French Revolution, of Germany during World War II, and of American women during the same period, they conclude that political participation does not necessarily follow from economic mobilisation, either during the national emergency or afterwards. They say each case 'documents the remarkable fluidity of circumstances and the innovative quality of the experi-ence that characterised these national crises; yet each also attests to the resiliency of traditional roles and structures and to the fragility of egalitarian reform. It is within this contradiction between the promise of change and the restoration of tradition that the experi-ence of women is to be located' (1980:p. 3).

Berkin and Lovett go on to document the persistence of patriar-chy during and after the revolutionary times by presenting five cases, the American, French, Russian, Chinese and Cuban revolu-tions. These five analyses demonstrate that even in situations of cataclysmic change, men and women, leaders and followers, fre-quently continue to advocate values and social arrangements disad-vantageous to any change for women. Yet their case studies go beyond the ideas of women as victims of their socialisation and social systems, suggesting instead that

with a few exceptions, women revolutionaries do not seem to have perceived such a conflict any more than did men. On the contrary, the behaviour of Parisian women on the bread lines and of Russian leaders like Smidovich and Liubatovich suggests that in their view revolutionary change would enable them to function better as wives, mothers, and providers. If this was indeed their self-perception (and further research is needed on this issue), the

preservation of patriarchal values and their rapid postrevolutionary resurgence reflected something more complex than a delib-
erate and callous exercise of power by male leaders over their
female allies. Perhaps it reflected the belief of revolutionaries of
both sexes that the effective performance of traditional duties,
especially child raising, by women was no less vital to the func-
tioning of postrevolutionary society and to the consolidation of
some revolutionary gains than was the actual direction of public
policy. Two essays in the third section of this volume do, in fact,
illustrate how nineteenth century French and Italian women,
while excluded from political power, performed an important
civic function within the family. The introduction to Section
Three shows this to have also been the case in the early years of
the American republic.(82)

Thus, for Berkin and Lovett and their colleagues the emergence to
patriotic motherhood (the belief that women best serve the nation
as mothers raising the future generations, an idea that restricts
women to the domestic sphere while attributing to that sphere a
political meaning) rather than equality or change is often the
outcome of wars and revolutions. Using essays on the French and
Italian revolutions and the World War I experience of American
women, the authors argue that patriotic motherhood appears frequently as a post-revolutionary role for women.

It has been argued that Republican Motherhood was indeed a
progressive development for the white American woman. It fell
short of any egalitarian goals, yet it was the first recognition of
women as civic figures, and it brought a dignity and a sense of
purpose to domestic duties previously without significance outside the narrow circle of the home. But in Napoleonic France the
establishment of the 'mother-teacher' identity for elite women
marked not progress but a decline in actual political influence and
participation. (209)

They conclude by saying:

The essays . . . explore the complex relationship between ideology and reality. Thorny problems arise in such an endeavour. To
what extent was Patriotic Motherhood in all its forms a social

rationalisation? To what extent was it a genuine personal identity? These essays suggest that its origins lay in the determination of political leadership to preserve patriarchy and to design legal and institutional structures that would make equality, by class or sex, an impossibility. Thus, historians must always examine the material basis for women's inequality within a society. The ideology of Patriotic Motherhood appears to be a construct of traditional beliefs that fortuitously justified a role policymakers created. Yet, as scholars in this final section remind us, ideology has no static reality; its internalisation often means its metamorphosis. The women discussed in these essays are proof of human versatility and the healthy drive to a mastery of circumstances. If, ultimately, historians judge for social change, or that it is not a satisfying explanation for historical realities, still no humanistic model of the past can be constructed without considering the impact of ideology. (pp. 212–13)

3.4 *Kenyan women and nationalism*

How does our knowledge of Kenya accord with these ideas? Previous descriptions of women's participation in Mau Mau contain the same double standard that critics of the watershed theory argue against. That is, Kenyan women's bravery and support, as freedom fighters, couriers, and mainstays of their communities during the revolt, is praised as a significant contribution to the struggle. Women like Field-Marshal Muthoni (no relative to the author of this book) have a prominent place in Kenyan memories of Mau Mau; the leadership she provided along with Dedan Kimathi and General Mathenge in the fighting in the Aberdare Mountains is cited to extol women's participation in the struggle. Nonetheless, the form of those contributions was essentially traditional and the innovative behaviours, attitudes, and ideas which women contributed are noted but were not built upon generally in the before and after Mau Mau. Nor did many other Kenyan women follow the early lead of Wanjiru, the woman who led one of the protest movements during the struggles of the early nationalist leader Harry Thuku in the 1920s and who was one of the first Kenyans to be killed fighting for independence. For example, while women partook of political leadership during the struggle, they did not achieve leadership positions in corresponding numbers afterward.

While women showed by their activities and statements that they operated as civic as well as sexual beings, their civic contributions have been minimised. And while women clearly struggled during Mau Mau for their families (as did men), they also struggled for their land and their livelihood (as did men). Women's non-familial aspirations, however, did not receive recognition during or after Mau Mau while men's aspirations were seen as a combination of familial, ethnic and national loyalties.

Passbook Number F.47927 both affirms the place of women in Mau Mau as it has been previously described by men, and extends the analysis of women's involvement by documenting the diverse motivations women had and the numerous tasks they undertook. Likimani's material does not dispel the doubts cast by commentators arguing against the watershed interpretation. Women's involvement in Mau Mau took traditional forms, made significant contributions to the struggle, and afterwards was transformed in another version of civic motherhood that continues to characterise the circumstances of Kenyan African women today. Lacking an explanatory ideology of their situation and an organisation capable of articulating it, Kenyan women today operate in a complex and often contradictorary milieu.

On the one hand, Kenyan women are internationally heralded for the extent to which they have taken advantage of economic and political opportunities, individually finding ways to be leaders and exercise influence. Publications like *Women of Kenya*, a 'Who's who' of Kenyan women; and *Viva*, a popular magazine which combines features on health, beauty and fashion with reports on women as workers, women's status and women's health issues, attest to the fact that many Kenyan women *do* break through existing barriers and achieve at high levels of politics and economics. *Maendeleo wa Wanawake* is one of the oldest and most prominent of the comprehensive women's organisations on the continent. *Maendeleo*, originally founded by colonial officers' wives to teach domestic and social skills to African women, undertakes diverse projects, teaching domestic science, farming and poultry skills, creating craft and trade options, and providing leadership training. Some say it was charged with the task of rehabilitating women freedom fighters and the wives of loyalists. The organisation grew beyond these original tasks as it developed both urban and rural branches. Its leadership has historically been tied to those in power, its politics are essentially those of reform and accommodation. There are now more than three dozen other women's organisations in Kenya, all of them addressing the issues of women's contemporary status in a variety of ways under the aegis of the National Council of Kenyan Women. For many Kenyan women, their achievements in the two decades since independence rest in women's mobilisation during Mau Mau. The Mau Mau experience, they claim, taught women the skills and gave them the confidence to participate successfully in contemporary politics and economics. The closing conference for the United Nations' International Women's Decade set for Nairobi in 1985, comes as a recognition of the status Kenya holds among the third world countries on women's issues.

On the other hand, Kenyan women frequently lament the severe limitations under which they function and from which they see little relief. Believing as they do in the primacy of the family as their social basis, they nonetheless seek to engage in work and politics. The debate Kenyan women carry on among themselves can be illustrated clearly through a brief look at a book of Likimani's fiction in which her central characters all try to reconcile the demands of men, marriage and work in the contemporary setting.[16]

In *What Does A Man Want?* women's roles are discussed in terms of whether and how women are social beings in their own right or whether they 'need a man' to be considered whole. Through the turmoil created by modernisation, the balance of women's traditional identities has been upset. Each character in the book is forced to search for a way to regain the emotional, social and moral equilibrium originally provided by traditional roles. Some characters respond to this challenge with despair, resigned to their inability to reconcile their traditional identities with the modern world. Others attempt to balance elements of traditional and modern ways. A few women deny and even degrade their traditional African identities in favour of a totally Westernised way of life. The question of how individuals redefine and reaffirm their psychological, emotional and social identity is central to the book. Without exception women take advantage of the educational, economic, and psychological opportunities offered by modernisation. The characters neither reject modernisation nor unquestioningly appropriate the past in order to redefine their identities. Instead, they accept the difficulties of a new dual identity. The difficulty of balancing this identity and the dangers of the duality become apparent when one sees how troubled these women say they are. It seems they are never sure how much tradition to accept in their lives: accepting too much leads to domination they cannot control; yet if they reject too much, they feel that they discard the good with the antiquated past.

In *What Does A Man Want* Likimani speaks through several women characters who express their seemingly futile efforts at being both a worker and a wife. These monologues express the lack of self-worth and personal gain that are women's 'wages' in their struggle for a 'respected' position in the work force. The degradation and hopelessness of female employment comes through in each monologue that discusses how work revolves around men and how women spend their lives catering to someone else's needs and whims. Invariably the women lose out and are left emotionally drained and confused. In one section an older women laments:

> I married him young
> My beauty he could not escape
> I married him poor
> What we've, I contributed
> It is my sweat
> My brain too.
>
> Now as weathered as I am
> Teeth dropping down
> Telling me to go
> To go where?
> Go to whom? (p. 184.5)

'Their' wealth becomes 'his' once she no longer appeals to him.

Another section in Likimani's book details the depressing results of a successful career woman's achievements. At a mature age she relents to social pressures and sets out to 'capture' a man. She suddenly feels unfulfilled as a woman without a husband or child. When she was younger she was full of confidence, stating:

> Those who wanted me
> I refused with pride
> I was earning money.

> Property I had
> And freedom to do
> What pleased me best.
>
> I thought they were enough. (p. 172)

Like other women in her society, however, she becomes disillusioned with career success and regrets the undesirable label it has placed on her:

> Work is too much
> All by myself
> Responsible work completely alone
> I dare not be seen
> I am respected.
>
> Where the young go
> I am not welcomed.
> Where the old go
> They are all in pairs.
>
> and they do not understand.
> Men are men
> Married or not
> They remain yet men. (p. 173)

Her endeavours have stripped her of her 'femininity.' Her ambitions and her pride must be relinquished for a husband – a man that will help her to eliminate the uniqueness she represents in her traditional society. When she finds a man who wants her he is young enough to be her son. He is the only one innocent and vulnerable enough to find her and her accomplishments appealing. She lavishes him with her wealth to keep him satisfied.

> My young man drove
> My car now at his disposal.
>
> The gasoline came
> From my account;

> The home was mine
> And so was its support;
>
> A comfortable home
> Where food was plenty;
> Drinks ready
> Ever in the fridge;
>
> For my man to relax
> Buying all to win his love. (p. 180)

Regardless of her own intellectual and occupational accomplishments she feels she must succumb to the male-oriented standards of society. After their marriage the young man takes her gifts but offers her no love or affection in return. Her support and her business achievements seem futile at the end. In her final statement she says:

> Loneliness and poverty
> Were all I had
> Now that he had
> Sucked me dry
>
> *   *   *
>
> You selected me
> You thought me worthy
> When you make me poor,
> Nothing more to be consumed
> It's time to remember
> I am old enough
> To be your mother. (p. 182)

4. Conclusion

The voices of Kenya's African women achieve a new outlet with the publication of *Passbook Number F. 47927*. Where previous descriptions of women's roles in Mau Mau have kept women in the shadow of men's accomplishments, Muthoni Likimani focuses directly on women's activities and ideas, demonstrating not only the roles they played but the assumptions behind those roles.

At the end of the colonial period, with the economic, political and cultural transformations imposed by integration into the world system already well begun, African women faced a double set of disadvantages. Not only were their traditional sources of power and influence severely undercut by the colonial system, but access to the resources of the new society were more limited for women than they were for men. Within those circumstances, African women acted during Mau Mau to further the goals of the movement.

Involvement in Mau Mau did not represent a watershed for African women. It did not alter deeply-held beliefs about women's place in the family and how the mother role defines power and position in the society at large. Women during Mau Mau linked themselves to the future through representing their families rather than directly assuming positions of leadership in the public arena as well. The nationalist movement has been an empowering episode in the history of Kenya's women. Yet it has not proved to be complete enough to resolve many of the issues faced by Kenyan women today. Without leaders and an ideology to articulate how women relate both to families and to the world of work and policy, the ability and strength women demonstrated during Mau Mau has yet to be fully tapped for Kenyan national purposes.

The unique blend of personal experience, keen observation and deep feeling that Muthoni Likimani brings to her accounts gives the reader a full appreciation of that untapped potential.

Duke University, Durham, North   Jean O'Barr
Carolina
October 1984

Notes

1. The exact origin and meaning of the term *Mau Mau* are unknown according to Ladislav Venys, *A History of the Mau Mau Movement in Kenya* (Prague: Charles University, 1970), p. 4. The colonial government records refer to Mau Mau events officially as an *Emergency*. Recent – particularly Kenyan – interpretations call the events a *Revolt* and interpret them as a part of the process of nationalism.
2. The social science literature on Mau Mau is extensive. The four key

sources for an overview of Kenya during Mau Mau are Carl Rosberg and John Nottingham, *The Myth of Mau Mau: Nationalism in Kenya* (New York: Praeger, 1966); Donald Barnett and Karari Njama, *Mau Mau From Within: Autobiography and Analysis of Kenya's Peasant Revolt* (New York: Monthly Review Press, 1966); Q. W. Furley, 'The Historiography of Mau Mau,' *Hadith*, Volume 4, 1972, pp. 105–133; and Sorobea Boganko, *Kenya 1945–1963: A Study in African National Movements* (Nairobi: Kenya Literature Bureau, 1980). These sources contain full references to government reports, to settler interpretations, to popular accounts of the revolt, and to the periodical literature on Mau Mau.

3. The following life histories have been consulted in this introductory essay. Reference to the statements about women in them does not imply that Muthoni Likimani endorses their interpretations. Rather they have been used to illustrate the limitations of previous accounts of Mau Mau with regard to women. The consulted works include Guen Gikoyo, *We Fought for Freedom* (Nairobi: East African Publishing House, 1979); Waruhiu Itote (General China), *'Mau Mau' General* (Nairobi: East African Publishing House, 1967); Waruhiu Itote (General China), *Mau Mau in Action* (Nairobi: Transafrica Publishers, 1979); Ngugi Kabiro, *Man in the Middle: The Story of Ngugi Kabiro* (Richmond, British Columbia, Canada: LSM Information Center, Life Histories from the Revolution Series, 1973); Bildad Kaggia, *Roots of Freedom 1921–1963: The Autobiography of Bildad Kaggia* (Nairobi: East African Publishing House, 1975); Josiah Kariuki, *'Mau Mau Detainee': The Account by a Kenyan African of His Experience in Detention Camps* (London: Oxford University Press, 1963); Maina wa Kinyatti (ed.), *Thunder From the Mountains: Mau Mau Patriot Songs* (London: ZED Press, 1980); Mohamed Mathu, *Urban Guerrilla: The Story of Mohamed Mathu* (Richmond, British Columbia, Canada: LSM Information Center, Life Histories from the Revolution Series, 1973); Karigo Muchai, *The Hardcores: The Story of Karigo Muchai* (Richmond, British Columbia, Canada: LSM Information Center, Life Histories from the Revolution Series, 1973); Joseph Muriithi, *War in the Forest: The Autobiography of a Mau Mau Leader* (Nairobi: East African Publishing House, 1971); H. K. Wachanga, *The Swords of Kirinyaga: The Fight for Land and Freedom* (Nairobi: Kenya Literature Bureau, 1975); Joram Wamweya, *Freedom Fighter* (Nairobi: East African Publishing House, 1971).

4. Five works by Ngugi wa Thiong'o (James Ngugi) deal directly with the Emergency time. These include *Weep Not Child* (London: Heinemann, 1964); *The River Between* (London: Heinemann, 1965); *A Grain of Wheat* (London, Heinemann, 1967); the play, *The Trial of Dedan Kimathi* (London: Heinemann, 1976); and the book of essays, *Homecoming* (London: Heinemann, 1972).

5. The most recent and comprehensive analysis of African Women from the point of view of many academic disciplines is Jean Hay and Sharon Strichter, *African Women South of the Sahara* (London: Longman, 1984). A review essay by Margaret Strobel, 'African Women' (*Signs* 1982 Volume 8, Number 1, pp. 109–31), fully describes the literature of the last two decades. Selected chapters in the following books provide useful

overviews of the ideas and research on African women: Christopher Mojekwu *et al.* (eds), *African Society, Culture and Politics: An Introduction to African Studies* (Washington, D.C.: University Press of America, 1977); Beverly Lindsay (ed.), *Comparative Perspective of Third World Women: The Impact of Race, Sex, and Class* (New York: Praeger, 1980); Filomena Steddy (ed.), *The Black Woman Crossculturally* (Cambridge, MA: Schenkman, 1981). Two earlier classics include Nancy Hafkin and Edna Bay (eds), *Women in Africa: Studies in Social and Economic Change* (Stanford, CA: Stanford University Press, 1976) and Edna Bay and Nancy Hafkin (eds), 'Women in Africa,' a special issue of *African Studies Review*, 1975, volume 18, number 3. Numerous books and articles on individual women, women of certain ethnic groups, and analysis of women on a country-by-country basis by both Western and African scholars are cited in the works listed above. Specific references to analysis of Kenyan women are found in all these sources.

6. Arthur Hazlewood, *The Economy of Kenya: The Kenyatta Era* (Oxford: Oxford University Press, 1979) presents a good overview of women's economic situation. Kathy Santilli, 'Kikuyu Women in the Mau Mau Revolt: A Closer Look,' *Ufahamu*, Volume VIII, Number 1, 1977, pp. 143–59, surveys women's participation based on secondary sources.

7. See Cheryl Johnson, 'Madame Alimotu Pelewura and the Lagos Market Women', *Tarikh*, Volume 7, Number 1, 1981, pp. 1–10, and Nina Mba, *Nigerian Women Mobilized: Women's Political Activity in Southern Nigeria, 1900–1945* (Berkeley, California: University of California, Institute of International Studies, 1982).

8. See the accounts of Filomina Steady, *Female Power in African Politics: The National Congress of Sierra Leone* (Pasadena, California: Munger Africana Notes No. 31) and 'Protestant Women's Associations in Freetown, Sierra Leone,' in Hafkin and Bay, *op. cit.*, pp. 183–212.

9. Margarita Dobert, 'Liberation and the Women of Guinea,' *African Report*, Volume 15, Number 7, pp. 26–28.

10. David Gordon, *Women of Algeria: An Essay on Change* (Harvard, Massachusetts: Harvard University Press, 1972).

11. S. B. Spies, 'Women and War,' in Peter Warwick (ed.), *The South African War: The Anglo-Boer War, 1899–1902* (London: Longman, 1980).

12. Cherry Michelmann, *The Black Sash of South Africa: A Case Study in Liberalism* (London: Oxford University Press, 1975).

13. Hilda Bernstein, *For Their Triumph and For Their Tears: Conditions and Resistance of Women in Apartheid South Africa* (Cambridge, Massachusetts: Internal Defense and Aid Fund, 1975).

14. Iris Berger, 'Sources of Class Consciousness: The Experience of Women Workers in South Africa, 1973–1980,' *Boston University African Studies Center Working Paper*, Number 55, 1982.

15. Carol Berkin and Clara Lovett, *Women, War and Revolution* (New York: Holmes and Meier, 1980).

16. Muthoni Likimani, *What Does A Man Want?* (Nairobi: Kenya Literature Bureau, 1974).

Passbook Number F.47927

Women and Mau Mau in Kenya

Muthoni Likimani

Passbook Number F.47927

Introduction

Passbook Number F.47927 was my own passbook. The passbook was an identity card the Colonial government required of people belonging to the ethnic groups suspected of deep involvement in Mau Mau. The ethnic groups branded as Mau Mau came mostly from the Central Province and around Mount Kenya: the Kikuyus on the south and west of the mountain; the Meru on the north; and the Embu on the east. Anyone from these groups was subject to continuous suspicion and scrutiny. If one lived in the towns, particularly in Nairobi, one needed a passbook.

To obtain a passbook in Nairobi one stood in a queue for hours, only to face a thorough and hostile interrogation. You had to have good reasons for wanting to remain in the city; without that you faced repatriation to your ancestral village, a place you might never have seen. To qualify for a passbook, you must be employed or involved in a legitimate business. A responsible person such as a district commissioner, a location chief or even a well-known loyalist must vouch for your loyalties. As a woman you must be the wife of a passbook holder or must be legitimately employed. Employers were important for the help they could lend a person in obtaining a passbook.

The government required considerable information from passbook applicants: date of birth, place of birth, village and district, house number in the locations, name of village chief, present employer, other references. All this permitted the

40

Colonial government to keep close tabs on you. You could not be employed unless you had a passbook and employers were expected to report their firings. The process ended much like in the police stations where they sat you down, hung a board with numbers around your neck and took a photograph to include in the passbook.

The passbook was a precious document. You never went without it for fear of homeguards stopping you. Even just outside your own house they'd cart you off to detention camp rather than let you go back inside to get it. Areas such as Kariokor, Bahati and Bondeni where the passbook holders lived, were subject to harrassment at all hours; to be awakened in the night, even in pouring rain and have one's house torn apart in search for weapons and other contraband became a familiar occurrence. This is why many women made a small bag with a strap, that they hung around their necks. It stayed with them always.

After getting your passbook you were entitled to continue working in the city. Yet it gave no real liberties; the passbook did not mean you were loyal. Rather it permitted the government to supervise you more closely. You could not, as a passbook holder, spend a night in anyone's home but your own without official approval. Some locations in Nairobi such as Kaloleni and Ziwani were off-limits to you; you could not live or visit there without written authority. After any new turmoil, you were subject to a curfew from 6 pm to 6 am during which time you could not leave your house even to use the communal facilities.

Travel for a passbook holder was difficult: when you wanted to go out of Nairobi you had to obtain the permission of the district office and upon arrival at your destination immediately report to a local officer. When returning, the same procedures were required. At times, travel restrictions were made ludicrous such as when a rule was announced forbidding more than one of the subject groups to travel in a car; this meant that a woman could not travel with her husband if they both had passbooks.

The loyalist homeguards who patrolled the locations had authority to shoot if you failed to stop when they commanded. They were strict and brutal; they gave no opportunities to explain. If you were out without a passbook or during curfew time, you might count on being detained or even repatriated.

Many women did not qualify for a passbook. They often turned for help to men whose own wives were living on farms. These city women would pretend to be wives to the single men, sharing the same houses. They became known as Passbook wives.

*   *   *

It was a Monday morning when the District Commissioner of Nairobi summoned all chiefs, subchiefs, and even all the District Officers of Nairobi to gather in his office at Nairobi's centre. The meeting was so secret that even the clerks were left ignorant of it. No agendas were prepared, no one knew why the meeting had been called. Even Kiarie, a senior clerk and secret Mau Mau supporter tried in vain to discover the meeting's purpose. It was a top secret meeting. Kiarie knew nothing; nor did the people attending this meeting. In any case this was part of the state of emergency, and anything could crop up at any time.

As the chiefs and subchiefs stood around outside the District Commissioner's office, they kept on whispering questions to each other, trying to find out more about the meeting. Those who were not sure of their loyalty, showed gloomy faces as they wondered whether this was a meeting to discipline them, maybe to mete out punishment, or worse still to sack and detain them, or even to kill.

Subchief Isaac wondered how he could live as an ordinary citizen. 'I think I can easily be persecuted if I am left loose among the other citizens. Think how I punished them, I fear what the revenge would be.' Subchief Isaac felt worried.

District Commissioner Steel entered the room dressed in his khaki uniform and big helmet. As he entered, all the chiefs and subchiefs stood to attention, all showing faces of obedience and trust; some with guilty consciences forced wry smiles to their lips, the smiles no more than a brief opening of their mouths. The chiefs' helmets were off, held in their left hands, as their right hands flapped aimlessly in agreement of I don't know what. Their hands tried to give reasons to a meeting yet free of any. They all, then, sat down at the far end of the table. The DC sat at the centre, presiding over the meeting. His face looked more serious than usual; and more unusual of DC Steel, on this particular day he did not ask questions or encourage talk of the chief's problems. He had a colonial face, full of authority. His District Officer I and District Commissioner II also came and sat at the centre of the table, one on each side of District Commissioner Steel. An *askari kanga* stood quietly by the entrance.

All the chiefs kept looking at each other with inquisitive eyes. Their heads, their hands and even their eyes expressed nervousness, and when nervousness was added to the state of fear, the lack of firmness in their minds was more noticeable.

Looking even more full of authority, DC Steel called for the attention of his chiefs, subchiefs, DO, and all the other officials by tapping a pen against a water jug. The local chiefs focused their attention on the DC, some clearing their throats as if requested to speak. The DC's interpreter stood by, ready to translate to the majority of the chiefs and homeguard leaders who did not understand English. 'I am sure by now you are wondering why I called this emergency meeting instead of having our usual weekly meeting. You should not be too surprised as this is emergency time, or call it war time if you like.' The District Commissioner went on as his rather poor translator continued to interpret wrongly and to exaggerate the DC's words to those less-educated chiefs and subchiefs. 'Yesterday, I am sure by now you all know, we had a long meeting with the Governor and the Provincial Commissioner. The meeting was to explain to us that the way things are going is not good, the trouble has gone from bad to worse. We have all tried our best to control the terrorists, but no matter how we curb Mau Mau activities, they seem to find another way out, and whether we like it or not, the security must be there and has to be tightened. Although we all know beyond doubt that nearly all Kenyan tribes are behind the freedom fighters, it is obvious that the Central Province people are the originators, the Mau Maus, the oath operators, the terrorist attackers, and the major planners of all those ambushes. The tribes of the Central Province are very well known to you; they are Kikuyu, Embu and Meru, all surrounding Mount Kenya, all believe in oath-taking, and swearing with their goats never to surrender.

'Gentlemen, I did not call you here for any further discussion, but to give you an order, and for that order to be taken. In our meeting with the Governor, it was passed that in order to enable the Government to maintain strict control over the Central Province tribes, the following particulars must be observed:

1. All members of those tribes, namely the Kikuyu, Embu and Meru, must have an identification in the form of a "passbook".

2. The said tribes must be isolated. They must not mix with other tribes in case they spread bad influence.

3. In order to have full control over their activities, they must all live in one place. It will be easier to have firm control over their movements and their visitors. And when it is necessary to punish them, it can be done easily without affecting innocent tribes.

As soon as we leave this office, I want you to see the City Council Housing Officer and ask him to give you all the names and houses occupied by Kikuyus, Embus and Merus in all locations; take their numbers, and with the help of the Housing Officer and *askaris*, tell all Kikuyus, Embus and Merus that they have been ordered to vacate their houses and must be relocated to camps.

'The City Council Housing Superintendant has prior knowledge of our operation, and I am sure by now the vacating plan is ready. Start with Kaloleni. Take all other tribes from Bahati and allocate to them the better accommodations of the Mau Mau tribes. And those oath operators living at Kaloleni, remove them to Bahati Location. Let them operate their oaths from there. After all, the Nairobi River valley by Bahati Location has enough banana trees for oath operations. Ziwani, too, could be used for other tribes, if all Kikuyus are stuck together at Kariokor Location.'

District Officer Wainaina did not seem quite satisfied with the decision. He raised the problem of the loyalists from the Mau Mau tribes. 'How can you mix them with their enemies? There are also some very good people who are neither Mau Maus nor loyalists. People who are just good, unconcerned citizens, some who are used to leading a clean life, why should they be punished? Doesn't such action make them feel bitter and even wish to become Mau Maus too? Surely not all Kikuyus are bad people, otherwise some of us would not have come here today as we belong to the bad tribes.'

'We have heard the same complaints before, but it is difficult to say who to help and who not to help,' responded the DC.

'Can you Mr DC, Sir, give another place for the Kikuyus, Embus and Merus? Some definitely need bigger places than those offered at Kariokor and Bahati,' Chief Kizingo complained.

'What about Bondeni?' subchief Wanzala asked. 'Bondeni' the DC repeated. 'Yes. Bondeni is the lower part of Pumwani, the Muslim area, they have better accommodations than Kariokor. Surely we cannot punish all the people from the Central Province because of the few bad ones?'

'What about the Civil Servant quarters and those of the East African Common Services – the Post Office and the Railways?' Chief Kizingo asked.

'Those should be left to their appropriate authorities, who can allocate them according to their wish,' Steel continued. 'They must know what residents are from the tribes surrounding Mount Kenya, Meru on the North, Kikuyu on the South West, and Embu on the East. Once they are in this city, they must be identified, these friends of the Mau Mau savages. That is the only way we can trace them.

'I now call on you all to go and hold public meetings in your locations, tell the tribes the following: All Kikuyus, Embu and Meru tribes are ordered to go and register for their passbooks. The procedure for obtaining a passbook is as follows: First, the applicant for a passbook must be interrogated by loyalists and the chief of each location. The interrogation must check on:

(a) who their employers are;

(b) if an unemployed woman, she must be living with her husband or her father;

(c) every single woman who is not employed or living with her husband must be sent back to her village and if employed she must get a letter from her employer;

(d) and, by all means, all those getting passbooks must be good and trusted people.'

DC Steel was not quite sure that all his juniors understood the order. So he went through it once again. The authority, the seriousness and the firmness of DC Steel left the chiefs and administrators with nothing to add – no questions, no comments. They wondered how they were going to approach the touchy and usually fed-up populace. 'Maybe they will mob us after we give them all these conditions,' some homeguards felt. 'Or they may think it was our own order,' Chief Kizingo thought.

'This is an order,' Chief Yusuf of Kariokor added to himself as he took his walking stick, and without knowing how to approach his people, walked briskly towards the government Landrover waiting to take him back to his camp.

The following evening the usual whistles were blustering all over, up and down the locations of Nairobi. The whistles were followed by the usual order to call all the people, young and old, to attend the chief's *baraza* at the local school compound or football field. The orders, the threats, and the whistles were followed by door-to-door calls. All over, all Africans' quarters in the city, the Mau Maus, the loyalists, and even the uninvolved; Kikuyu, Embu and Meru, they all must assemble for this urgent meeting.

At Bahati Location the meeting was to start at 5 pm on Tuesday. The chief of Bahati was a coward man, he dared not face the public without security; he called the District Officer and some administrative police to stand by in case of trouble.

By 5 pm, the Bahati Location football field was filled with bitter people: some badly dressed wearing an assortment of torn coats, ragged hats; disgusted, pregnant women, some with suckling babies, barefoot, dressed in old calico dresses and head scarves. All stern-faced and quiet, they sat awaiting for yet another boring speech as the sun went down.

The DC stood to attention and started to give orders to the gathered crowd: 'As from now, all members of the Kikuyu, Embu and Meru tribes will be required to carry an identification in the form of a passbook. A passbook will only be given to those in genuine employment or married women. Don't say I never warned you, you have ten days to register for your passbooks. Go now, see your employer, get a letter or identity card from them and at once go and register at the Labour Office. The offices will be open and ready tomorrow morning at 8.15. When the ten days expire, do not come crying to me; you have no choice other than face the consequences.'

Similar *barazas* were held in each and every location in Nairobi. The African Broadcasting Services repeated several times the information on the passbooks, the news made the headlines of all the local newspapers and in no time everyone was well informed.

At 7 am on the following day, people started to pour into the labour office at Delamere Avenue for the passbook. Panicking faces, worried faces, young and old, men and women, all rushed to be registered before the deadline.

By 8 am the scene outside the labour office was unbelievable. The *askari kanga* arrived earlier and ordered all people to queue before the officials arrived. Two queues were formed: one for the women facing one office and one for men directed towards another office.

At 8.15 am some office clerks arrived, their faces looking unapproachable, full of hatred, and full of forced officialism and authority. They refused to look at the crowd. One by one, the officials entered the labour office, the chiefs, subchiefs, the DOs and many other officials. The crowd stood still, the officials at the office entrance closed the doors, stayed unconcerned inside while the people outside waited. The December sun started to shine brightly on the faces of fed-up and tired Kikuyus, Embus and Merus – all who waited patiently, wondering if they would qualify.

At long last, at 10.30 am, one clerk opened the door of the office and shouted, 'Keep in the line! Stand still! Have all your identity and employment cards ready.' Some nervous headmen with the help of *askari* came out to help line-up the crowd which by now had become vast.

'First one,' the clerk at the desk of the first office called. The forms were ready on the table, beyond the table was another little table, where yet another man sat.

'Can you read?' the clerk asked Mr Nyagah.

'No, I cannot read.'

'Your name?' continued the clerk.

'Mr Nyagah – Nyagah son of Mbogo.'

'Where were you born?'

'I was born at Runyenjes in Embu District.'

'Which year were you born?'

'I do not know.'

'You do not know?'

'No, I do not know, but my father says I was big enough to take care of calves during the famous earthquake, and I was one of those who first got circumcised during the *ndururu* age group.'

'God almighty! Which age group is that? And when was the famous earthquake? I better leave that space blank until I check on the age.'

'Where do you work?'

'I am a gardener at Nofka Hotel.'

'Where is Nofka?'

'Over there, the big hotel down there.'

'You mean Norfolk Hotel?'

'Yes, Nofka. That is where I have worked for many years now. Even the Manager knows me.'

'Do you have any work identity card?' the clerk asked Mr Nyagah.

'What is that?' Mr Nyagah asked.

'Do you have any papers?'

'Yes, many papers,' Nyagah answered as he pulled out a bunch of dirty decayed papers, folded together and tightly tied inside a little leather bag which was hung under his right arm, covered by his rather dirty coat. Mr Nyagah placed them all on the clerk's table.

The clerk, looking very disgusted, went through all the papers, some were very old indeed, some were old letters from his relatives, some concerned land disputes, others were tax-cards and finally he found a dirty, torn employment card. The clerk took the number from the employment card as he asked Mr Nyagah where he resided and other personal matters. 'Move to the next table.'

The clerk there was busy rolling something like a piece of steel or wood. He added some ink to it, then rolled it again.

'Give me your right hand!' shouted the man by the small table at *mzee* Nyagah. No explanation. He later pulled Nyagah's left hand. 'Left hand I said!' the clerk shouted again, after finishing the fingers on the right hand. The clerk added some more ink, rolled once again on the plate, then with the clerk's help took the print of both palms of *mzee* Nyagah's hands. After finishing with fingerprints, and without a word he took Nyagah's shoulder roughly and showed old Nyagah into yet another office. He then turned to attend to the next man waiting by his table.

Inside the next office, another man waited for Nyagah.

'Remove your coat and hat,' the clerk demanded. 'What is that dirty leather bag hanging on your shoulder? Put them all in the corner. When did you last wash them?' The rude clerk kept on insulting Nyagah. 'Here, over in that corner; it's not all that cold, you can do without them for a while.' The man then brought out that famous little board with numbers. The one used for convicted prisoners. He hung it round Nyagah's neck. 'Here, look at my hand!' the man shouted again. 'Shut your mouth. Open your eyes. Here! One, Two, Three,' the snap was shot. 'Another one!' the man shouted again, 'I want to shoot another one.' Then he led Nyagah to the door and told him to wait outside. One by one many men entered and went through the same routine. Women too entered, one by one on the female side and went through the same routine as the men.

For several days the street outside the labour offices was always filled with worried Kikuyus, Embu and Meru trying to get pass-books before the deadline of ten days. The clerks, the chiefs, the subchiefs, the administrators, and even the administrative police became fed up from being overworked, even at lunch time they had to work on shifts so as to finish registering these tribes before the ten days deadline. Days passed very quickly, yet the crowd seemed to increase.

* * *

For a long time Wacu had been employed as an *ayah* at *bwana* Captain Evans' house. She had a nice room in the house at Kilimani, just near the King George VI Hospital. Captain Evans' home was quiet. Men dared not enter his compound because of the many fierce dogs. Captain Evans was also known to be in possession of guns, and that he had been a captain during the Second World War. Captain Evans was unlike the other whites. He did not like others bothering him in his compound. Apart from his many dogs, he had a lot of servants, and unlike many other Europeans, Captain Evans trusted his servants very much. He was nice to them, paying higher salaries than the other Europeans, providing good accommodation and looking after his servants' welfare. Therefore none of his employees would welcome any danger for Captain Evans, or assist any intruders, as the servants too would suffer. Just before the passbook requirement was announced, Captain Evans' long leave fell due and he and his family left for six months' stay in England.

A new European came to deputise for Evans and resided in the house. This one was a very bad man. He said he did not want any of the known Mau Mau tribes at his house. He had his own servants and his *ayah*, and as a result of this Wacu found herself without a job or a home.

For Wacu, life in the village would be impossible. Her brothers had never liked her after she had run away from her husband. When she left her so-called husband, all the cows and dowry had to be returned as she had no children by him. Wacu did not like to keep on meeting her divorced husband, who was still very jealous of her good looks. Since her ex-husband was now a famous homeguard, she thought he was likely to fabricate a story just to put Wacu into trouble. 'This is emergency time,' Wacu thought. 'I better hide in Nairobi until my employers are back.'

Days passed and the days for getting passbooks were getting fewer. Luckily the administrators had extended the deadline by a few days. This was allowed due to pressure of work on the administrators.

'How can I get a passbook? What shall I do? What indeed?' Wacu wondered. The days were going by, the threatening warnings never ceased to sound. Every time she heard a whistle, it made her tremble with fear knowing that this was really a threat to her.

The sight of any authority, police, the chiefs, homeguards, gave Wacu sleepless nights. 'Where else can I go? Where indeed? What then shall I do?' A problem such as this is difficult to face alone, Wacu felt as she tried hard to think of what she could do. 'Living in Nairobi is impossible without a passbook. To get a passbook I have to get a letter from my employer, or have a husband to sign for me. My employer is out of the country. A husband I don't have. And to go back to the village, I would rather die.'

With all these problems, Wacu decided to talk the matter over with a friend. Men are even more clever with these things than women, and at the thought of this Wacu decided to call on John Irungu and explain her problems to him. Irungu was a bus conductor and had lived a long time in his one room at Shauri Moyo Location. Wacu called on Irungu to seek his help and ask whether he could help her, or at least suggest some ideas.

'Here I am Irungu, your old girl friend,' said Wacu. 'You know my husband, a jealous man who kicked me out, and since he knows I have a better job and he is jobless, he is even more jealous. He calls me a prostitute. He swears that the next time he gets hold of me, he will kill me. And now I understand he is a homeguard in the village. My brothers hate me, they complain that because of me they had to return all the dowry to my husband's family. They are very bitter. And now with these passbooks coming when I haven't a job, without an employer and without a husband, no one can recommend me for a passbook. What can I do? Please tell me?' Wacu repeated as tears ran down her cheeks.

Irungu looked at Wacu with pity. He helped her wipe the tears and comforted her. 'Leave it to me; I am a man and we have to do something.'

'Something? What can you do? Only three days are left before they start to arrest us, then they will send me to the village to those brothers of mine and their wives who think I deprived them of their riches. To go and be hunted day and night by that ex-husband of mine, who is very jealous of my smooth skin, and complains and calls me a prostitute. They will definitely enjoy seeing me in trouble.' Wacu at this point burst out again in tears. Irungu made her comfortable in his bed, and begged her not to cry any more.

Wacu from that day stayed at Irungu's house. Irungu's wife was living in the village taking care of their piece of land and the children. At least they had enough space for their eight children and they managed to grow some food on their *shamba*.

Neither Irungu nor Wacu got any sleep for a whole night. They kept on listening to every movement and sound. They slept in fear that Wacu would be caught in Irungu's house. This would get Irungu sent to the detention camp or to prison. The same could happen to Wacu or she could be sent back to the village.

The sleepless night made Irungu think deeply about Wacu. He turned several times and with the help of the moonlight which broke through the partially drawn curtains, he studied Wacu's beautiful face, covered in tears. Wacu was just starting to fall asleep, as Irungu took this deep look at her.

Just before 5 am Irungu woke up, Wacu was still asleep.

'Wacu, Wacu, Wacu, wake up. Don't forget that I am a bus conductor. I start work at 6 am, and I have to report to the bus station by 5.45 am. Before I leave, let me give you the answer to your problems. You have lived in Nairobi for many years. I know you definitely know a lot of people, but it is me you trusted to solve your problems. It is me you thought would give you the right advice, and I hope you will accept it.

'Now Wacu, in the whole of this block nobody knows my wife. She never comes here. Before the state of emergency was declared, my children occasionally came to visit, but no one knows my wife. I suggest you go and bring your belongings here. Relax here as my wife. Tell everybody who asks you that you are my wife, and talk less about yourself. I am going to ask for an off-duty so that I can take you to have a passbook. Why should you suffer? After all Kikuyus can have as many wives as they want. And having another wife is not a crime indeed, it is a bonus.

'Wacu, there is food in the house, tea, meat and everything. Just eat and relax,' Irungu continued.

The following morning, Irungu and Wacu readied to go to the

passbook office. She woke up early, put on a very nice dress, given to her by Captain Evans' wife. The dress was old, but very well made, and of good quality. Mrs Evans used to give a lot of her old clothes to Wacu, and although old, no one else had such good clothes. Wacu and Irungu took a bus to the Post Office, just opposite the labour office.

The female line was quite long, but the males' line was even longer. Wacu stood in the female line while her 'husband' who already had his passbook went to find out the proper procedure for his 'wife.' The rude, unsmiling clerk just shouted 'Put her in the queue and wait.'

Wacu took her place in line. Irungu stood by her side waiting to see the outcome. The line was long and the clerks were slow. The longer the lines, the more they got fed up, and the more they became difficult and rude.

'Next one!' This time was Wacu's turn. As she entered, Irungu followed too into the room.

'What is your name?' the clerk asked.

'Wacu is my name.'

'Wacu who? Don't you have a father, a husband or somebody?'

'Wacu Irungu,' Irungu answered.

'Wacu Irungu?' the clerk repeated. 'Is she a child that she cannot speak for herself? First of all you are a man, do you see the males' line? Look, all the passbooks for this line are green and marked 'F' meaning female. Do you want a woman's passbook?' the clerk mocked! 'Over there in the office is where men are lining.'

'I know, sir,' Irungu answered as he pulled out from his pocket his own passbook. 'I have mine, I just came to help my wife to get one.'

'Where were you born?'

'I do not know, my mother cannot read or write.'

'Age group?'

'*Ndururu* age group. The group circumcised when the five cents coin was introduced. Which year, I do not know.'

'Where were you born?'

'Maji Mazuri, Rift Valley province, my parents were working on a European farm.'

'Your husband's home?'

'Mangu, near Thika,' Irungu answered quickly as he was not sure if Wacu knew his home.

'Why didn't you come to get your passbook when your husband came?'

'He came from work, and he had no spare time to come for me.'

'Wacu?' the clerk looked her over with suspicious eyes. 'Tell me Wacu, why is it that you are more clean than any other wives I have seen. Your cleanliness, the way you dress, the way you shine, you don't look like somebody's wife. Your looks are like those of a free woman, or a working woman. Where did you get that smart dress?'

'I bought it from Burma Market, at one of the second-hand shops there, sometimes you can get some very nice cheap second-hand clothes.'

'OK, mother of eight children go to the next table,' the clerk shouted. 'Next.'

At the second table, Wacu's fingerprints were taken, each finger starting with her left hand then her right were pressed hard on the signature board, already smeared with purple-looking ink. Next, her palm prints were taken.

'This way.' The man pulled Wacu by her shoulder to direct her to yet another room.

Sitting on that stool, like Nyagah, Wacu had the narrow white hardboard bearing numbers hung round her neck. The numbers were 47927. It was hung below her neck.

'Look here! Here! Look at my hand! Don't you hear? Shut your mouth. Open your eyes! One – two – three.' Snap. Wacu, without knowing, smiled slightly, then furiously the photographer shouted, 'Who said you could smile? Stay still as I ordered you. Shut your mouth, open your eyes, look at my hand again, one, two, three.' Snap. 'Off you go, wait outside.'

The passbook took very long to process, but at last Wacu, wife of John Irungu, became a passbook holder. She was very happy, passing as a wife of Irungu, the bus conductor of Shauri Moyo Location, Nairobi. The 'mother of eight children', while the real mother, and the rightful wife was left in the village. You are very kind Irungu, Wacu thanked Irungu as they celebrated their unintended and unplanned marriage.

Wacu's passbook, number F47927, green in colour, was well-kept at the bottom of her box. Luckily, Wacu was always around her home. She was happy at the thought of how she managed to trick the officials. She laughed as she looked at her passbook stating Wacu wife of Irungu, the mother of eight children.

It was not long when during the daytime the homeguards were seen patrolling in the location. They were stopping and talking to people they suspected of not being residents of Nairobi. The sight of them made people go back to their rooms; some frightened children hid in their rooms looking at them through the key-holes and other open gaps.

One morning Wacu was busy washing at the communal water tap, just next to the communal bathrooms and toilets. So busy she was that she did not notice the patrolling officials approaching. Somebody tapped her back with a stick. She was shocked, stood and turned her face quickly. But ah! There stood a group of homeguards, the police, the chief and some policemen holding police dogs.

'Mama, where do you live?' an *askari* shouted.

'Over there, that block there, door six' the frightened Wacu answered.

'Do you have a passbook?'

'Yes, yes.' Wacu stared in fear.

'Where? Show us quickly.'

'It is there, over there in my room, well-hidden in my box. I can bring it in a minute.'

'In a minute?'

'Yes, yes in a minute. Yes, just wait.'

'Wait for what?' the *askari* repeated, calling two other *askaris* to take Wacu to the camp. 'Take her there; these are the prostitutes who stay here without passbooks. Prostitutes who feed Mau Maus. Take her away.'

'Please, I beg you. My passbook is just here, give me one minute to prove it to you. I am Irungu's wife. Please, please I have a passbook.'

'Do you think you have a passbook for decorating your house? Or your box? Every Kikuyu, Embu, Meru must always carry their passbooks.'

'I had gone nowhere. This is my house. Please, please, I beg you.'

'Shut up or you will regret it.'

Shortly, Wacu found herself being pushed inside the barbed wire compound. The door was locked and the guards left to go and arrest some more people. Wacu was barefoot, in tears, looking around her.

There were many people. On one side were women, and on the other were men. All sat not knowing their next destination. Towards late morning, the coolness of early day vanished. The sun began to warm, soon the heat was unbearable in the open detainees' camp. As the time went by, the heat increased even more. Inside there was nothing, no grass to sit on, not even a single tree that could shade the sweating detainees. It was all bare. Detainees sat on the empty ground, the sun burning them fiercely. The lucky ones were those who happened to be wearing head-clothes or men who had on their hats. They all sat quietly showing bitter faces, as people kept on coming in from all directions.

When homeguards were at a distance, the detainees explained to one another how they came to be arrested. Some like Wacu had done nothing at all, they even had their passbooks. Some were found having tea in another's room, others were outside their houses, coming from the toilets, bathrooms, shopping centres. But at the came compound, people whispered, one woman was said to have hidden suspected freedom fighters, others were hiding from the village, some were found without passbooks. All sorts of stories.

All day long the passbook offenders were given nothing to eat or drink. At about 4 pm Wacu was very thirsty. She sat there wondering whether her passbook had really solved her problems. 'Here I am, "wife" of a man I do not love. I'm with him for the sake of getting a passbook. Yet, here I am, locked in a hot camp as a passbook offender, when it was just inside my house. Was it really worth the trouble?'

Irungu was busy all day, he knew nothing of what was going on at his house. This day he finished his duty just after seven. Irungu came straight home. Coming near he was first struck by the darkness of their room. Would Wacu be in bed so early? Irungu asked approaching the room. The door was open. 'Wacu, Wacu, Wacu,' Irungu called. 'Where are you?' No answer. 'Wacu, Wacu, what is all this?' Irungu shouted. 'What happened?'

'Sh-sh-sh,' the man next door quitened Irungu. 'Don't make any noise. Many were taken to the chief's camp. She was washing clothes at the tap, and did not carry her passbook. And not she alone, they are all there. Irungu, we had a very bad day.'

Irungu lit the hurricane lamp to find the room was just as he left, using his torch he checked the water tap where the pail full of soaked clothes still stood. Irungu brought them back into the house and locked his room. As a bus conductor, he had a night pass, so taking Wacu's passbook he headed off to the camp. He explained where he worked. The chief rang the manager of Kenya Bus Services, and after a long discussion, Wacu was let out.

From that day on Wacu never left her passbook behind. Smart
Wacu made a little bag big enough for her passbook, then made a
strap around it, and from the day she was arrested it always hung
like a precious jewel round her neck. In the toilet, in the bathroom,
in bed, in church, everywhere, Wacu's passbook always hung
around her beautiful neck.

*   *   *

The problems of emergency continued to grow bitter. The Mau
Maus became more active, as the administration became even
tougher and more ruthless. Wacu remembered when one time she
went to buy vegetables at Burma Market, near 6 pm, just before it
closed. As she was approaching the exit of the market to go home,
she heard a pistol shot from the side of Donholm Road, near
Nairobi City Stadium. People ran from all directions, some falling
down as stronger men ran over them. Wacu too ran for her dear life,
she entered and locked her room worried and trembling. It was a
frightening sight. Wacu decided not to light her lamp in fear of
people noticing her room. Irungu had not come back from work,
and there was Wacu, worried and full of fear. Wacu did not dare
even open the door that evening. She could not cook in fear of
lighting her charcoal stove, the charcoal was outside the room and
Wacu alone would not dare even open that door.

Later her hungry and tired 'husband' returned home. Frightened,
Wacu opened the door after making sure that it was Irungu.

'Why are you in darkness?' Irungu asked.

'Sh-sh-sh . . . Get in bed and keep quiet. Things are not all that
good around here,' replied Wacu.

'What is the matter? Please give me food, I am hungry.'

'Keep quiet, please. Here, take this cold sweet potato and that is
all I have.' Wacu then narrated what happened when she went to
buy vegetables at the market. 'After hearing the shots I was scared,
everybody ran away and entered their rooms, and that is why the
whole location is in darkness. Please, Irungu I beg you to eat quietly
and get into bed.'

Sleeping was difficult under those circumstances. Wacu finally
fell asleep, so did tired Irungu. Soon after though, they were
awakened by very frightening bangs from the other rooms. The
sounds clashed over the whole of Shauri Moyo. Bang, bang, bang

spread like wild fire. The shouts of 'Get out' were heard, screaming children, wailing mothers and frightened males. 'Come out all of you, come out all of you. Come and stand outside your doors before we break them.'

Everybody, frightened, came out. There was no time to dress, in a room without electricity, and with no chance to light their lamps, they could not see their clothes. Shivering children stood outside naked, men in their underwear, some managed to get bedsheets, *kangas* or anything just to cover themselves. Wacu who was sleeping in her underwear managed to pull her *kanga* on. Her passbook still hung round her neck. Irungu wrapped himself in his blanket.

'Hands up! Everybody must show his passbook.' The authorities were making a house-to-house search, each room invaded, turned upside down. Dirty boxes were emptied to see what they contained, beddings were turned over. Everything was checked, as the owners stood in the bitter early morning cold, some covered, others naked.

'The shooters must be found. Any place you find guns, pistols, *simis*, or anything let the owners be arrested. Those the strict orders.' Even the babies were searched properly. The chief operation officer shouted, 'Take the napkins off, you might find bombs hidden in them.'

In Irungu's room they found nothing. Wacu's passbook hung round her neck while Irungu's passbook was held as they inspected him thoroughly.

'OK.' the inspector said as Irungu and Wacu returned cold to their room.

The following day, all the newspapers had the shooting news on the front page. The African Broadcasting Services also reported the incident as a special announcement: 'The terrorists had attacked a group of homeguards on Donholm Road, very near the African Stadium. The shots came from a fast moving car. The car was believed to be carrying five terrorists, one driving while the others shot through the car windows. The authority will leave no stone unturned, and those responsible are expected to be brought soon to trial. . . .'

Noon was the time for the Kikuyu language news; many people of the said bad tribes were eager to listen. Those without radios went to nearby kiosks where owners kept radios, or to their neighbours. All expected to hear important news. Soon the news started, as the groups of the tribes who understood the Kikuyu language listened attentively, some sipping a glass of tea bought at the kiosk, others just listening.

'Mau Mau terrorists have been active in the African Location of Nairobi's Eastern Division. New emergency rules have been introduced to block the Mau Mau terrorists' new tactics. The Governor of Kenya this morning met with the European farmers who had called on him to discuss the emergency problems.

'Yesterday just before the 6 pm curfew, a car full of terrorists opened fire on a group of homeguards near Nairobi Stadium. The homeguards were caught unaware on the crowded street, leaving one homeguard dead, two badly injured. The homeguards returned fire. The car was damaged and was later found abandoned in Nairobi's Industrial Area. The terrorists disappeared into the crowd. Responding to increased terrorist activity, the police have expanded their patrols and the Government has been forced to tighten their emergency rules. Lately many of the dangerous forest fighters' activities have been carried on by people who later escaped by bicycle, car or motorbike. Therefore from today:

(a)   no members of Kikuyu, Embu and Meru will be allowed to ride a bicycle or a motorbike without a special permit;

(b)   no car shall carry more than one individual from the said tribes;

(c)   members of the Kikuyu, Embu and Meru must report their movements.'

This sounded very funny on the radio. 'What will those who live near Nairobi, who sleep at home and ride to their places of work do? Do they have to stop working? Suppose one drives, do they want to say that one cannot give a wife a lift in case there are now two Kikuyus in one car?' All these sounded like a dream to Wacu until she decided to go home and see her sick mother. First she had to seek permission from the chief, and the local DO. Then she had to explain the day and the place where she wanted to go. Her passbook must be stamped that she is leaving Shauri Moyo, door six, with the name and signature of the chief and DO of Kariokor.

When she arrives home, before she sees her mother, she must report to the local chief and have her passbook stamped that she is there and at those hours. Again before leaving to go back to Nairobi, her passbook was to be stamped, and after arriving she must report that she is now back in her Shauri Moyo room, for yet another stamp in her passbook. The passbook was so precious, it had to have a special plastic bag, and permanently hang round Wacu's neck, like a precious gold chain, that green passbook number 47927.

Forced Communal Labour

Introduction

During the Emergency, the Colonial government instituted a programme of forced communal labour for the people left in the villages. During communal labour projects new roads were built, providing access to remote villages so that the homeguards could easily drive there for emergency operations. And with many men in the forest, and others in prison or in detention camps, the majority of those forced to labour were women. The trouble was that those in charge of communal labour were power-hungry people. Loyalists and homeguards misused their power, mistreating the workers. Women and the few men left would be forced out to work very early in the morning, before they had even given their children breakfast. To miss a communal labour, one had to give a very good reason. It was a deadly slavery. At forced communal work, people stayed there hungry all day long and had no time to attend to their gardens where they got their food. Neither did they have time to care for their cattle and goats; children were left unattended. In many cases such communal work was followed by a curfew. No one should be seen moving after six o'clock, but what surprised the colonialists was that despite this sort of punishment, the gardens still grew, the children were still getting milk, and the children continued to study. Many colonialists wondered how these Central Province women worked all day at communal *unpaid* work followed by a strict curfew, and yet still survived. The secret of everything

60

was that traditionally these women were very hardworking, and with the emergency problems they had learned to survive. That one spare hour from forced communal work, it was enough for a woman to weed one line of potatoes, collect water and vegetables or even firewood, things she could not do when curfew started. Things like cooking and washing she could do inside the house at night. Women during emergency time survived because of unity and the sense of sharing. Those in one village would share whatever they had, one would run to the river for water, the other would collect the firewood or vegetables, and each would exchange whatever the other did not have. They would still have a spare minute for weeding their gardens, and for feeding their animals. The chapter displays the authority the homeguards had – mistreating of innocent women – and the way the women were forced to work no matter what their physical condition, whether feeding a baby, pregnant, or sick. But the glory of the women was continued.

*   *   *

Phee! Pheeee! Pheee! The sound of the whistle was heard blowing wildly from the direction of the Chief's camp. Children sprang to their mothers' sides, sucking their thumbs and clinging to them for safety. The bigger children, trembling with fear, quickly hid themselves under the beds and behind the doors and some big boys even climbed up into *itara*. These homeguards came terrorising them and beating their dads and mums!

Pheeeeee! 'Come out of your huts, all of you!' Pheeeeee! the whistle went on. 'Men and women, young and old, don't say I never told you! Tomorrow at noon you are ordered to attend the DO's *baraza*,' Pheeeeee! 'at Kamuri Market! Kamuri Market at 12 noon! Friday at noon.' Pheeeeee! 'You dare not miss or you shall face the consequences!' Pheeeeee! 'Or dare be late. I would rather not repeat!' Pheeee! 'Tomorrow on Friday DO's *baraza* at Kamuri Market!' Pheeeeee! 'Market Kamuri, DO is coming tomorrow at 12 noon.' Pheeeeee! 'Young and old, men and women!' Pheeeeee! The headman went round the village announcing the DO's *baraza*. His hoarse voice was so loud that one thought he had a microphone, blowing his whistle, announcing the meeting and repeating.

This headman, Gikandi, was dressed in a mix of Western and African clothes. He was wearing a pair of khaki shorts, a sheet wrapped around his shoulders, a heavy second-hand overcoat needed for the up-country weather. On his feet he wore sandals made from old car tyres and on his ears he still had his *nyori* – earrings worn by Kikuyu leaders. His gourd, containing tobacco, was slung around his neck like a woman's beads and the *nguri* for plucking his beard hung alongside his snuff container. Under his arm was stuck the rather dirty-looking leather bag in which Kikuyus carry their personal belongings.

This strong, healthy looking, middle-aged headman was impressive and had a commanding voice. His authoritative behaviour indicated his confidence and satisfaction with life. His personality is usually found in well-to-do people who don't have to stoop down and beg favours from anybody. In fact, many people hated him for his arrogance and women would show their contempt by folding their lips in disgust, throwing their folded fingers in hatred as they shouted abuses at him and even spat like a poisonous snake in their bitterness. These expressions by Kikuyu women were signs of disgust and helplessness when face-to-face with somebody they could do nothing about. They had no power to act; otherwise their wish would have been to tear oppressors like Gikandi into small pieces.

They grinded their teeth and were ready to bite. But bite whom? And bite them if they dare! When and where indeed! So in the end, the angry women had to listen and obey.

Friday came, and Friday was a market day at Kamuri. In fact, this was a big market, and very popular because it was at the centre of the division, easy to reach and the main road passed through, though that road was not a good one.

Women worked tirelessly to prepare enough goods to sell, so they could buy what they did not have. Traders arrived to buy. Sellers and farmers brought in their products. Women looked forward to the market day. They came from all directions. Villagers from the lower part would bring pigeon peas and millet to exchange for bananas, arrow-roots and yams. The lucky ones who had farms by the riverside had their fresh maize and vegetables, but needed dry maize to mill for *ugali*.

Market day was a social event; a day to meet friends, a day to hear news, a day to gossip, a day everybody looked forward to.

Friday morning started as usual. Town traders arrived in their old vans to buy vegetables; women's voices sounded like thunder, bargaining their products by the shops surrounding the market. Traders were busy weighing in tin cans dry products, maize and a dozen types of beans. This too added more noise to the market.

Pheeee! The whistle was heard once. Those farmers from nearby knew what it was for, but for those busy traders from outside, the significance was lost on them. They thought it was probably one of those market *askaris* who kept an eye on what went on. The *askaris* were a bother. They whistled, shouted and interrupted for a lost child, for a woman crying for her lost basket, even for an elderly woman who might have misplaced her cowhide strap. People reported things to the head of the market to be announced. The outsiders went on bargaining, shouting and exchanging goods, vans hooting and driving around the market pretending they were ready to leave. Turn-boys shouting as they swung outside their moving vans 'We are going, be quick, we are off!'

These turn-boys were really amusing. They swung outside their moving vans like acrobats singing, shouting and cracking jokes, ever dirty with their torn clothes and old worn hats. Anyone else trying to swing like that would surely fall, but not the turn-boys. And as for accidents, they were the last to be hurt.

All the nearby villagers were already assembling under one big tree, as others continued bargaining and sometimes stealing unattended goods. Pheeeeee! the whistle went again, but the shop-traders were still buying unconcerned with anything else going on. Suddenly the *askaris* started harrassing them, hitting them with their clubs, pushing and abusing them. 'You town people, Mau Mau gangsters, must you come here to steal and spoil our innocent citizens. You have no regard for your leaders. You only sign for Mau Mau leaders. You stupid people, better obey before I handcuff you. Then you can call your leader to come to your rescue!'

One rich man was caught unaware just when he was counting some coins from his heavy money bag. His hand holding the money was hit hard by one *askari*, and the money was thrown all over the ground. Children tried to help themselves to the scattered coins until one homeguard came and struck at them and chased everybody away. And believe it or not, the *askaris* and homeguards helped themselves to the money. This was a lot of money; it could easily have been hundreds of shillings in copper and silver coins.

Everybody was chased to the meeting, leaving all their goods and uncollected money unattended. The *askaris* and homeguards helped themselves liberally while goats and cows strayed all over eating, tearing, and overturning everything.

Some butchers left their slaughtered goats half-skinned hanging in their slaughter-houses to attend the meeting. Only the turn-boys, their drivers and the passengers already inside the vans managed to escape this onslaught of trouble.

The troubles arose because the *askaris* tried to stop people too early, well before the meeting was to start. By 10 am these *askaris* had asked people to assemble when they knew very well the DO's party would not arrive before noon. An hour or two passed while they talked with the chiefs and the headman; while they tried to put others into trouble; while they showed off by pretending to be the most loyal, offering drinks and food, and, of course, a lot of gossip to the leaders. All this was an effort to keep people busy while waiting for the meeting. No one ever heard of a meeting starting on time, but harassing people went on long before a meeting.

If only those homeguards had anything of importance to do besides showing off, if only somebody could remind them that time was money, they could have made life a little easier even in those days.

All those visiting traders were thrown like heavy, unwanted sacks into the crowd. They sat packed very close on the hilly side of the market. Those lucky ones and early assemblers had a chance of sitting by the only tree, the best side of the shade was, though, reserved for the officials. Others had to sit close together in the blazing sun, their shaved heads glittering in the noon light. Women carrying their babies gathered green tree branches to protect them from the worst heat of the sun. Scarves were pulled to cover their faces and old torn hats were also pulled over the faces. Jumpers and coats were removed because of the heat. The crowd looked fed-up; and bitterness and hatred stretched across their tired, sunburned faces.

At the front of the crowd stood a cheap table borrowed from the nearby primary school. Around it were a few chairs for the officials. *Askaris*, the chief, the headman and the homeguards looked their best, wearing neat uniforms and helmets. They looked very busy moving here and there, pretending to organise the crowd although it was simply more harassment. They had to make themselves busy otherwise they would be regarded as unworthy of their job. These *askaris* kept on moving the crowd here and there, striking them on their heads, pretending to be disciplining them and asking them not to talk. They really enjoyed badgering people.

At 12.30, two Landrovers arrived. In the first was the DO and a few homeguards and in the other were the police. The drivers drove with an air of arrogance and the way in which they applied the brakes created real excitement. You could hear the screeching of the vehicles; tyres and the dust created made one think that a helicopter had landed.

The nervous chief, his headman and guards came to attention to be introduced. The way they stood indicated that we were at their mercy and any action they ordered, we were ready to execute.

The chief welcomed the DO, introduced him to the *askaris* who were all lined up outside the chief's barbed wire camp. Then the chief lead the DO to a welcome inside the hut, where leaders from the women's clubs were all standing by with tea and home-made buns. They really showed how clever and loyal they were, different from those dirty market women who were Mau Mau savages. These women who must have been in the homeguards' good books entertained the visitors with confidence. They looked cleaner than other villagers and, of course, happier. These women were the wives of the loyalists, wives of chiefs, headmen and homeguards. But other men or husbands were either in the forest fighting or in the detention camps, or in the village, jobless and unhappy.

Mrs Stephen, the wife of a DO, who was also employed by the Community Development Council and Mau Mau Rehabilitation Department, came to teach them home economics. Their embroidered table-cloths were displayed on the tables during the meeting.

At the tea party the buns and cakes made for the DO and his group showed that these women were, indeed, above the others. The party took a very long time, while the audience waited, thirsty, hungry and tired.

It was now nearly 2 pm when the chief came and announced that he was ready for the meeting. Headman Gikandi blew his whistle once again, then with his walking stick banged the table to make people pay attention to the guests. In a minute, the chief rushed back to the office and escorted the party to the *baraza*.

With exaggerated behaviour, jumping here and there, ordering sub-chiefs and *askaris* to leave the young children unmolested, he ushered the DO and his party to their seats. The DO was dressed in a khaki jumper coat, khaki shorts and sun goggles. He really looked too young to be a DO

The chief, addressing the meeting in Kikuyu, said how they must welcome the DO with happy faces and they would be treated as good people, but if they welcome him with their dull swollen faces, no one would listen to them. They must remember that the curfew had been lifted due to the valiant efforts of loyalists who had tracked down the few people feeding the Mau Maus. More should be like these loyalists and all would improve. 'So let us try to impress our guest today and things will be easier for us,' he concluded.

The young Mr David Clifford, District Officer of the Location, was called to address the meeting. Clifford was a young boy who had just finished school at Prince of Wales in Nairobi. He had never worked before, and his father was a wheat farmer at Mweiga in Nyeri District. This was his first public address; the only audience he had addressed before was in a school debate. His contact with Africans was limited to the *ayah* and servants at his parents' house, though sometimes during holidays he would accompany their farm manager on pay-day, when he would help hand over to the Africans employees the already counted money.

Nevertheless, he had learned how to give orders, and to expect them to be obeyed. He could speak a little Swahili and a bit of Kikuyu. The boy was really arrogant and hated these dirty black servants who thought they could take and manage his father's farm and even rule the country homestead of that great Queen.

Mr Clifford looked at those dirty bare-foot Kikuyus and wished he could shoot them all as they sat there sweating and full of bitterness, gazing at him. With a displacement of contempt he put his pipe on the table, then said: 'Today, I did not come here to give any speech. You have heard enough speeches from your chief, your headman and from others. But today as DO of this division, I came to give an order. The order comes from the head DO, who got it from the DC and the DC got it from the PC and the PC got it from the Governor and it is therefore something which has been decided from the top. The order is, obey if you want peace, or refuse to obey and you know what to expect. And I know you people think you are very clever and, of course, we have traced a few home-made guns made by your so-called clever sons.'

At this point he pulled out his sten gun, turned to the other side of the field where there was no one, and shot at the empty ground. 'Can your home-made guns shoot like that?' he asked. The frightened crowd shouted 'No', as a cloud of dust blew up from the shots. 'You people who don't even know how to make a match stick, think you can fight with those home-made guns! If that is what your leader tells you, then try and I shall show you. Can you? Answer me, can you?' Then bitter faces forced themselves to say 'No Sir!'

'Now! Now listen, all of you of Kamuri division. From tomorrow morning you have been ordered to do communal work. The first work to be performed is to dig a road between this market and Kagwa Shopping Centre. This road and bridge must be finished. We need this road to help trap Mau Mau terrorists. You all know this hilly countryside, full of valleys and bushes. Evil-doers find it easy to murder you. Women cannot go to the market or fetch water and your children on their way to school are in great danger. And, of course, the homeguards who are here to protect you from those Mau Mau savages cannot protect you properly. If such internal roads were here, at least jeeps could go through. Those girls who were recently kidnapped by terrorists and taken to the forest to fight have been rescued. Such roads can be used to patrol the areas easily, and those women who pass food to the terrorists can easily be traced. Look at your dirty and bitter faces. I can tell that you are not in favour, but as I mentioned before, the order did not come from me, it came from the Governor right down to me. This is just the first communal work. Much more will follow soon. No questions! I am sorry. Just action. Full stop.'

Then the DO turned to the chief and asked him if he had anything else to add, and also asked him to translate his speech into Kikuyu. The chief stood and translated everything for those who did not understand Swahili. He knew very well the the chief exaggerated the speech. Gikandi even added things which the DO did not say. That was to make his work easier. At last he concluded, 'All of you go and prepare for early Monday morning communal work. I shall be standing here at 6 am.'

'Six am, my God!' one young man shouted. 'The DO said 7 am.'

Poor young man, even before he finished, *askaris* went for him as if their blood was burning for action. They rushed towards the young man, manhandled him and pulled him out of the crowd. This young man was bitter, hungry, tired but also strong. When two *askaris* grabbed his hands, he bit their arms, and kicked at them.

This young Kamau was really stubborn. He refused to stand and refused to walk to the chief's centre. The DO's police came to the rescue of the *askaris*. One struck Kamau on the head with a *rungu* and he started to bleed badly, as all these other men were boxing and slapping him. Women screamed, men dispersed.

Kamau's mother shouted and joined in the struggle. 'Are you killing my son? Are you killing my son?' she screamed loudly. Kamau's younger sister, Njeri, heard her mother's angry voice and ran to see what was going on. Finding her brother bleeding and being dragged towards the chief's camp, she punched one *askari* and scratched him with her nails. As the *askari* turned to her, she put his fingers in her mouth and would not let them go. His fingers were almost severed. The struggle was very bad. Some people came to help; others ran away.

The chief blew his whistle to call other *askaris* for help. There was real commotion. People fought with anything they could find. Food was thrown all over. They overturned bushels of beans and millet, they struck at each other with calabashes filled with porridge. Stones were thrown from every direction. Cows and goats wandering through the market ran away frightened. Shopkeepers locked their shops not knowing what trouble might befall them. Children and women were crying.

This went on for a short time until Kamau, his sister and a few other young men who came to help had all been overpowered and locked in the chief's camp, half-dead.

Meanwhile the DO was nowhere to be seen, nor was his Land-rover. Only his frightened driver remained. Mr Clifford himself had sought refuge at the chief's camp as he could hardly trust anybody. This young DO was so cowardly that he could not wait. When he got back to his office, he dialled 999 and said that a very big trouble had started at the Kamuri homeguard centre. One young Mau Mau was shouting at the meeting, and at present the whole place is in chaos.

'Any casualties?' the man on the other side asked.

'There must be many; the whole crowd was fighting the loyalists. They were wild and even the women were battling. Send the Army or the GSU quickly to reinforce the homeguard. Let us pray that the chief is not killed.'

In a very short time, other homeguards, police, the Army and men from the famous General Service Unit arrived. The last were known as the '*askaris* who covered their heads with steel.' All were well-armed and had their tear gas ready for action.

When they arrived, Kamuri Market was dead. There was not a soul to be seen. People had dispersed. Some simply left their belongings behind at the market; the shops were closed and a few injured people were quickly removed to a small crowded cell. Cold water was poured into the cell to make the prisoners even more uncomfortable. This small unventilated cell had neither chairs to sit on nor beds to sleep in. It was nothing but a cold dark room, with a small window cut just where the wall and ceiling joined. It was the only source of light for the cell. Thanks were given to the builder who for some reason known to himself alone had left an inch gap between the floor and the door. Without that gap suffocation could not have been avoided.

After this disturbance, the whole of Kamuri Division was once again put under curfew. This time it was even worse, for while other curfews started at 9 pm this one began at 6 pm. This was unfair for busy farmers, and housewives who fetched water usually at six o'clock. Six o'clock was also the time to drive herds home, time to collect firewood, time to prepare meals, time to milk, and lock up the animals – but who could explain all this to the authorities.

The week following the DO's meeting was a sad one; the prisoners had nothing to eat all day on Friday and were given nothing at night. Kamau's mother was not allowed to see to his injuries or even to look in on him.

On the following day, Kamau's mother begged to be allowed to see him, all in vain. She asked to be allowed to pass some porridge to him. But instead one homeguard took the gourd and smashed it to pieces, spilling all the porridge. This nasty homeguard threatened to lock her in if she kept on creating trouble. They shouted at her and chased her away.

Kamau was the youngest son of this woman, Wambui, and being the last child, there was a special attachment to the mother. This was all the more since Wambui's other sons had died and her husband's whereabouts were unknown. He could have been killed; he could have been detained or imprisoned. Poor Wambui wished that she was a forest-fighter. This would satisfy her, even if she got killed, at least she would not die like a sheep, not like a woman, but like a man fighting for the land. At the thought of her son, Wambui looked in disgust at the *askari* standing by the cell door and refusing to let her know how Kamau was. In anger she said,

'Are you going to allow me to talk to my Kamau or not?'

'No!' the cruel young *askari* answered.

'Are you or are you not?'

'I said, no! Don't you have any ears? See a doctor if your ears are bad.'

'What is there left for me?' Wambui cried. 'What do I live for if you take Kamau? Take me too!' She screamed loudly and bitterly. She went near the jail and started to bang on the door, calling for Kamau: 'Kamau, my son! Are you alive? Kamau did they hurt you?' The *askari* shouted at Wambui and told her to shut up otherwise they would lock her in.

'Lock me in! What is there left for me? Lock me in now! Now!' she went on screaming. Wambui's screams had made her son angry. Kamau could not stand it any longer. He, too, started to bang at the cell door from inside despite being very weak. He was cursing those who locked him in. Open the door if you are a man! You cowards, silly stooges. Leave Mama alone!'

Others in the cell got hold of Kamau, they placed hands over his mouth as they all knew very well that this was not going to help get them released, but only add to their troubles. Others struggled to hold him firmly as this hot-tempered Kamau tried to rip their hands from his mouth.

By now their noises had attracted other homeguards at the centre. The mother was dragged to the homeguards' post where two *askaris* kept a close watch over her until the chief came. Wambui, whose nature was known as that of a quiet hard working woman had changed. To her, death was preferred to living the way she did. Threats to kill her were very welcome to Wambui; this would have solved her problems.

The chief came, as arrogant as ever, not knowing how much agony Wambui's mind was experiencing. He started to threaten her in his usual way.

'I have nothing to say.' Wambui said. 'What do you want?' Then Wambui threatened to strip herself naked in the presence of the homeguards, *askaris* and the chief. 'I am going to show you my body. I shall stand in front of you the way I was born – naked.' Then one *askari* slapped her and Wambui thought that this probably was the end.

Without another word, Wambui bent in front of these men, took hold of a handful of soil. She smelt it as if it was something precious, like a woman smelling a new perfume. She looked at all these bitter men wanting to put her into trouble. Then she smelt the soil in her hands again, put it in her mouth and chewed it. Then said, 'Whatever I go through, no matter how I suffer, I suffer for this soil. The soil is ours!'

One homeguard slapped her face again and the chief ordered another slap. Flushed with pain and anger, Wambui slipped off her top *shuka* and threw it on the ground. But by the time she was untying her skirt, all the *askaris* had run away. They disappeared, for an old woman stripping herself naked is the nastiest abuse one can expect from a Kikuyu woman. It is the worst curse one can expect.

'Leave the mad woman alone,' the chief said as he covered his face with his helmet, and turning facing the other way to avoid seeing her naked body. 'Let her go, but the son must be detained. Send him to *bwana* Clifford. He must be thoroughly interrogated. He may be able to tell us more. Maybe he can tell us where his brother is, for he may not be dead. I don't want to hear of this family again.'

Wambui left and went home shouting 'And feed my son.'

*   *   *

Sundays were spent quietly at Kamuri Division, and although unhappy faces were everywhere, there was no talk about what had happened. Women knowing of the next morning's forced communal labour worked hard to prepare enough food to last their children all day on Monday when no grown-ups would be seen at home.

Being late for communal work was not a joke. Kamuri people had experienced enough problems not to want to see any more. There was the 6 pm curfew, communal labour from 7 am to 5 pm, leaving just an hour for all their personal business. There was water to fetch from the river, firewood to collect from the field, vegetables to gather, yams, bananas and corn to be brought from the gardens for cooking, arrow-roots, and sweet potatoes to be dug, animals to be fed, cattle to be milked, gardens to be hoed, and, of course, children to be cared for. And all in just one hour before the curfew. What could be more inhumane? What could be more mad than this?

Monday morning at 6 am people began assembling at Kamuri Market. Digging equipment of all kinds accompanied them. Some shivered with the cold of the morning; barefoot, wetted with the morning dew, they stood waiting orders from the chief and his people.

Each person was asked to show what he had brought to work

with, and all were asked to see whether there was anybody left behind. 'Not everybody is worth coming to do communal work.' Wanjiru answered.

'Who is worth?' the headman asked, and without waiting for any answer, Gikandi put another question, 'and who has the authority to decide who can work and who cannot? Tell me, who is left behind?'

'You see my mother-in-law is very old. She is over eighty years, and for a long time has been suffering from backache, and I know she cannot stand for a long time, I left her behind.'

'Go home and bring her here at once!'

'She is also keeping an eye on my baby.'

'Will you go and bring her and your baby too! Quickly, bring her in a minute. Anybody else?' the headman went on.

'Only another woman, co-wife, she had just delivered a baby.'

'So what! Tell her to come here. It is for me to say who can work and who cannot.'

After these orders, anybody left behind was brought to join the communal work. Strong, young men and women were given heavy work to do, and those not very strong were put to light duties, such as removing soil from the road, cutting grass instead of trees. The strong ones were told to do the digging. The weak and the aged served as baby-sitters, but only by the communal site. They had to be there to answer Gikandi's roll call and sometimes they were useful for fetching water for the thirsty workers. There were lactating mothers, their breasts swollen and dripping with milk which should have been fed to their children, but they had to work. Expectant, underfed mothers had to cope with the forced communal labour. From 7 am to 5 pm, Monday to Friday, from the first day of the month to the end, the communal work did not cease. From the hunger and from the heavy work, many of the pregnant women had miscarriages. But that did not stop them from being forced to work day after day. The road was to be made.

It was not long before it rained. This heavy rain caused soil erosion, and it was worse in the hilly countryside around Kamuri. With the rains came another order by the chief. He said that the rains had come and the Agricultural Office had ordered him to tell the people that all the gardens must be terraced so as to stop soil erosion, and this would benefit the gardens with better crops.

'Better crops?' one man repeated. 'Better crops planted by

whom? We spend all our days digging you a road to make it easier for you to kill our sons. Our gardens are nothing but bush when they should be prepared for crops. Our cattle are dying for lack of care, our women are dry and weak, and you talk of our gardens.' This man, Kibunja, was manhandled, and badly beaten. He later died.

There was forced labour to make the roads, terraces had to be made in every garden and grass was to be planted by the slopes of the main road. Each day women had to fetch water for the homeguards' camps.

It is very hard to understand how Kamuri people survived. Children being helped by their elders, and at the same time sisters and brothers continuing to go to school. Women grew to like each other. There was no room for gossip, no room for back-biting, and no time to be wasted. People lost their selfishness, and the thought of hatred by women because they loved the same man disappeared. Care for others grew. Children were cared for communally, housework was done together. At five pm, when forced communal labour was finished, some women went to fetch water, others went for firewood, and yet others rushed to collect food from the gardens. All these activities were to be done between five and six. To be found outside one's hut after six meant certain detention.

These problems were so many that mothers were forced to become friendly with each other and care for each others' welfare. The one with food readily fed her neighbours and the children, the one with water gave to her neighbour; firewood was shared; milking was done for everyone. And yet, as tired as these women were, they used their spare minutes to dig their gardens, even if it was only for ten minutes, to grow vegetables and other crops. It is hard to believe how close to death the women at Kamuri were. It is unimaginable how they survived. Their legs and arms grew thin, their veins were showing all over and the women's softness was replaced by cracked, rough hands and feet.

The curfew time went on for a long period. Thanks to one old man at the African Court, women were never charged for breaking curfew laws. He used to say women were late trying to feed their children. They had no watches, and the only way they could tell the time was by the shadows and by looking at the sun. This made them make mistakes, and to be a few minutes late was inevitable.

Day by day the forced communal work continued. Before one task was finished, another one was ordered to be started. Kamuri villagers had suffered too much. They kept on, wondering why they didn't surrender their lives. The curfew and communal work did not pay for their children who were left uncared for each day. The DO and other officers used to come with camera to take pictures as gloomy faces dug the road of suicide, making easier the bringing of their own deaths. Visitors from overseas were brought to see the magnificent work, and the Colonial Office had reports supported by pictures that this was the spirit of self-help here, and not forced communal labour.

What a boldfaced lie! Officers got promotions and they got honours for fostering such high communal spirit. Women continued to have miscarriages, children got *kwashiorkor*, animals grew thin, the milking cows dried up. The dry flabby breasts could no longer suckle the infants who often died. Those who lived, laboured alongside their mothers. Sometimes they laboured with the few men who were somehow left behind. Thus at forced labour, the families toiled in speechless bitterness, while the London Officers commended them on their self-reliance.

Kariokor Location

Introduction

Kariokor was among the oldest African locations in Nairobi. It was first used to house members of the African carrier-corps (hence its name), during the First World War. The buildings, now torn down, were built in long lines. An entire family might live in one of these small rooms, often not more than 10 feet by 6 feet. In these tiny, ramshackle rooms, children would sleep on the floor or under the parents' beds. There was no privacy except for the odd kanga screen that people constructed. The toilets and water were communal and in sad shape.

The story of Kariokor is true although I have changed the names; I knew a woman who was smuggled out of Pumwani Maternity Home as homeguards were searching for her in another ward.

The account shows the life people had to endure during the Emergency. Even the most innocent were subject to constant suspicion and harassment. Homeguards played on the slightest irregularity to demonstrate their loyalty and power. These guards often got innocent people into trouble. Women and children particularly suffered. Pregnancy and illness were no proof against harassment, and husbands taken away to detention camps could leave families without money for food and housing or even lead to their repatriation.

The personal jealousy of homeguards put many people into problems. A well-to-do person could be put under suspicion of where he or she came by the riches. This could end in prison and the wealth be split among the homeguards. A beautiful woman could be framed so that the homeguards could get a chance to molest and rape her. Most people suffered through such people – and they had no one to hear their complaints.

*   *   *

'It is nearly 7 pm,' the chief of Kariokor location exclaimed, glancing at his big but cheap watch. 'Another night! Oh, what a life, and for how long will this kind of life continue?' he thought as he yawned, wiping his eyes as he woke up. 'Another night, and yet another night after night! In any case it was me who applied for this job. I was very proud when they announced me as a chief of Kariokor Location. And of course, they promised me a good job when we have wiped out all Mau Maus. I might be honoured or even knighted. And the way they trust me, I am sure I will be on the list of those who will be nominated to visit Britain next on one of those British Council Bursaries. Oh!, what a thought! Flying to Britain, and seeing all those wonderful scenes with my own eyes. London, House of Commons, and, by good luck, I might shake hands with the Queen of England.'

'Maria! Maria!' Chief Yusuf called his wife. 'Why didn't you wake me up? How can you let me sleep so much when you know I have a lot of work to do? You women, you never bother about your husband's responsibilities. The only thing you know is to eat and produce children, but even where food comes from, you don't care to know.' Yusuf said this as he started to wash his face and make ready for the busy night.

His shy wife apologised for not waking him up, giving him the excuse of feeling sorry for her overworked husband. 'I know you men think we don't think of you, you may go as far as thinking we don't care or we are not interested in your work. But I only wish you knew how happy I was when listening to you snoring like a bat who had suffered all night with sickness. Chief, for your information, it is I who covered you with the blanket. I closed the window, and ordered the children to play outside far from your room, and made sure that no noise was created nearby. I wanted you to sleep, sleep and rest, and you definitely needed that sleep. I was so happy listening to you snoring away like a baby! You needed rest after all these night duties.' The word 'night duties' reminded Maria of her lonely nights, night after night, all by herself. 'I live like a widow.' Maria said. 'True, an emergency widow! What a life!'

'*Askari*!' the chief called, ignoring all that his wife was saying.

'*Wapande*!' the *askari*, who was standing erect, well dressed in a khaki uniform, waiting impatiently for orders, saluted in reply.

'I want you to gather everyone here at once – homeguards, *askari kangas*, and all those who can help us. At once *askari*!' the chief called again.

'*Wapande.*'

'You must know that things are not well in this area, and I am already late. Quick go and ask all the homeguards to come. I have got bad news in this area. Tell them to be well equipped'.

Askaris came and lined up outside the chief's centre, standing erect and ready for action. After a few minutes, the chief stood outside the house, well dressed in his uniform. To this he added a heavy dark green coat, like those British coats worn during World War II, and his helmet. His subchief stood next to him, also in uniform and wearing a heavy coat.

'None of us enjoy going round all night,' said chief Yusuf. 'Where we would like to be is beside our wives, eating hot meals and relaxing with our family. I tell you now homeguard and all of you *askaris*, it is your duty to wipe out Mau Maus, wipe them all out and at once! Then you shall soon enjoy a good night's sleep, and a safe sleep – the safety we are all looking forward to. And listen all of you, yesterday I went to the DC's *baraza* where all chiefs in the district met, and I was ashamed to hear that the Mau Mau movement in my area is being reported by other chiefs, just because you people are lenient. You just walk up and down without looking into details, without being ruthless to those Mau Mau heathen. How long ago was a forest fighter arrested in my division? Tell me!'

'One week, chief,' one homeguard replied.

'Who spotted him? Tell me quickly!'

'A homeguard from Kaloleni area.'

'Where were all of you? That terrorist has been living in this area, fed by those women. You people can be killed by him, walking all day and night, but you never spotted him. Thank God none of you or your family got into his hands. Now you all know that there is a curfew in this area, a punishment they must get for hiding and feeding that terrorist. Now go, scatter all over, walk in twos, but don't go far apart. Listen to what is going on. Listen to the talks if you can. Headman, do you see that business man in Block 29? Watch him, check him closely. That big car of his – we do not understand how he bought it. Keep on checking his movements, and the whispers in his house. Such rich anti-Government men are very dangerous. Off you go! I, too, shall walk in one group. Scatter all over the location, and let us have results!'

By 9 pm, Kariokor Location was dead quiet. Many rooms had already put off their lights, and for those few rooms whose lights could be traced, they were not bright enough to bring life into the location. In fact, the area resembled a town of ghosts. Frustrated husbands lay down on their beds, tired and fed up with being surrounded by women and children all the time because of this curfew. What a life for a man! You cannot go out for a drink! You cannot go and chat with your friends! Wives, however, were happy to have their husbands back early in the house. Nevertheless, 9 pm was rather early, even for the eager woman.

This locking in of men made them frustrated, angry, despondent, fed up. Many said, 'I would have been better off fighting like a man in the forest, or suffering with other men in a detention camp rather than being locked into a one-room house, eating like a pig, like a ram being fattened for the marriage ceremony'.

Wanjiku was alert like all other careful women in the location. She prepared her family for curfew early enough, since no one is allowed even to open the door after the curfew starts. The trouble with locations such as Kariokor was that one family was living in just one room; father, mother, and all the children. Toilets, bathrooms and water were communal, and at quite a distance, too. A mother had to count carefully all her needs before curfew started.

There was water to store, charcoal to be brought into the already small and crowded room. And just in case one needed to go to the toilet, there had to be a bed-pan or an old bucket ready, but where could one use it? In a room with children, and children with the father, where do you keep that bucket? No privacy anywhere. Opening the door was a grave danger; you were never sure who was behind it. And if caught, no one had an ear to listen to your story; a homeguard's story was always right.

Wanjiku was careful. She made sure that food was ready early and that children were fed and sent to the toilet before curfew time. 'Better locked early than late.' was Wanjiku's motto.

For the careless ones, the time before curfew at 9 pm was a mad rush, trying to get the last needed – things like matches and toilet buckets. Some were never sure of the correct time, but who could run the risk of being wrong? In any case, by 9 pm every door at Kariokor Location was closed tightly. No movements were heard outdoors, and the narrow, tight spaces inside did not encourage movement. The dirty hurricane lamp or just a tin kerosene lamp known as *shika nitandike*, meaning 'Hold that I can make the bed,' cast only a dim light inside, adding to the fearfulness of living. The little gap in the wall, called a window, was well covered with charcoal smoke on the inside and full of dirt on the outside. Light had little chance of being noticed from outside, yet, no matter how dim the light was and what the outcome, schoolwork had to be done.

There was much to say, but not much to do during curfew time. Energetic men went off to sleep early like babies, frustrated and full of bad temper, missing other men's company and remembering their girlfriends whom they couldn't visit and here they were locked in a room with wife and children. Wanjiku's husband, and others like him, resigned to their fate, took off their shoes, pushed them under the bed, then closed the *kanga* screen and lay down in bed. This was the only way to get any privacy.

By now all the homeguards had spread out through Kariokor Location. Some started their check-up routines from Quarry Road, others from the market, yet others from Ziwani side. Homeguards, well armed as they were, were known to be cowards. Just one noise of dropping leaves, a dog's shadow, or even a dropped tin inside a darkened house would scatter them in all directions. They'd fix their guns, look around in a hurry, turning their heads here and there, ready to shoot any time. Young people used to mock them. Frequently, they'd drop something noisily and enjoy watching through the tiny windows as the panicky guards ran to call for help as if they had spotted something serious.

This night was quiet and still. Most in the Location were fast asleep, not knowing if homeguards worked outside their rooms. Some homeguards were tired and sleepy and not one of them welcomed these all-night vigils, patrolling in the cold. Some even sat under trees or on people's porches for a rest after 2.30 am when the morning cold began to make itself felt. Jakado, a homeguard well known for his cowardice, was on duty. He used to get excited for nothing, and had once or twice called the police for things just imagined. Now, early in the morning, he suddenly jumped up and ran as fast as he could towards the chief's camp. He was too excited even to remember that there were two of them on patrol and that he should have sought the opinion of the other homeguard. Ajaya, the other homeguard, thought Jakado hysterical and, indeed, no one would doubt it if he was.

'Here I am,' thought Ajaya, 'with him on patrol, and there he is running like a mad man without even warning me. Shall I follow him?' Ajaya wondered. 'What did he see? This stupid mad man did not tell me anything! I may run where danger is. I hate working with these half-mad people. Stupid people like Jakado! A woman would have been a better companion. Yet, you never know. I had better hide by the corner of the communal bathroom. Let me watch and see. If only he had pointed or whispered to me about what he had seen, this silly man Jakado! His stupidity, I have never experienced before. What a man to call himself a man, dressing in trousers like a man and yet getting excited like a woman and running off.'

By now Jakado had reached the chief's camp; a few homeguards were still guarding the camp and chief Yusuf was back, too. Many knew that though the chief started patrolling, it wouldn't take him long to go back to the camp where he could have hot coffee and a nap in his office chair.

'Chief! Chief! Chief!' Jakado came calling in an excited voice, breathing fast and sweating. 'Mau Mau! Chief, Mau Mau and oath. Come quickly! Quickly! Come, they are there! I have seen them with my own eyes! Quick,' Jakado went on as he was trying to reach the telephone to ring for the Army and the police.

'Sh sh . . . Sh sh . . .,' Chief Yusuf quietened the homeguard Jakado. 'Speak slowly man. I have told you this many times. They may hear you and even run away and make our oath operation ambush fail.' Chief Yusuf calmed Jakado as he took the telephone from his hands, than rang 999.

'Chief Kariokor here, Sir,' he said in his rather broken English. 'Mau Mau oath is being given in my location. I have scattered most of my homeguards in the location, and it is difficult to call them back without much noise. Also, I do not want many movements around; this might scare the Mau Maus, or we might be attacked. So please, Inspector Snodding, please act quickly. I suggest you come from Ziwani side. Ziwani people are rather quiet and religious. Act quickly, please.'

Jakado was by the door, ready to run out again when Chief Yusuf grabbed him by his coat and asked him to explain exactly what he had seen.

'This is Mau Mau oath, Chief, a real one. And they are so bold, they think no one is around. There is whispering in the house, the sound of whispering cries. I had a feeling that somebody was being strangled. It was a woman's cry I heard, and the sound of somebody dying. I am sure they strangled her. She must be dead, and a woman indeed.'

'What signs did you see?'

'Chief, these people are bold, so bold that they even dragged somebody from another room, and so bold that this man, whom I think must have been from the forest, had a torch. I wanted to shoot him, only to find my pistol was not loaded.'

'Then why didn't you strike him with your sword? Put it through his heart as I have taught you?'

'No, I feared that if I struck I would be killed. All these people taking the oath might have come after me.'

'And where is your patrolling companion?'

'You know, tonight I had this sleeper Ajaya, Chief. He never acts quickly. He argues first. I hate working with him.'

As they talked, Inspector Snodding arrived with a lot of well-armed police. Over his khaki uniform he, too, had on a dark coat and wore a hat. Inspector Snodding asked the chief to explain where the Mau Mau oathing was taking place. As the chief started in his poor English to explain Jakado's story, Jakado kept on interrupting. Inspector Snodding, answering in his poor Swahili, went on asking for more information about the oath taking.

Jakado really had nothing much to say but had no patience to wait. He proudly turned to Inspector Snodding and said, 'Come, come quickly! I will show you the house. It is over there! Follow me.' Jakado, feeling very proud of his night's achievements, walked briskly. By now he was shaking and sweating, ready to act. They pounded at the house door; the man inside hiding his rather dirty hurricane lamp, opened it. Jakado pulled his pistol ready to shoot but his hand was held tightly by Ajaya who had come up behind him. The man from the house asked, 'What can I do for you at this time of the night?'

'What can you do for us?' Inspector Snodding repeated. 'You can do a lot! You can give us the Mau Mau oath takers. And shut your mouth and get out of this room before I shoot you dead off!'

Jakado had given up his pistol to Ajaya, then in a temper he slapped the man so hard in the face that the man dropped by the door. Inspector Snodding landed his heavy booted foot in the man's stomach. And the chief added yet another slap and grabbed him by one leg to clear him from the doorway. One policeman holding his gun ready for action placed a leg on the man as a warning: 'Move, and you're a dead man!' In horrible pain, the man tried to open his mouth to explain, but no one was ready to listen. The answers were more and more slaps: a bleeding nose, two broken teeth and a swollen face. While some were hitting him, others were busy searching the room demanding everyone to come out with hands up. Others busied themselves opening his boxes, one hunted for any money in his coat pockets. Only ten shillings.

The real reason for the cries Jakado heard, no one seemed to care about. First children were dragged out, then another woman who said she was not a wife of this man and that her room was next door. As they went on interrogating this woman, asking why she was not in her room where her passbook was, another cry was heard in a bed surrounded by *kangas*.

'Oh ahh ... ohooo,' the cry went on. The woman being questioned ignored them and quickly slipped behind the *kanga* screen. The chief followed to see who was being strangled. To their surprise, they found themselves staring at a woman having a baby, and she was crying because she was in labour.

They sent the woman off to Pumwani Maternity Hospital, but only after inspecting just to make sure it was no trick. And no matter what the reason for the lights at night and the strangling cries, the interrogation had to continue. The children were ordered back to bed, but their battered father and the woman helper were ordered to the chief's camp where they were locked up until the following day.

On the following day the two endured more interrogations. The worse case was that of this kind woman who had been helping another woman in labour.

'What is your name?' Chief Yusuf asked.

'My name is Nyambura.' she answered.

'Where are you from originally?'

'I am from Location 14 of Muranga district.'

'I see. I say that is where Mau Mau run through forests like monkeys!'

'No, Chief, I never lived there,' the woman went on, 'since my childhood I have never lived there. My father parted with my mother and all my life I have been here in Nairobi. My mother used to live at Pangani then moved to Shauri Moyo.'

'Do you know that it is an offence for Kikuyus to leave their room even if it is to go to the toilet without a passbook?'

'Yes, I know that, Chief, but . . .'

'Shut up! I have not finished. Do you know that this is curfew time and no Kikuyus without a special pass are allowed even to open their doors after 9 pm?'

'Chief, can I explain please?'

'You are a cheeky woman,' the chief cut her short before she finished. 'I told you to shut up until I finish and hold your mouth tight, otherwise you will find your teeth on the floor just like the man you were visiting last night.'

'But, Chief!'

Slapping her face, the chief went on, 'Did you hear? Dare you open that big mouth of yours again! That is another very serious offence! And do you know that no Kikuyus are allowed to sleep in any house other than the one entered in the passbook without special permission? Now, my dear woman, count your offences as three – all three are very serious offences.' A few seconds passed and the chief repeated, 'Roaming about without a passbook, not observing curfew laws, and sleeping in another house without special permission; each one of these can send you to prison followed by detention camp!'

'Askari!' The askari came in and saluted. 'Remove this woman from here! Put her in cell 2. I think she has a lot to tell us and these city women brought up by prostitutes are very daring and dangerous. They know a lot!'

Now, the husband of the woman who had the baby had a swollen face, his lips were swollen and two of his teeth knocked out. This *mzee*, called Kamau, was carrying a bad headache and when he thought of his wife dragged out of the house in labour pain . . . 'Whatever happened, God knows. I only pray that she gets a safe delivery, God bless her. And my children? All alone in that room, no food for them. Oh God, those unreasonable *askaris*, whoever bore them? So unreasonable.' Kamau felt sad.

Jakado entered his cell. Kamau was taken before the chief; there he stood with hands folded over his chest, his face showing innocence and his eyes begging for mercy. Jakado gave him a sharp look.

'Yes, this is the one who was walking around with the torch knocking at other people's doors, and he dragged that woman from her house.' Jakado declared.

'But I was calling her to help my wife who was having a baby.'

'Don't tell me! You can explain to the magistrate when the time comes.'

'What about my wife? Has she got a baby?'

'That, too, the magistrate will tell you. Askari, put him in cell number three! Oh no, wait, that is too near to that prostitute. Make sure that they are apart so they cannot communicate!'

By then Kamau's wife had borne a baby boy. Kamau himself never knew. He worried and wondered what had happened to his wife. Pumwani Maternity never used to feed mothers who had babies, and Kamau worried what his wife would eat. Luckily, other women at Pumwani Maternity shared some of their food until a friend of Kamau knew and took care of her. Thinking of all these unnecessary problems, Kamau grew very bitter. In his heart he was not an active Mau Mau, though he had just taken a Mau Mau oath. 'If this is what an innocent man has to suffer, from now on,' he thought, 'I'm going to be Mau Mau number one.' After all, he was a Kikuyu and whether a Mau Mau, he suffered like the rest. 'Let them beat me, let them drop all my teeth. They will put me in prison, but I am sure this magistrate of theirs will go to sleep knowing that something was wrong.'

The day came for the case to be heard in the court. The magistrate was rather young, calm and intelligent looking. He was not one of those Kenya-born Europeans, those brought up by their parents to hate Kikuyus. He did not know Kikuyu or Swahili, so was not a local white. This was good, thought Kamau, maybe he then had some hope.

The magistrate read the charge: That on a certain night the defendant was seen moving outside his house. On that same night he allowed into his house a woman who was not supposed to be in there without permission.

With no lawyer to defend him, the defendant pleaded not guilty and requested to be allowed to explain to the magistrate. With the help of the interpreter he began: 'Mr Magistrate Sir, I am not going to cheat you that I have never taken a Mau Mau oath. Most of us have taken it, not because we want to, but because we are forced to, and so to be on the safe side we take it. But I have denounced the activities of the Mau Maus to the chief and the homeguards. In fact, I have never been involved in any Mau Mau activities, Sir.'

'Could you ask him to tell us what happened on Monday, the 10th of December? This is why he is here at present.' The interpreter translated.

'Yes, Magistrate Sir. On Monday, after my wife had prepared everything, and as usual put everything in the house before curfew time, we all went to bed. But around midnight my wife, who was pregnant and due any time, started to have labour pains. I woke up, lit the hurricane lamp and started to comfort her hoping she could wait until morning. At about 2 am, the labour pain was rather too much, and she told me she could not wait. Mr Magistrate Sir, I am a father of five, but I have never seen a baby delivered. So the only thing I could think to do was to call on Nyambura, this woman here, to come and help. As she was helping me, I heard somebody knocking on my door so hard like they wanted to break in. I offered to open for them, but though asking me questions, they did not wait for answers. By opening my mouth to explain, that is how my teeth got knocked out, my face swollen from being pulled by the collar like a goat being taken to slaughter.'

'Tell us what you have been doing. You are being accused, now that you want to accuse us. You can well do so later.'

'My story, Mr Magistrate Sir, is short, the reason why I broke curfew was to call the woman from next door to come and help my wife who was having a baby. My wife's was the cry these homeguards heard. It was nothing more than those of labour pains from my wife.' And then the magistrate asked, 'Nothing more?' The magistrate looking at this man decided to acquit him. There was simply no case.

Just as Kamau was walking out of the court a free man, Chief Yusuf decided to arrest him again for more questioning. In fact, they felt let down, embarrassed, by their abortive case; that is why they decided that they must hold Kamau as a suspected Mau Mau.

The cells at Kariokor homeguard post were not big enough and Chief Yusuf decided to transfer Kamau to a bigger interrogation camp at Langata to await further interrogation.

As for Nyambura, Kamau never saw her again. She too was

locked in for one week then 'recommended' for repatriation to her village. They branded her as a very dangerous woman, living in Nairobi pretending to be a businesswoman at Kariokor market.

'From now on,' said the chief, 'you are going to go back in the village!'

'Oh, no, Chief,' Nyambura cried. 'Since I was young I have never lived in the village! I know no other home than Shauri Moyo and Pumwani. I have nobody there, Chief!' She was in tears and continued crying. 'Who do I go to in my village? Send me to my mother's place. I know nowhere else. Please I beg you, Chief, please I beg you.'

'Chief, I beg you,' Chief Yusuf mimicked. 'Those clean fingers of yours are now going to scratch the soil making roads and digging fields. That plaited hair of yours will fall off by carrying water and firewood on your head. And these beautiful dresses of yours will rust and decay from carrying sweet potato leaves for the goats. Your pretty soft feet used to wearing shoes will crack walking barefoot. The heavy work will be good, reduce that fat in your body. And of course, the homeguards too will enjoy themselves having a well-fed woman like you around them. And that sweet smell of yours will soon change to a smell of cow-dung and smoke. Jakado!' Yusuf called. 'Be ready and make sure that this woman is dumped at the homeguard post near her home village.'

'My home is Shauri Moyo, Chief! I know no other home. I have nobody there. Please chief, please, I beg you. Let me take a few things from my house. Let me at least say good-bye to my mother, Chief! I beg you. I will not run away. My suitcase is unlocked, my business at Kariokor market is unattended! Please, I beg you in the name of God who created you. Please, Chief!' Jakado slapped Nyambura and told her to shut up as the Landrover rolled away from Kariokor post to an unknown place.

'What had happened to my wife, Wanjiku?' Kamau kept on worrying as he sat helpless at Langata interrogation camp. Many more bitter-faced men sat scattered around on the dry dirt of this barbed wire camp. The police remained standing, confidently satisfied with their achievement and authority. Their sharp eyes, full of hatred and looking here and there, showed how they were ready to satisfy their masters' needs. Kamau hated them; in his mind he was swearing, 'The day I am allowed out of that gate, if I ever am, I shall take all the oaths there are. I shall fight until the end. If they can arrest me for doing nothing wrong, I shall prove to them that one person was very annoyed with them. Here I sit, my children left in a house without care, my wife's fate in the hospital is unknown.' Kamau felt the gall rising inside him as he bit his lower lip. He scratched his hair and shook his head.

All this time the *askari* and guards were watching him. Later one came to where Kamau was sitting, bringing his leather whip down across Kamau's shoulders and, then, against his face. The mark of the whip left its sign. The *askari* shouted at Kamau, 'Behave yourself, or else . . .'

Kamau's bitterness was aroused further, but fellow detainees advised him that those who pretended to be good were let off easily and if he showed any bitterness he may suffer forever or even be killed. 'Just try to be friendly, Kamau,' he thought finally.

By this time, news of the ambush of Mau Mau ceremony at Kariokor Location was all over the place. One midwife at Pumwani Maternity went home for lunch. She decided to listen to the news, and to her surprise, she heard: 'This is African Broadcasting Service, Nairobi. Here is the news, read by Husein Abdallah. A new trick for operating Mau Mau oaths has been discovered by the chief of Kariokor Location. The King's African Rifles have discovered a Mau Mau hideout in Meru forest. A group of Embu women were found transporting food to the forest fighters near the Ena village. At Aberdare Mountain, the officials are still flying over the forest calling on all the Mau Mau forest fighters to come out of their hiding carrying a green leaf to show they have surrendered.' Midwife Eunice was very much concerned as she ate and listened attentively to the news as it continued: 'The Mau Mau operations were discovered at Kariokor Location by a homeguard. The chief of Kariokor Location and DO Snodding arrived on the scene well-armed. The oath operator gave the excuse that his wife was in labour. The man has been arrested and is now waiting further interrogations. The woman who was helping him has been repatriated to the village as a dangerous person. More interrogations of those involved are expected and officials anticipate more information to be forthcoming.'

Midwife Eunice listened to all the news and she wondered whether the news did not sound like the same story Wanjiku, who just had a baby, had told her. That her labour pains were connected with Mau Mau ceremony, and that both her woman friend who came to help her and her husband were taken away by the homeguards. Poor Wanjiku had thought that after finding that it was a baby being born, they would at least release her husband and the friend. She did not expect her husband to be arrested. He had done nothing. In fact she was very bitter that he did not come to see her. 'Shall I tell her?' Midwife Eunice asked herself. If I tell her she may be worried, and this is no good before she is better. Eunice looked at her watch and found that it was time to go back to work.

It was late in the afternoon when the telephone rang on Ward II at Pumwani Maternity Hospital. 'I hope they're calling to say they're bringing more patients today,' Eunice thought as she walked into the office to pick up the telephone.

'Hallo,' the male voice on the other end said. 'Pumwani Maternity Hospital? Is this ward two?'

'Yes, it is Ward two,' Eunice answered.

'Can I speak to the midwife in charge?'

'I am in charge. What can I do for you?'

'Listen carefully. I am Chief Yusuf of Kariokor Location.'

'Yes, Chief. It is Eunice here.'

'Oh, Eunice, I am glad it is you on duty.'

'Chief, don't tell me Maria is having another baby. How is she?'

'She is all right and your baby is a big boy now.'

'So, is she having another baby?'

'Now listen, Eunice. I am glad it is you on duty. I do not know whether you have heard about the problems we have been having here at Kariokor. Problem-makers are getting out of hand. Please, Eunice, you know very well. Try to help me.'

'Help you how?'

'Now there is that woman who was brought there the other night by my homeguards.'

'You mean Wanjiku?'

'Yes Wanjiku Kamau. She is very much wanted by the Government. She and her husband have been operating Mau Mau oaths. She is considered very dangerous. Her husband has already been arrested and she is wanted for interrogation.'

'So what do you want me to do? I am only concerned with her health and that of her baby. What you do after she leaves my hospital is up to you.'

'No, Eunice, I do not need you to do anything. But we would like to know when she leaves, then we can bring her here to answer a few questions. It is good for us as well as for you. Please try to co-operate. I have already spoken to the matron and she, too, is with us.'

'All right, Chief.'

Midwife Eunice began her afternoon rounds. Soon the visiting bell rang and relatives of the mothers flocked into the wards. The midwives-in-training were busy showing eager husbands and relatives the newborn babies. In the meantime, midwife Eunice stood quietly looking through the window observing the visitors as they flocked in carrying presents for the new mothers. Through the glass separating her office from the ward, she could see Wanjiku looking sad. Wanjiku was alone. Some visitors, noticing Wanjiku's loneliness would go and say, '*Jambo Mama.*' This made Wanjiku even sadder. No visitors came to see her that afternoon. She then decided to cover herself with blankets as if she was asleep until she heard the bell telling visitors to leave.

The bell rang and all the visitors were chased off by the *askari* for they were always slow to leave. During this time, Eunice was thinking about the chief's telephone call. She remembered how that poor woman was brought in by the guards, the baby almost dropping out. There she was, not knowing where her husband was. Since she came to the hospital, no one had brought her anything. Poor Wanjiku, she did not even know where her children were, neither did she know that her husband was in the news at lunch time; that he was awaiting interrogation. 'Poor girl. And for me to allow her to get into more problems! Not me! I would rather die! I am not going to betray a woman like myself. And a mother, too – an African mother. Not me!'

After all the patients had finished their dinner, midwife Eunice went round handing out medicines and giving injections to those who needed them. Coming to Wanjiku, she asked her to wait in her office for there was something she wanted to check on her health.

In the office, Eunice faced Wanjiku looking directly at her, point blank. 'Listen, Wanjiku,' midwife Eunice said, 'I understand that things are not well at Kariokor Location.'

'Have they arrested him?' Wanjiku asked with shock.

'No, not about arrests. In any case, even if he was arrested he was one of many arrested. The rich are detained, so are the poor, the educated and uneducated. Once you are a Kikuyu, Embu or Meru, we all know one can anytime be inside that cell.'

'After all,' said Wanjiku, 'he had stolen nothing at all.'

'Now, if your husband is locked in, that we cannot help. But what I want you to know, things are not good, even for you. You see, Wanjiku, you have just had a baby, and we must protect you and the baby. And the other children? Leave them alone for a while. Listen, Wanjiku, you must be brave and you must know that what is going on is not happening for you alone. You must face any problems bravely, and give us a chance to use our heads. You are weak and you still need care as well as your baby. Now, Wanjiku, because I am from one of those unpopular tribes, and a woman like you, that is why I am telling you this. I just had Chief Yusuf from Kariokor Location on the phone.'

'What does he want?' Wanjiku asked without waiting.

'Don't get worked up.' Eunice said to her. 'This can get me into trouble too. You know I refuse to use my Kikuyu name. I prefer using my Christian name. I make people wonder where I came from. Many don't even know I am a Kikuyu. My father was working with railways at Mombasa station and I went to school in Mombasa and learned my midwifery at Lady Griegg Maternity, Mombasa. My Swahili is very good and there is no trace of a Kikuyu accent, and I shall call myself Eunice John. Many people think I am a Taita or a Giriama. I never say anything. So, Wanjiku, listen. I want you to run away from here because these people want you for questioning, and you know even if they do not find anything wrong with you, some guards are never satisfied before they lock you in.'

'How can I run away? And will they give me my clothes from the stores?'

'Clothes are nothing. I can give you my own clothes or even give you a nurse's uniform.'

'What about the gate man?'

'Don't worry for that one. We can just send him to check on something and at that time you can just go. In any case, the man at the gate is himself a Meru. He is a Meru Muslim; his Muslim name is Saleh Mohammed. These are those Majengo people, but I have to check whether he is a Mau Mau supporter, but I suspect he is. To be on the safe side, we'll just send him off for something.'

The next day, Eunice began her night shift. At 8.00 pm, she started working after taking a report from another midwife. At about 9.30 pm, women were asleep and lights went off. Eunice then called Wanjiku to her office, gave her another dress to wear and wrapped her baby nicely in a blanket ready to leave. She, then, went to the gate and asked the man there to check around the building as she had heard some funny noises. When he went to the other side of Pumwani Maternity, Wanjiku walked through the gate and disappeared.

Poor Wanjiku did not dare go back to Kariokor Location to see her children. Carrying her newborn baby she walked in the dark, hiding behind buildings and by the Nairobi river. She walked by the river until she reached Bahati. Bahati was well known for its Mau Mau activities, in which only Kikuyus, Embu, Meru were allowed to stay, and no one of the other tribes was allowed to visit them. This made Bahati very safe for Mau Maus as no one would ever disclose the whereabouts of anyone who was hiding there.

Wanjiku entered the location slowly going through the fence, and entered some friends' room. She told them all that had happened and they told her what had happened to their husbands. Wanjiku was hidden for several days at Bahati. Other Mau Maus helped to send food to her children at Kariokor.

Chief Yusuf kept on ringing the maternity ward, asking when the Mau Mau mother would be discharged, until the matron discovered that Wanjiku had disappeared. A search for her was mounted; the African Broadcasting Service and the newspapers announced that whoever saw the woman should make a report to the nearest police station or the Homeguard Camp.

Wanjiku bought a black veil like a Muslim to cover her head. And to anyone asking her name, she said, 'Fatuma.' She continued hiding, being helped until when her hisband was released. He was later repatriated to his home village, where Wanjiku and the children joined him.

Komerera – Lie Low

Introduction

Komerera is a Kikuyu word meaning 'lie low, keep out of trouble'. People used it as a slogan during Emergency time. The advice most often heard was *komerera*, to keep quiet, stay out of the way. Even the richest Kenyans were advised by friends to keep quiet, it did not matter who you were, talking would still get you in trouble. And then who would take care of your business and family?

This is a sad chapter, telling of three women from rural Kenya who could not *komerera* and walked about 100 miles in search of freedom and news of their husbands in Nairobi. Without official permission, they were forced to travel with great caution through dangerous byways of the country. If caught they faced both assault and imprisonment. Yet the forced communal labour at home and knowing nothing of their husbands was worse than the dangers they might meet in their flight to Nairobi.

Here I demonstrate the determination and cunning that women demonstrated during the revolt. I also try to convey in this chapter the strong feelings all had for the soil, for the land taken by the whites. The soil was their lives, giving them strength as they grasped handfulls, smelling it as if a precious perfume and repeating: 'The soil is ours.'

The story illustrates the extremes of suffering women endured when separated from their husbands, working desperately to keep their families together and being forced into more

92

and more communal labour. Tears and disappointment became the order of the day. Yet out of each person's terror and frustration we see growing a sense of community, of the need to work for all if any one was to survive.

*   *   *

It was early morning when a few select young women carrying their tins and barrels ran down the hill to fetch water for the homeguard camp. After this chore, they joined the others at the forced communal work.

The homeguards had chosen these young women for their strength, health and beauty, but these were never enough for the daily uncertainties. The homeguards' harassing soon drew sadness on their once happy faces.

These women had children to worry about, and their food, their clothing, and the daily forced communal labour. Their skin roughened, and the early morning dew hollowed their feet with cracks as big as those of black murram soil during the dry season. Lack of nutritious food made their skin peel off like a snake's. Worries of their children's future, worries of their husbands in detention camps, worries of those fighting in the forest, even anxiety over those lucky ones working in Nairobi, no communication with their husbands or sweethearts, wives living like widows.

Nduta felt emptied as she filled her water barrel. She then pulled it up by the side of the river, closed it tightly with a cork, wrapped it with a cow-hide strap and, without asking any help to lift it on her back as other women did, swung the barrel up. With one part of the cow-hide strap in the middle of her forehead and the other supporting the water drum, she silently started to walk away.

'What is the matter with you, Nduta?' Nyakio asked.

'What is the matter?' Nduta repeated. 'Just leave me alone.'

'To leave you alone? This is not a time to talk of leaving anybody alone,' Nyakio continued as she stretched her hand and stopped Nduta from leaving them behind. 'Nduta, you are not yourself this morning, you seem worried. And you must tell me what is the matter with you. Put your barrel down and tell us what has happened that you are behaving so mysteriously early in the morning? Tell us the problems you have that others don't! This is war time, Nduta. That is what you should remember. Then tell me now what has happened, why are you so miserable? Tell us, which one of us has annoyed you?'

'Leave me alone.' Nduta went on as tears ran down her cheeks. She pulled the corner of her head-scarf and wiped the falling tears. Her nose too started running as she stood still, looking at the water flowing down the river Kabuku. Nduta got hold of some soft *maigoya* leaves and used them to wipe it.

The other women got worried too, and Njeri pulled her slowly to another side and begged her not to behave like a child. 'This is war time.' 'We know why we are all going through these problems, at least we are lucky to be alive so that we can comfort our hungry, lonely and miserable children. And unless you have something especially terrible that you are going through, the suffering is common to all of us, Nduta. Do you have any special problems?'

'Problems? Which one do I start with? You married before me and at least your husband left you with four children. Nyakio has three sons and two daughters. You have had time to be with your husband. But as for me – what was the point of having a husband? My husband is not even in the forest fighting like other men. He is not killed so that I can forget him. The last time I heard of him was when he was working for a European, as a house-boy, somewhere near Dagoretti Market, that big area where those rich Europeans lived.' Nduta started weeping afresh and this interrupted her description of where her husband lived.

'That sounds like near Mtoni,' said Njeri. 'It is also known as Karen. Yes, it is Karen! I just remembered the Dagoretti Market where I used to go to buy some food. Now, believe it or not, after I married my husband, that European said he does not want any visitors, or even relatives near his home and anyone ready to work for him was forced to send his family away in the village. That *mzungu* said visitors can bring Mau Mau into his compound; except for his employees, no one was allowed nearby. I was just newly married and five months pregnant, and since then three years have passed and I have never again seen my husband. And my husband has never seen his child, neither does he know whether I produced a boy or a girl, or whether this child has died. This is a living man, just there in Nairobi. I wish he was fighting in the forest, maybe he would have been killed or detained. And here I am I've had just five months of married life. I need another baby. In case my husband is killed, at least somebody may revive his name. And here I am destroying my youth by carrying water for the homeguards, cutting wood for them, being scolded, doing communal work, being raped by these ugly fat old men! I have to see my husband. I must see him! I have to! No matter what happens. I miss him, and so does our child. I want him!' Nduta went on.

Nyakio then recalled that she too had a problem. Her husband was also somewhere in Nairobi. He was a labourer at the Railway goods shed. His mother was a dying woman, and her constant cry was: 'I shall die before I see my son. God help me live until I know where my son is.'

'My mother-in-law never stops crying,' said Nyakio.

'Me too, I have problems and wish to see my husband, if I can ever trace him,' Njeri began. 'The last time I heard of him was that he was employed as a head cook at one of those European Clubs. The trouble is that I have never visited him openly, as none of them allowed a wife in the servants' quarters. And when I went to see him I used to hide in a friend's house during the day time, and at night, I would sneak to my husband's house, unnoticed, like a thief, leaving early in the morning before they wake up, or waiting till *memsahib* was either out shopping, or until the afternoon when she usually took a nap. The trouble is I could never take my child there. I once made him lose his job by my mere presence when *memsahib* heard my child crying. And now, do you know that piece of land where I live is not completely paid for, and the owner is really bothering me. He has threatened that if I do not complete the payment in two months' time, he will return what was already paid and take back his land. Think of that! That piece of land is my only wealth, it is the only place where I can get bananas for my child, the place I grow beans, maize and sweet potatoes, without that land I am as good as dead. And now, Nduta, as you see me here, I have sent several messages for my husband, but have received no answer. No one knows whether he gets the letters which my son writes. This man of mine could have been killed, he could have been detained, or he could have been taken to the forest, or he may be just hiding somewhere – who knows? But I must keep on living and hope that one day I will see him again.'

'Then what shall we do? Shall we sit here with all these problems without knowing what to do next?' asked Nduta.

'Not me,' Nyakio answered. 'I was born once and I shall die once.'

'Then what do you think we can do?' Njeri asked.

'Sh-sh-sh-sh . . . Please speak softly and let us walk back slowly, planning as we walk. We don't want anybody to suspect and don't forget Kikuyus are not allowed to be seen talking together. These stooges always think we are planning on how to attack them. And you, there Njeri,' continued Nyakio, 'you have to keep your big mouth shut. I know you are a coward, so coward that if a homeguard slaps you once, you will start crying and tell them all. So promise you will never say anything.'

'I swear,' Njeri responded.

'Swear by your father's name who bore you that you will never disclose anything.'

'I swear, Nyakio, this talk will never go beyond us I even swear by my own son. Let God kill me if I ever say anything!'

'And you, Nduta?' Nyakio asked.

'Me too, I promised when I took the oath I shall never disclose!'

'Now ladies, as I said before, no one who was born will live forever, anyone will die, and die once. After all none of *iregi* age group is still surviving. Let us try to go to Nairobi and look for our husbands,' said Nyakio.

'But who will get us passes? You know, no bus conductor will allow you to get on without passes, they don't want to be put into trouble. And there's that law that no car can have more than two Kikuyus, men or women. No one will give us passes! And when we get there, we are not allowed to sleep in anybody's house without reporting to the authorities there, and proving to them that we have been allowed to leave our village. We must also have reasons why we must see our husbands, and give the name or house number of where we're going to stay. I don't see how we can make it. I prefer at least to be comforting my child at home than try to do things which I know are impossible.' Nduta looked relieved that she could think up so many reasons not to leave the village.

At this time Njeri interjected, 'There is one new homeguard who likes to talk to me. I cheated him that I am not interested in Mau Mau, and he believes me. If you allow me I can try to get passes from him. I know he likes me, and he had promised that if there is anything he can help me with, just to let him know.'

'You are very stupid!' Nyakio whispered. 'That is how you make things leak, and that is why I even fear you knowing too much. You women, you seem not to know what we are going through! These homeguards are only interested in our bodies, the beautiful young bodies of us lovely women, but by any chance if you go on their wrong side, that is when you know you are dealing with a homeguard.'

'Now Njeri, it is OK to have a pass. Then you can pass through homeguards, police, and the army. But you forget that the worst of them all are the forest fighters, and if we travel with passes, that is a clear indication that we are friends of the Government and we could be spies, homeguard or anything else, then what will happen to us? I prefer being in the good books of the fighters than in these books of the homeguards.

'Sh-sh-sh-sh . . .' Nyakio went on as she tried to quieten the others: 'We are now near the centre, see all the people are assembling for communal work! We cannot have another meeting; I think when we go home this evening, you should prepare for a Nairobi journey! Cook as much food as you can. If you have any money, bring it with you! Don't carry anything bulky, just a barrel of water strapped on your back. If you have a few dresses, wear them – three or even four! Also you should carry a *panga* for weeding or a *jembe* for digging, and market basket, it will be alright. Don't tell anybody, only your mother if she is told not to talk.'

'Where do we meet!' asked Njeri.

'Just here: Come earlier than today!' said Nyakio.

'We cannot get there without getting ourselves arrested,' said Nduta. 'How can we pass all these homeguards and forest fighters? Where are we going to spend nights? What do we eat and how do we know whether we shall be able to meet our husbands?'

'Nduta, you are the one who had tears in your eyes a few minutes ago, crying that you need another child, that you are missing your husband. Do you want to try to come with us or not? After all, is this digging, going hungry everyday, better or easier than walking to Nairobi? For me, I am leaving and if either of you want to join me, so much the better. We have to plan and, as I said, we die just once. If you want to come then let us be here tomorrow all prepared; leave the planning to me.'

The forced communal work went on very well, the bad and unkind homeguard, Kamenju was sent for some meeting or another. Mwangi the officer in charge, at least was human. He used to allow the women to rest, feed their children and even used to send people to fetch water for the very thirsty workers. Another thing which made Mwangi very popular was that he would give women a set piece of work for the day and if one was a hard worker and quick enough one was allowed to leave once he was satisfied with the work done.

This day each woman was given a piece of road to dig. Nyakio, Njeri, and Nduta were a little bit late as they had gone to fetch water for the homeguards' camp. They also said that one of the barrels lost its stopper and the water poured out and Nyakio was obliged to return to the river to fill it. This being a lonely valley and so early in the morning, the others had to wait for her.

Mwangi understood the problems and excused them for being late so they were asked to help on removing soil from the piece of road which had been dug the day before. Njeri, Nyakio and Nduta were very happy as this gave them a chance to plan more as they were at a distance from the others. And they indeed planned. By lunch time they had almost finished clearing the soil. They were really hardworking, that everyone knew.

Then Mwangi called Nyakio and asked her to go for drinking water.

'Oh yes,' she said, 'but I do not know why I am so scared of passing through a lonely bush path alone. We are nearly finished, why don't you let us clear just this which is left, then we three can go for water?'

'Very good, Nyakio,' Mwangi said. 'No wonder your mother named you Nyakio – as *nyakio* means a hard worker, and I like you because you are very intelligent.'

'Thank you for your compliment.' 'I am not joking,' Mwangi said 'And if you continue proving to us how cooperative you are, I shall soon recommend your name to the chief that you should be put in charge of other women and make them work like you do.'

'Thank you, Sir,' Nyakio added as she carried her load of soil to dispose of it.

When Mwangi turned to the other workers who were watched over by the *askiri kangas*, Nyakio pinched Njeri and Nduta, she winked at them, and using her fingers, gave them a sign of departure. Nyakio also whispered to them, 'Take your *pangas*, your dirty baskets and off you go!'

As soon as they left the working place, Nyakio called them together and said, 'Do you know girls? This is the best time to escape, everybody is busy making the road – all the men, homeguards, chiefs and all the informers are busy. They know no one is in the village, and therefore not worth guarding. After all, the whole location has been very quiet. No Mau Mau incidents! So don't be fools. This time is better than early in the morning when we shall meet a lot of people going for communal work, and we might be suspected.'

'But I have not washed my dirty clothes,' Njeri cried.

'Wash dirty clothes?' Nyakio repeated. 'Take them as they are! Wash them for what? Don't forget we are walking from Rwathia to Nairobi, going through the bush.'

'What about food?' Nduta asked. 'I have nothing in my house.'

'I have some boiled sweet potatoes,' Nyakio replied, 'and I think if the children didn't finish them, I might have one or two boiled arrow-roots.'

'I hope my mother-in-law put the beans on the fire as I requested her to do.' Nduta commented. 'If she did, then it might be ready. Otherwise, she always keeps some sweet bananas at her old bee-hive.'

'I think it is high time we went.' Nyakio said.

'What about the money?' Njeri inquired.

'Money for what? Run home quickly, put on as many clothes as you can. Carry them on your body. Don't pack anything. Bring any cents you can put your hands on, and just tell these old ladies that if they don't see you not to worry, you have to run somewhere. Tell the children that you are not dead, you have to go and get them something good to eat, and they should pretend to the homeguards to be very sad, and let them suspect that we have been abducted by the forest fighters. That will help our families from being victimised by the homeguards and the Government.' Nyakio gave her final directions to Nduta and Njeri, and they all moved quickly back to the village.

By 2 pm, Nduta and Njeri, led by Nyakio, each carrying a water barrel and a dirty basket for moving soil, left barefooted from their village for Nairobi, the journey which would take them through the forests, crossing big rivers, climbing steep hills, walking down steep valleys in search of their husbands.

Nyakio led the other two with confidence. She thought carefully on the possible dangers and problems. Her intelligent mind made plans for escapes, and she told the others that if they met any problems, just to keep quiet and let her speak. 'Pretend you are shy.'

'We have a saying,' said Njeri, 'Once you undress to take a bath in the river, whether you find the water ice cold or not, the best thing is just to take it.'

'Let us go!' announced Nyakio.

Young Nduta, still in doubts, followed quietly as Nyakio led the way. The afternoon sun shone brightly as the three women followed a narrow footpath down the hill. The heat of the sun was not all that brutal; their home was high up near the Aberdare forest. But the many dresses they had worn made them feel heavy and sweaty. The three ladies walked briskly and without a word to one another. They crossed the river Muthioya, went up the hill, down the valley, and crossed several streams and rivers. All the time they avoided highways and crowded roads in fear of being spotted.

Avoiding crowded roads made their journey even more danger-ous, particularly when they walked at the edges of the forest, and when they crossed many large rivers without proper bridges. And of course, passing through narrow roads where they had never passed before and at the same time too scared to dare ask for directions for fear of getting into trouble.

At about 4 pm, the sun was getting cool and they had just crossed a little clear stream with cold, blue water as they left the Nyandarua rocks, better known to Europeans as Aberdare Mountains. They unloaded their barrels of water, went to the river, and, using their hands, drank a lot of water. They were really thirsty. Two of them also cooled their clean shaven heads with the cold stream water. Nduta was the only one who had not shaved her head, and she did not like to wet her hair. She just washed her face, and as hungry as she was, she opened one basket, pulled out a sweet potato, peeled it with her dirty *panga* and started to eat it. As she sat there eating while the others were still enjoying pouring cold water on their heads, she saw two men peeping at them from a bush just near where the others were washing. The sight was so frightening that her sweet potato dropped on the ground. For a moment she did not know what to say. Very frightened and shaken, she jumped into the stream without caring about her clothes getting wet. She went between Njeri and Nyakio.

'Men! men!' she went on as she held both of them tightly to her sides.

'Where?' the shaken Njeri asked.

Nyakio slapped Nduta, pushing her off her waist. Nduta fell in the water with her clothes.

'Stupid fools, bring your barrels and let us fill them before dark. We have to go and cook for our children,' Nyakio spoke loudly. She was pretending that they had come from a nearby village to get water. Nyakio untied her barrel and started to fill it as she sang *citiro*, happily as if nothing had gone wrong. The hiding men came closer. They had long hair, plated heavy and thick. Their clothes were torn and the sight of them was really frightening.

'Any insects among you?' the first one asked.

'No insects,' Nyakio answered.

By then Nduta was holding Njeri very tight, her whole body shaking with fear. She really looked terrible with all her clothes dripping wet. Njeri's tears coursed down her cheeks. But Nyakio, hearing that first question from the strangers and seeing the way they looked and dressed, knew immediately that they were forest fighters. She smiled and showed confidence and hope in them.

These fighters too laughed and hugged each other when they heard Nyakio's answer which showed that she was a Mau Mau supporter. She answered the sign very confidently. The forest fighters came closer and although Nduta had only spotted two there were several of them.

They had come to hunt something to eat. Their food suppliers had not fulfilled what they were supposed to do. There was neither food nor messages at the appointed place. Nyakio felt sorry for them and offered what they had brought with them. Luckily they had enough beans, some sweet potatoes and ripe bananas. The men ate some and left a bit for the women.

'Pass me some water,' one fighter called to the fear-shaken Nduta while laughing at her cowardice. Nduta turned and cut an arrow-root leaf, folded it nicely, filled it with water and passed it to the thirsty frightening man. As he drank the water supported by Nduta's hand, he warned her, 'Your cowardice can land you into trouble. By the way, how many oaths have you taken Nduta?'

'One,' Nduta answered.

'Just one? Why is it that living in a bad village like yours you only took one oath?'

'I have not been married for a long time, and I was living with my husband in Nairobi. My husband's employer was very bad and a homeguard leader of the Europeans. He had a very close watch on us. Our movements were always followed. And later, everyone who was not working for this European was asked to leave. And in my village, since I came back we live by curfew, and although some leaders wanted to give us more oaths, it was too dangerous.'

'And you, Nyakio?' continued the forest fighter.

'Me? Any oath supposed to be taken by women, I have taken. It is me who drives women to take the oath, and near my area, it is me who organises food and medical supplies to be delivered to our forest fighters.' Nyakio went on as the fighters nodded with happiness, 'Did you ever hear of the *githeri* operation when women carrying food were ambushed by the homeguards at Marimera forest?'

'Oh yes, I know of it.' one man answered.

'It was me who was leading it, and no woman was caught.'Nyakio said proudly. 'And have you ever heard of Major Ndubi?' He operated near Murang'a and Njeri forest.'

'That is right! The name rings a bell, but I have never met him.'

'That is my brother.' Nyakio went on.

'Shake my hand.' the forest fighter said. 'We must leave now and we thank you for the food. Have a safe journey.'

'Anything we can do for you?' Nyakio asked.

'You are with us, and you are intelligent women, so use your heads.'

'Hold on,' Njeri interrupted, 'I have some few aspirin tablets I was given by the Red Cross. You better take them as I don't think I need them. You may make use of them in the forest.'

'Thank you very much, and good luck to you all.' The leader bent down, got hold of some soil, and shutting his eyes and in deep feelings, smelt the soil as if expecting it to be well perfumed. He held the soil in his hand and gave it another good look, then shut his eyes again. He put it in his mouth and started to eat it, as he said: 'The soil is ours.' They then disappeared back into the forest.

Nduta had to borrow a dress from Nyakio she folded her own wet clothes and put them in the basket.

By now it was cool, the sun gave a sign known to Kikuyus as *mirugia aka*. This is the time when women start being busy before dark. It was now easier to walk and as the forest fighters gave the women some short cuts and good directions, it was easy for them. Even when the darkness started to appear, these women continued walking. Luckily Kianoru division had many good Christians, and although there were Maus Maus, they managed to bluff the DO, and by now the curfew in the area was lifted to 9 pm. This allowed

Nyakio, Njeri and Nduta to continue with their journey until late. Towards 8 pm still walking in the dark, but enjoying the coolness of the evening, they decided to enter the nearby Gituamba village. This village was on the other side of Kianoru Division.

Then they went down the river, filled their barrels with water, and managed to pass through the gate. One *askari kanga* asked them: 'Why should you three women decide to come home so late? Suppose you get into trouble?'

'It is the homeguards from the next door division who made us so late. They even asked us to take water to their post first, and by the time we went for our own water, we were too late.'

'Didn't you tell them that you belonged to Gituamba village?'

'Oh, do homeguards ever listen to women?' Nyakio asked in confidence as she continued walking as if she belonged to that village.

By now everyone was inside their huts. Nyakio suggested to the others that they go and knock at the houses in the middle of the village and not near the gate for they might be spotted.

'Don't forget, it is breaking the law to spend a night in another person's house without a permit. This will make both you and your host get into trouble.' At last they knocked at one hut where they were met by another lady. After she heard their story, she decided not to keep them in her hut as her husband was already detained, but directed them to one old lady's hut where they spent the night.

On the following morning, the old lady gave them some breakfast and sweet bananas for them to eat on their way. They would like to have left early, but since the curfew ended only at 6 am, it was impossible to pass through the guarded Gituamba village gate. But at exactly 6 am, Nyakio, Nduta and Njeri were already at the gate ready for it to open before it was opened.

'It's rather early,' the gate-keeper commented.

'What can we do when one is to live up for all-day communal work? We have to fetch water for the family,' Nyakio said as they went past the gate. This *askiri kanga* watched suspiciously as the three ladies passed through the gate. He felt like calling them back then he decided to leave them alone.

Still carrying their barrels, the three ladies continued their journey to Nairobi. All the way, it was pretending and telling lies. By now Njeri and Nduta had great respect for Nyakio's quick thinking. Any time the three of them met a stranger, they would first pretend they belonged to the same area. If they met somebody near a garden, they would pretend to be the owners and start digging. If near the bush, they would pretend to be collecting some firewood, and by the river, they were drawing water, and this made people less suspicious of the Mau Mau travelling lonely ladies.

On many occasions Nyakio would give a Mau Mau sign, but if the stranger did not respond, she would automatically know they were in danger. If they responded to the sign, she would explain their problems and they would be told of the possible dangers and where not to pass, and thus got much help.

The second day was a lucky one, there was less trouble. Chief Githanga of Mukuru division was a very good man. In fact he was a big Mau Mau supporter, but in a cunning way so that no official suspected him. If he met with Mau Maus, he used to ask them just to collect their food and go, and if any of the homeguards aroused the alarm, he would send them in the opposite direction. The fame of Chief Gathanga was known all over, and this made the three women walk over to his division in confidence.

The night fell and the three ladies spent a night at Karia village which was at the edge of Mukuru division. At night one local woman went, after seeing the three at another woman's house, to report to chief Gathanga who was, by now, really fed up with informers. And this woman, Nyaguthii, was a well-known troublemaker, in the village. The European DO had made her to be a woman community leader. He had suggested her name to the community Development and Rehabilitation Officer as a most intelligent and loyal woman. Most village women hated her. The only thing she could think of was how to put others into trouble. This, the European liked in her.

Nyaguthii had no time for her own children. Her children's toes were deformed by jiggers. Her seven-year-old girl was left all day in charge of the other children. Her garden was like bush and although she spent time teaching others how to take care of their children and homes, she did not care for her own. She looked clean, while her children wore torn clothes. Why she hangs around with homeguards riding on their Landrovers, no one knows. Neither did anyone understand how her husband disappeared. In fact she was the most unpopular woman in the area. Even the homeguard had become tired of her. Chief Gathanga sent Nyaguthii back and asked her to bring any guns if they had them, but if she did not find any guns to leave them alone. Nyaguthii left rather ashamed, and she was not seen at the camp again.

The third day of the Mau Mau trip to Nairobi was not as easy as the second. By now they were not far from Kiambu town. They had started early enough since it was best to walk when the weather was cool. At about 7 am, when going down to cross Nyataara river, they saw a big crowd of villagers coming down carrying working tools.

The headman was shouting names as the crowd answered. 'I am here,' came the answers from tired faces. The weather was chilly and it was drizzling. The old men stood with their dirty and torn coats. Women had dirty sacks, folded to cover their heads and back as they worked. Nyakio for a moment did not know what to do. It was too early to think.

'You fools!' one homeguard shouted at Nyakio.

'Nduta and Njeri,' said Nyakio, 'come and take your place.'

The homeguard shouted, 'This bridge is to be finished and I want to see a Landrover patrol car cross it before the end of this week.'

At such an order the three women started to work with the other women. Nyakio gave a Mau Mau sign to another woman, but she did not seem to understand. The only thing this woman said was, 'I do not seem to have met you before.' On hearing this Nyakio did not feel safe and decided that they had better work at an isolated corner. Their heads, covered with kangas as it was cold, were well hidded and they avoided anyone who did not respond to the Mau Mau sign.

After sometime the headman saw water barrels placed down by the three ladies and asked them who was the owner of those barrels. 'Tell them to leave making the bridge,' said the headman, 'and start drawing water,' The homeguard passed quickly giving his orders. 'And they must walk quickly,' he continued. 'Before mid-day, they must take four trips of water. Fill all the big containers there. '

'Alright chief,' Nyakio answered.

'And you women dare bring these barrels of water from your home during communal work. Go and draw water for the post!' The three travelling women picked up their barrels and as soon as they were out of sight of everybody, they sped off heading for Nairobi. This time it was easy as everyone was busy at communal work.

The headman and homeguards waited for a long time for the women to come back with more water, but there was no sight of them and they were never seen again. Checking the post, no woman was seen bringing water, then a search was mounted. No one knew anything about the women who by this time were heading to Mutoni near Dagoretti.

When the three women arrived at Dagoretti Market, Nduta started to smile. She remembered a young girl who used to make her dresses, and she had some friends around Karinde and Mutoni. Nduta asked about her old friend.

'She is alright.' replied the girl. 'Since her husband was detained she has a boyfriend who is a homeguard. Anyway why don't you talk to her? She now lives at Mutoni village.'

'I better not,' Nduta said. 'I would rather go to Karinde near Ngong Forest, where we can hide, and of course I know the people at Karinde are big Mau Mau followers.'

'Yes, Nduta, you are right, but there you will easily be caught. After all, you know our friend Wanjira, she just pretends to like that man for what she gets from him. I don't think she would betray you. She comes here to get dresses made. Even this dress I am making is her's. Wait, I will send a child and tell her I have something for her, she will come.'

The tailor sent for Wanjira, Nduta's friend. Luckily she was at home and came promptly. She was surprised. Nduta hugged her and asked her how she was after such a long time. Nduta then told Wanjira all their problems. Nyakio did not feel safe with her, but there was not much she could do. For one thing she was very tired and hungry and they had to find somewhere to go. At that moment, Nyakio knew that their choices were few.

Do you ever see my husband?' Nduta asked.

'Oh yes, I see your husband often. He is still with that Kaburu.' Wanjira answered as she invited them to the back of the dress-shop and ordered tea and slices of bread for them.

'Does he know you are coming?'

'No, he does not. For more than five years, I have heard nothing from him. In fact I came to check whether he was detained or killed. If he was killed then I can declare myself a widow.'

'So he does not know that you were coming,' Wanjira repeated showing a worried face.

'Wanjira,' Nduta asked, 'Tell me the truth! Why did you show that face? Tell me how is it that with all these troubles, my husband is still with that Kaburu and safe.'

'That is not the point as your husband is a good double crosser.

And so all of us are! Nduta, you have to leave. What do you want to get in a detention camp? What do you or your family gain when you are killed? And what life is there to go and live like a beast in the forest? We have to play it cool, on both sides. Nduta, we used to be good friends, and I must tell you the truth.' Nduta listened as her heart raced faster. Nyakio was suspicious. Her eyes looked at Nyaguthii Wanjira as she continued with the story. 'By the way, do you have passes to come here?'

'No my old friend, we could not get any. If we did, Mau Mau fighters would have killed us.

At this point Nyakio decided to tell the whole story and how they came. 'Poor ladies,' Wanjira commented. 'Unbelievable. You are really brave. You are women like men and I shall do what I can to help you. But I too must tell you my story. My husband went to sell milk; he was a milk distributor in Nairobi. He used to collect milk all over the place, and he would deliver milk door-to-door. One day my husband left in the morning and that was the end of him. Anyway, his bicycle was found in the bush near Dagoretti corner. Just as he was passing Ngong Forest on the way to Karen, he might have been snatched. But Nduta, believe it or not, I am a hundred per cent sure, my husband was not killed by forest fighters. He was a good helper to them. He even used to give them money. I know one of the homeguards used to hate him very much. Anyway, when the Government say it is Mau Maus, with whom can you argue?'

'Oh, I am very sorry,' said Nduta as tears ran down her cheeks. Wanjira cried too when she remembered her husband. 'And would you believe it,' Wanjira continued, 'I now live with that guard. I hate him. He reminds me that one of them killed Mwaura's father. My son Mwaura was left without a father before he even knew what life is. We are helpless, but I have to live and take care of him.'

She wept, and at this point Nyakio scratched the soil on the uncemented floor and put some in her mouth and said, 'The soil is ours!' Other women followed and did the same and said, 'The soil is ours.'

'We cannot sit here just like this, Wanjira, Where can we go from here? Help us.'

'Now Nduta, you have been my friend for many years, and I must tell you the truth. Sometimes the truth hurts, but the truth has to be spoken. Nduta,' Wanjira began.

'Oh yes,' she answered.

'Have you ever heard of passbooks? No. You know all women without passbooks are returned to the villages or detained, and the only women who are allowed a passbook are those who are married to people working in Nairobi, or those who have genuine employment.'

'Is that so? Yes, so I can get one because I am married?' Nduta asked.

'Wait until my story is finished.' Wanjira continued. 'This law has made many women move into men's houses and pretend to be their wives; now many prostitutes live with men as their wives. These men sign that these prostitutes are legal wives.Wanjira stopped to pour more tea for these ladies and persuaded them to drink. 'Many legal wives have no chance to obtain their passbooks.'

'So I have no right to my husbands passbook. Tell me, Wanjira,' Nduta excitedly asked her heart beating faster, her hands shaky and sweat pouring from her forehead. 'You mean Maina, my husband is one of those who registered prostitutes as their real wives?'

'I am afraid, my friend, that is right' A prostitute for Maina? Yes, and a terrible prostitute too! She drinks all day, and when Maina is at home she's still whoring with other men. She spends all day in bars; she even brews her own. Our only fear is that she might get him killed one day. She goes with all sorts of Europeans. Oh, that is not a woman! And Nduta as your friend, I tell you not to go near her. She can put you into trouble, she can call her homeguards friends to arrest you, or you may be shot for her benefit.'

Nduta's tears flowed as Nyakio listened to the story and she was thinking on what to do next. Njeri too was wondering which type of a prostitute her own husband might have.

'Then where do we go from here?' asked Nduta.

Wanjira said, 'We are married to survive. Wait, I am going to Karen, and I will try to tell Maina you are here. I think the best thing is just to sit here behind the tailors shop it is safer than people's houses. I will tell Maina that I have some eggs I want to sell. I sometimes do that.'

'Good luck,' Nyakio told Wanjira.

Wanjira bought some eggs and vegetables at the market and headed to Karen. While bargaining with Maina she told him that his wife was hiding at the tailor's shop.

Maina said he would see what he could do and showed as little emotion as possible.

Meanwhile Maina's prostitute was looking through the window of the servants quarters with suspicious eyes, then she came out and greeted Wanjira saying, 'Are you selling vegetables?'

'Yes.'

'You are lucky to be allowed here as they stopped vegetable sellers.'

'I must have been lucky'

'And as a woman, I have never seen such a clean and smart vegetable seller,' the prostitute commented.

'There is always a start for everything.' replied Wanjira cleverly.

After the talk Maina reported to *memsahib* that he was not feeling well and he would like to see a doctor. *Memsahib* wondered if she could help but Maina insisted that he preferred going to Kikuyu Mission Hospital. He was better known there and they give very good treatment.

'Wait until *bwana* comes. He can drop you there then you will not be in Mau Mau problems, and you can be attended to quickly.'

'No, don't worry, I just feel bad. People there are good Christians, and I know the Dagoretti homeguards.'

'OK Maina, I don't like to drive through these Kikuyu villages alone in fear of attack. Take care, Maina.'

'Thank you, *memsahib*.'

In the late afternoon Maina arrived at the dress shop. He hugged his wife and his tears ran and mingled with Nduta's, the children of both happiness and bitterness. They sat quietly without words for a while until Nduta asked her husband how his new wife was.

'Wife?' Maina asked.

'And how many sons has she given you since I left?' Nduta continued furiously asking her husband.

'Nduta, it is five years since we met, and I request you to be responsible and understanding. Wait until we talk.'

Nyakio turned to Nduta and said, 'This is not the kind of discussion which brought us here. Is it?' Nduta did not answer, but kept on weeping. Her husband looked at his wife, who used to be a beautiful woman, young and tender. Her skin had been smooth, her feet were soft. Her long fingers and soft hands were now dry. The soft skin was peeling. Her clothes were torn, rusty and dirty as if they had been washed in muddy rain water. Maina felt sorry to his wife and asked, 'How is the child?'

'Child?' Nduta repeated. 'He is big enough to look after goats.'

'Boy or a girl? Guess a boy.'

'Yes a boy.'

'Oh my son. What does he look like?'

'As ugly as your family,' Nduta said.

'Are we ugly?'

'Don't you have a mirror to see yourself?'

'Then why did you love me?' Maina asked.

Without any answers, Nduta asked, 'And where do we go from here?'

Maina turned to the other two women and asked them if they knew where their husbands lived.

Nyakio said, 'I am not sure. The last time I heard of him he was working at the Railway Location.'

'Which section is that?' Maina asked.

'Don't even ask me. What I know is that he works where they deal with railway machines. He used to be dirty and oily every time he came home. What he does, I don't know. He used to share a room with three other men at Muthurwa Railway Quarters. One man I remember was Mbogo, he comes from Ndia area Sagana, and he was a cleaner. I never liked to visit him unless there was something very urgent. I could not stay in a room 10 foot by 10 foot, shared by four men. Not me, Thank you.' Nyakio said. 'I am in my own hut in the village:'

'And you?'

'Mine used to work at a European club,' said Njeri. 'No black people were allowed as members to this club!'

'Do you know where the club was?'

'Yes, it is not far from that big hospital where Africans go.'

'You mean KAR Hospital?'

'Oh yes, that name sounds like it.'

'Then I guess, this should be Jibikana Club. Oh yes that must be Jibikana, just before you get to that Army Camp, KAR,' Maina repeated. 'Now I suggest you spend the night here, and tomorrow I have a day off, and I will pretend that I am very sick and I have to see a doctor again or I shall ask the hospital assistant to give me a letter that I have to be seen by another doctor in Nairobi. This will give a day off, and a free movement pass to Nairobi.'

On the following day, Wanjira warned the three about the dangers of travelling by bus to Nairobi without a pass. The best way was to travel by train, but how will you buy a ticket? The Station

Master would definitely ask for your pass before he gives you a ticket.

'Oh no, not more problems,' Nyakio said. She was getting fed up wondering whether all this was worth the trouble.

While Nduta stayed behind, Nyakio and Njeri went down to the train station. The train for Nairobi arrived at Dagoretti Station. Nyakio stood as if not sure what to do, and when the whistle blew for the train to start, she just entered. Njeri followed and off they went to Nairobi by train without any tickets. Dagoretti and Nairobi are so near that the ticket examiner never really bothered to check. People would rarely travel by a very slow Kisumu train for just one station. The ticket examiner relaxed, and the two ladies hid in the train lavatory, avoiding many eyes. After Kibera Station the ticket collector, an Asian started to see to it that everything was alright.

Nyakio peeped through the key-hole as the ticket examiner walked down the side satisfied, looking forward for a nice rest after a long all night journey. Nairobi buildings gave the ladies a hope.

Maina, Nduta's husband, travelled by bus. He had come down to the platform to meet his 'relatives'. Maina gave each woman a ticket and they walked through the station gates unnoticed.

The station was near Muthurwa Railway quarters, and Nyakio went to look for her husband. To her shock among people she asked, they all answered by looking down. Nyakio went on, 'Tell me, what happened to my husband, Karanja? Tell me please! Let me Know.'

'Are you his wife or his mother?'

'I am his wife, though I look very old. I am, tell me.'

'I am very sorry, but one day we were just sitting here. It was a Sunday afternoon. . . .'

'Then what? Tell me quickly,' Nyakio shouted urgently. 'Tell me what happened.'

'He was called by another man, and that is the last time we saw him.'

'Is he killed? Is he detained? Is he jailed? Or is he in the forest?' Nyakio went on asking without pausing for answers.

'Listen your husband was sent to interrogations like all of us, and one of the homeguards who was there that man I hear he has been having a land dispute with.'

'You mean, Njagi?'

'Yes, that is his name.'

'Did he ever sell you some land?'

'Yes, his father sold us a little piece of land, that is where I live and all the time his sons have been wanting it back. That is the reason why I came, to get some money to pay it off. So, go on, what has the land dispute got to do with the whereabouts of my husband?'

'Now this man Njagi was always after your husband. He had accused him of being a Mau Mau oath administrator. And when your husband was called for questioning, he was very badly beaten up. In fact I saw him bleeding at the nose and mouth.'

Nyakio screamed and went to the hospital to ask for him. The hospital staff said he was dead. She asked whether he was buried, but no one knew. In any case, The Hospital mortuary was needed for other bodies. There was a limit to where they could keep unclaimed bodies, and in such a case, they sent prisoners to bury the unclaimed bodies.

'Karanja, Oh my Karanja,' Nyakio screamed as she went back to Muthurwa Railway Quarters to collect her husband's few belongings. Whether he had money, that remained a mystery. 'How can I go back home?' she thought. 'Where does one go? How safe will I be on the way? How will the homeguards take me? They will definitely kill me for running away. They will think I was in the forest fighting. Oh my God, of Mount Kenya, help me, what do I do?'

Back to the Muthurwa Railway Quarters, one of the men offered Nyakio a hiding place. He later managed to make arrangements for her passbook, signing as if she was his wife, and for this, as tough as Nyakio was, as strong-minded as she was, this was emergency time and she had to lie down, and become one of the famous passbook wives.

Njeri was taken to Jibikana Club, known to Europeans as Nairobi Club. Here she, too, learned that her husband was detained, no one knew in which detention camp, Njeri decided to *komerera* using the same tricks that brought her here, to get her back home. There she cheated the homeguard that they were kidnapped by the forest fighters and she had just managed to run away, and the others lived in the forest. Njeri promised to show the guards where the terrorists were hiding, which she did, but no sign of a terrorist was traced.

Maina by now had gone back to Karen, leaving his wife hiding in other people's houses. His passbook prostitute was already fed up, and she started to quarrel and drink more. Maina talked to Wanjira on the problems which he had with his two women, and that he did not want that prostitute. Wanjira arranged with her homeguard husband, and the prostitute was detained, her passbook was torn, and Maina begged to be allowed another wife as hunting for a girl-friend was very dangerous. With help of *memsahib*, who hated the other woman, a passbook was arranged for Nduta, and luckly Nduta and her husband were re-united. And later they managed to get their son to live with them.

Unforgotten Flames

Introduction

In this chapter, I treat the sense of unity shared among the freedom fighters and those other people called upon to assist in many different and often dangerous ways. Feelings of commitment drove each to participate, pushing individuals to acts of bravery beyond what they thought they had in themselves. Here, a lonely but intelligent woman assists in hiding some freedom fighters. Her brother-in-law, thought by all to be a loyalist, helps the fighters survey the homeguard post for the best points of attack and escape. For both, their acts mark those feelings of belonging and ownership of the land summed up in the famous slogan: *The soil is ours.*

Without women's contributions in hiding and feeding the freedom fighters, nothing could have been achieved. It was the women who transported arms and food to the forest edge. It was the women who steered loyalists into the fighters' traps; it was the women, even the prostitutes, who stole guns and bullets from those fighting their brothers. And it was the women who spied for the freedom fighters. The women as much as the men hazarded their lives to gain back a country.

The account also illustrates how the colonial government would retaliate against an entire village. Villagers, even loyalists, were forced to flee to friendly neighbouring areas or into hiding in the forests where they might join the freedom fighters. Communal punishment spared very few.

*   *   *

'If only we knew!', that was the unceasing cry of women in Mukoigo Location; a cry they always wept after very bitter and unforgetful punishment. They wished it was better to die than live, that was the cry of the day. Deep feelings for their community, strong feelings of freedom, and kind-hearted motherly feelings, ended these tears of everlasting suffering.

Soon after the day's communal work ended, Mumbi decided to run to her garden near to the river to collect some vegetables for dinner. She also wished to check whether her arrow-roots were ready so that she could bring some to cook for a change. Eating beans every day had become boring. She took her basket, a rope for carrying sweet potato leaves for her goats, and an empty barrel for fetching home water from the river. What a lot to be done by one tired woman in such a short time.

As she collected these things, she always wondered and asked herself, 'What a life! Do all women have to go through life like this? Here I am, young and beautiful, all day engaged in forced communal labour, and now as tired as I am, as hungry as I am, and as thirsty as I am, I have a duty to perform for my family. Outside there, my mother-in-law sits beside her empty grain store, ragged, old, thirsty, looking at me to attend her. Also outside stands my daughter with her younger brother strapped on her back, also gazing at me, expecting me to satisfy her hungry tummy. Oh my dirty daughter looks so beautiful, and a promising future mother. There is my plump son kicking happily for seeing my face again after a long day apart.'

Mumbi looked sadly at them; the baby smiled happily, Mumbi smiled too. She decided to pull him out of the carrier and played a bit. But just as playing with her son was bringing back her gloomy face to smile again, she remembered what she had planned to do. So she kissed her baby son once again, patted him with a friendly hand, then placed him next to his grandmother. She left him laughing, his hands stretched out begging for more friendly mother's companionship. His grandmother tried attracting his attention with her beads and bangles but he was almost in tears.

Mumbi left them hurriedly, entered her hut and collected what she needed. As she walked out through the gate, Mumbi looked at the sun, then checked with her own shadow to find that there was little time left. I should have not played with my baby first, Mumbi thought, as she walked briskly down the hill to the river Gaita. Thank God the curfew has just been lifted. A few minutes after six and not yet dark – I can finish what I want to do.

Arriving at her riverside garden, Mumbi was happy to find some arrow-roots ready. She pulled some out, cut them off and replanted the main stalk near the riverside. She also dug some sweet potatoes, trimming off the leaves for her goats. At the corner of her garden there were bananas and a little closer some pumpkin plants. Mumbi loved pumpkin leaves and, in dry weather like this, they served as wonderful vegetables for mashing with *irio*. Mumbi decided to pick some pumpkin leaves, checking to see whether they had any pumpkins yet. Next, she looked over her bananas. It was always good to know what to expect next time you came to the garden.

By now it was getting dark, the sun was slowly sinking behind the Nyandarua Hills. The coldness of the evening started to creep across her body. It is getting late, Mumbi felt, as she stood observing her banana plants. That one there should be ready for a meal before long, but it needs a pole to support it against winds. I must tell my brother-in-law to bring a pole soon. As Mumbi was bending to pick pumpkin leaves she heard the rustling of dry leaves, as if someone was walking on them. Mumbi stopped for a while, stood up and looked around, but saw nobody. She decided to pick some more leaves in a hurry and leave for home before dark. After all, over there Kamau's goats were still grazing, his younger son tending to them. Young women and girls were still coming for water; but this is emergency time, I should be home before dark.

As Mumbi pulled her basket to fill it with vegetables, she heard yet another rustling of dry leaves. Her stomach felt as if turned over with fear, and in haste, she threw vegetables into her basket. As she took her barrel to fill it with water, she heard a whisper coming from the middle of her thickly planted banana trees, 'Mama! Mama!' Hearing this, Mumbi dropped her basket and the barrel of water in fear and just before she screamed for help, she heard yet another noise, 'Sh...sh...sh...' She turned her head and looked toward the noise, and in the middle of the banana plantation, well-hidden by dropping banana leaves, stood a tall forest fighter. His face looked anxious, waiting to see if Mumbi would yell for her neighbours. Before she could open her mouth, the terrorist gave Mumbi a sign to shut up or else. Mumbi, a Mau Mau herself, returned the sign with a smile; she also answered with a Mau Mau secret sign, proving beyond all doubt that she, too, was one of them. 'Come closer,' the forest fighter demanded. Mumbi hesitated, wondering who might be watching her and what to expect from this stranger standing there in the twilight. At the thought of that, Mumbi remembered how well-disciplined Mau Maus were; rape was punished by death. So, she moved closer. Leaning near one banana plant, and pretending to be busy attending to her banana plants, Mumbi was surprised to see several other freedom fighters all hidden in her banana plantation.

'Can I help you?' Mumbi asked in a very willing tone.

'Yes, Mama. A big help and a dangerous help we need, too. Listen, I am General Gaitangi and my battalion operates by the slopes of the Aberdare mountains. Things are very bad with us these days, last month food and supplies were completely cut off. We now live on wild animals and wild fruits. Don't forget we are many, and even the wild vegetables and fruits are finished. Although we can still feed on game meat, we fear to shoot animals in case the sounds of our guns are heard. This would give us even worse problems. All these difficulties have been brought to us by that new DO, transferred from Kinangop to here. One of his uncles, who was a good helper for us, has changed; he is now one of these people who wear *gakonia* for interrogating. You know, those who cover their heads with a sack with two holes for eyes. But his head is covered so that you cannot tell who the hell is interrogating you; your friends are now enemies. If they like you they shake their heads that you are not a Mau Mau and if they hate you, they nod that you are one, and there and then you are arrested. This same man, who pretends to have taken Mau Mau oaths, is such a coward.'

'The trouble, Mama, is that when you have such a man as a homeguard leader, it is a big trouble. He already knows us, he has been one of us, he has been involved in giving oath to Mau Maus, and he is sure of who has and who has not taken the oath. That character never missed any oath takings. In fact, he was in charge of dragging people to take the oath, and now over there he stands comfortably next to the DO and the chiefs pretending to be a loyalist. I only hope he told the truth of what he had been before.'

The forest fighter scratched his long twisted hair, shook his head and bit his lips in a temper, as if ready to tear the traitor to pieces.

His breath was fast, as if he was face-to-face with this nasty loyalist. He started to shake all his body with fury, sweat poured down his face as if suffering from malaria. His long, uncombed beard and dirty, twisted hair made him smell of murder, his handsome face with big round eyes betokened his imagination for killing, and smelling blood.

Mumbi got the feeling of fear; she, too, was shaken. Unlike the freedom fighter who was shaken with fury, Mumbi was shaken by fear, fear of all these strange-looking men, too furious for any lonely woman to stand before, as the dark started to fall. Unknowingly, her urine escaped from her trembling body. Her tears, too, ran profusely as if a tap of water was suddenly turned on. Mumbi was near fainting when the freedom fighter realised her fear. The freedom fighter came back to his senses, he tried to control his fury as he felt sorry for this poor, scared woman. He comforted Mumbi and made her feel he was just like any other man, but that this was war, and his forest fighters were experiencing hard times.

At this moment Mumbi eased a little, she was ashamed of her behaviour and the way she wet her underwear. Looking at her legs showing lines of urine dripping from her, she bent down trying to hide them from the strangers, but it was too late. They had already spotted it.

'Now,' the freedom fighter went on, 'we are here on a mission, and our mission is to attack that Mukoigo homeguard post. We want to leave it in ashes, ashes which are not even useful for smearing the walls of our huts. Our biggest aim is to see that head of the homeguard, that former Mau Mau oath operator, now the biggest traitor, eliminated. Eliminated without a trace. Not even his descendants will ever see his grave. Let his sons never have the honour of carrying his body to be buried. His bones should be destroyed as they are not even worth feeding to the ants or the birds of our country.'

'Now what can I do?' asked Mumbi, her fear rising again.

'This can be a very dangerous thing for you and your family too. If such a thing happens in this village, everybody will suffer its repercussions! Curfew will be added and we shall be badly victimised. We know all that Mama, and perhaps better than you think, but this will have to happen, with your help or not. Now our first demand is that you shut your mouth about us, tell no one about us. Second, you must find us a hiding place and feed us, failure to help us will put you in the group of traitors.'

But Mumbi, on hearing this and being a Mau Mau follower herself, just bent down, took a handful of soil, smelled it. She then put some in her mouth, chewed it and said 'The soil is ours.' Mumbi bravely looked at the freedom fighter with a confident, smiling face, and said 'Brother just wait there, just here. I shall come back after dark,' Mumbi then filled her barrel with water, then swung it on her back. On top she placed the sweet potato leaves for her goats, and yet on the top of the leaves she put her basket filled with vegetables, arrow-roots and sweet potatoes, and off she went. Mumbi was late in returning home, which was unusual of her. She found everybody worried, her mother-in-law had already sent Mumbi's daughter to go and call her brother-in-law to go and search for her. Lucky she got back when she did.

'Why did you stay so long?' her mother-in-law asked.

'Oh, you know, I found too many weeds in my garden, and I decided to cultivate a little before I came back. The garden was so green, and the beauty of the young plants made me forget it was getting late.'

Mumbi sliced the pumpkin leaves in a hurry, added them to the already boiling beans and potatoes which she later mashed to make *irio*, a favourite Kikuyu dish. While food was cooking, she quickly roasted a few sweet potatoes to quieten her children's and the old lady's hunger. But, unusual for Mumbi, as soon as dinner was over, she sent the children to bed and ordered everyone to sleep. The big girl had a lot she wanted to tell her mother, but Mumbi said she was too busy and tired for any further talk. Grandmother offered to tell the children stories of giants and the cunning rabbit, but Mumbi this night refused and ordered everybody to sleep. The children fell asleep first, Mumbi's mother-in-law stayed awake wondering at Mumbi's behaviour, fearing that she had found herself a lover.

This could have happened as Mumbi's husband had been working in the town for a long time, and no longer came home or even wrote. There was fear he might have been killed or detained, no one really knew. At the thought of this, tears ran down the old lady's cheeks. Oh my son, she lamented. His father died young, leaving me a young widow. I decided never to marry again so that I could care for my two sons and their sisters, now all married. A year has passed without even hearing news of my son, leave alone seeing him. If my daughter-in-law loves another man, that is the end of me, and the end of my homestead. I only wish her interest is nothing more than wanting another baby, after all she always cries and wishes to have

another son, just to name after her dead father. That is reviving him.
And who can blame her, she is still young, and my son's fate is
unknown, Mumbi's mother-in-law thought as she wiped her tears
and covered herself with her blanket, drifting between sleep and
concern.

After sending the children to bed, Mumbi took her porridge pot
and decided to cook some sour porridge at night while everybody
was in bed. She ladled it into a big gourd, then set it aside to cool. As
she was cooking, Mumbi's mother-in-law lay in her bed awake. The
movement of her daughter-in-law so late at night worried her even
more. The movements and the noise from Mumbi's room made her
wonder if Mumbi was packing her belongings to run away. Curious,
she lay awake for a long time.

When Mumbi knew everybody in her family was asleep, she
walked slowly to her brother-in-law's house, and knocked by the
window, 'Kamau, Kamau,' Mumbi whispered.

'Who is that calling me at this time of the night?'

'It's me, Mumbi, your sister-in-law.'

'Mumbi? Kihara's mother?' asked Kamau. 'Anything serious?
What is the matter?'

'Don't ask too many questions, why don't you just come out for a
minute?'

'Mumbi!' Kamau called again. 'Did you forget this is emergency
time and curfew started at 9 pm?'

'Yes, I know. But Kamau, don't ask too many questions. You just
come! Have you ever seen me calling you at this time before? This is
emergency time so just come and listen to what I have to say.'

Kamau woke up, hurriedly dressed, then slowly opened his door
and followed Mumbi into her hut. Her mother-in-law who was
awake and quietly following her daughter's-in-law movements was
little happy when she found Mumbi calling her son. And Kamau's
wife was jealous of Mumbi, wondering why a lonely wife should call
her husband out of bed at this time of the night? The way these two
people talk, she cannot trust them together.

Kamau quietly entered Mumbi's hut, and whispering, Mumbi
started to explain. 'Kamau, today was a very unusual day for me.
When I left communal work, I rushed to the river to fetch water, and
see what I could bring back from the garden. Everything was alright,
my vegetables were fresh and green. I dug a few sweet potatoes and

picked some leaves for my goats, then I uprooted some arrow-root, and to my surprise, just by that big banana plant in the garden...'

'Which banana plant?' Kamau asked.

'The only plant at the east corner of the garden.' Mumbi answered.

'Oh yes, then what happened?' asked Kamau.

'I got the shock of my life.' answered Mumbi. I was looking at those bananas, wondering if there were any nearly ready to eat.'

'Then what? Come to the point, then what?' Kamau was getting edgy, sitting in Mumbi's house, away from his wife and after curfew.

'I saw some forest fighters, many of them hiding among the banana plants.'

'Oh what shall we do?' Kamau asked in a hurry.

'Wait until I finish,' interrupted Mumbi. 'No matter how we would like to help them, their request is hard to fulfil.'

'Why? What do they need? Tell me whether that means death or not, I have to help where I can. I took the oath and swore that I shall die for our country. Tell me all, my sister-in-law. Explain their needs, let me hear all, I am ready to serve, with my hands and with my soul. I shall be ready to offer and suffer, let my blood flow, if my country needs it. The soil is ours.' said Kamau bravely.

'Now listen, they want a hiding place,' Mumbi began her story, 'Somewhere they could hide without being traced. They are to be fed, too. And not only one day but for several. Don't suggest that they stay in my house. As much Mau Mau as I may be, I don't feel ready to suffer, leaving my children orphans at God's mercy. I am not ready to risk my children's lives for the country. Poor children of mine, even the whereabouts of their father remains a mystery.' As Mumbi said that, she looked sad and thoughtful; tears gathered in the corners of her eyes.

'Look Mumbi, this is not time to think of your sadness. But tell me where these brave people are now.' Kamau said gently.

She wiped her tears. 'I left them hiding by the banana plants at my riverside garden.' she finally said.

'Which banana plant?' asked Kamau.

'Look here, you know very well the family riverside garden, in my piece which is next to the bush on the east side, there is only one lot of banana plants, the only one in the whole area. People said riverside gardens are for arrow-roots, sweet potatoes, and off-season vegetables. They all thought I was crazy to plant it in that area, even mother complained that I was wasting my vegetable garden when bananas are easily grown on the hills.'

'All right.' Kamau impatiently cut Mumbi short, 'Tell me where, it is getting late.'

'Just there, at the corner of our garden,' she replied. 'When you go there, cough, flash the torch quickly. Make sure to direct the torch light inside the bananas to avoid attracting the attention of the homeguards. Then whisper "The soil is ours." This will give them confidence.'

'Shall I take Kinga with me?' wondered Kamau. 'No, not yet. My wife is a bigger talker, and I know she is one who can never keep a secret, news burns inside her head as if a heavy burden were placed on her. To let it out she goes on whispering to neighbours telling each one, this is just between you and me, and the news will spread like a bush fire.'

'Look here Kamau,' continued Mumbi, 'you were born once and once you shall die. This must be a top secret, so just go and do what I told you. Bring them back, let us feed them, they are human beings, fighting and suffering for our interest. We can have them stay at your mother's. She would be the last person to betray you. She should rather die than put you in trouble. All these homeguards don't bother about such old ladies. She has not many friends. If some come during the daytime, they can sit in my house. I cannot see a better place to hide them. The strangers best be hidden in your mother's hut.'

At this time Kamau was getting a bit impatient for waiting, and wanted to get going.

'No,' Mumbi said, 'Wait. I know these homeguards are very active during the early hours of the evening, but after midnight, they fall asleep. They are no longer active, but they are tired and sleepy. Most of them just sleep by the fence of the homeguard post. So wait until later, but we must now inform your mother of the expected guests.'

Kamau at this point decided to go back to his hut and rest until after midnight when everybody would be asleep, and the homeguards tired, and hiding back by their compound, fearing for their lives. As Kamau entered his hut, his wife was sitting up, and she remarked 'Has your brother been declared dead? Are you now taking over his family?' This came from jealousy, for some time now, she has been feeling that her husband was too much interested in Mumbi.

'Yes, and so what?' Kamau answered furiously. 'You women, your minds think of nothing else even during emergency times. You don't even care to know if there was any problem. If it wasn't for women, the world would have been great!'

Kamau's wife was stung by the answer and wondered if she was not jealous for nothing. Kamau as he was, and without undressing, and with his shoes on, lay down on the top of the bed. He was restless. His wife became worried and hated herself for her words. She later begged him to tell her what was the matter, but Kamau said to leave him alone and go to sleep. But Kamau's wife could not sleep.

At midnight, Kamau put on his old heavy rubber boots. He took his coat, a *simi* from under his bed, and a heavy *rungu*, and started to walk out. His wife jumped out of bed and begged him to tell her where he was going. 'Are you going to join others in the forest? Tell me please. Your brother's fate, no one seems to know. Look at all these children with no one to take care of them. You want to leave me to be raped daily by those homeguard savages? You go there to be killed, that will finish the whole of this home-stead. Your mother will definitely die of sorrow.'

'You just leave me alone, and keep your mouth shut. The more you are sobbing the easier it is for the people to pay attention. You never know who is listening to our whispers at night.

'Anyway, I am just looking for something. Keep very quiet, in less than half an hour I shall be back and tell you all.' Kamau, without even telling Mumbi, left quietly. The whole of Mukoigo location was dead asleep. The midnight cold was even more bitter than it used to be. Kamau had not been outside his hut so late for a long time. The moon was nowhere to be seen. The stars could be traced here and there, but most were covered by clouds, testifying that rain was on the way. A light was seen at a distance flashing here and there on the Mukoigo Hill. This was from the homeguards.

Kamau did not follow the common path. Instead, he passed through the bush and gardens. In fear of being followed and hunted down, the cowardly homeguards never dared walk in the bush at night.

Kamau moved slowly to the banana trees. General Gaitangi, who was waiting impatiently, had spotted him at a distance. General

Gaitangi was by now thinking maybe that the woman was a traitor, maybe she was organising a homeguard ambush. We must be ready to fight in case they come. General Gaitangi had already ordered his men into different corners, ready for any attack. Just then, Kamau quietly arrived. Kamau stood near the banana plants, quickly flashing his torch, then waited for the answer. General Gaitangi answered with a little cough.

At this point Kamau whispered, 'I am sent by the owner of this garden. The woman you talked to early this evening. So you just follow me. We are now ready. Try to walk on the east side of the village, our home is up on the hill, the safest, and the furthest from the homeguards. As they walked, light was seen flashing here and there from the homeguard post, but the place was rather too far for them to be seen. Homeguards' interest stayed around their post at night, just in case freedom fighters might decide to attack.

Arriving at his home, Kamau pointed General Gaitangi to his mother's hut. Then Kamau ordered everyone to take off their heavy boots quietly in case somebody else noticed their footsteps. 'Don't forget. There are as many enemies here as there are friends. You never know who might betray us.' Kamau then led them to hide behind his mother's hut. One by one, they entered the old lady's hut.

For a few days the General and his group lived in the hut. The hut was small for so many men. Kamau's mother was a clever lady and very secretive, too. She knew if, by any chance, her hut was reported as a Mau Mau hiding place, that would be the end of her homestead.

The hut was small, dark and smoky. On one side stood an untidy bed made of sticks, the bedding dirty and in rags. She stored firewood to dry in the *itara*. This was black with smoke, and the soot showed a place that had not been cleaned for a long time. In the middle of the hut there was a fireplace with three stones facing each other, and two more stones at one side, used as a side fireplace. A few calabashes and clay pots were piled in one corner. Several three-legged wooden stools, some broken, were set out here and there.

Kamau's mother decided to hide the terrorists up in the *itara*, and to avoid smoke, Mumbi brought all the food she had cooked earlier to her mother's-in-law hut, making sure that her movements were not noticed. Kamau's wife was the only one who, during all this time, kept awake wondering what was going on.

The guerillas' appearance showed that they had not eaten food for a long time. After eating, they climbed slowly to the rafters of the house and slept. The *itara* was not inviting, and worrying about the homeguard made sleep for the fighters even more difficult. Still, it was a warm hiding place compared to the cold winds on the slopes of the Aberdare mountains. There they were safe from wild animals, if not from the homeguards.

During the day, the tired forest fighters stayed indoors. They used the time to rest and sleep. The old lady locked them in and sat outside by her daughter-in-law's door to keep a watch. Several old ladies came for a chat with the old lady, but Mumbi's mother-in-law showed no interest. She pretended that she was not feeling well, so that they would quickly leave her alone. And the old lady made sure that no one went near her hut, not even her grandchildren.

Mumbi left early for communal labour. That day the headman had decided to set a quota, and anyone who finished their piece to the satisfaction of the person-in-charge was allowed to leave early. Quietly, Mumbi worked very hard on her piece, and by not resting, she was finished by 3 pm. She rushed for water, and came home quickly. Arriving home she was happy to find her mother-in-law putting beans on the fire. This would make for an early supper.

The guests had had enough rest by now. After the old lady locked the room and sat on guard, the forest fighters had climbed down, and slept comfortably in her bed and on the floor. Mumbi waited until dark to serve them food, and they were happy to eat *irio* and drink sour porridge, things impossible to make in the forest.

After midnight, the forest fighters decided to start the survey for their mission. They needed to study the best way to attack the Mukoigo homeguard compound. The routine for the forest fighter was sleeping during the daytime, and doing their work at night.

On the following day Mumbi prepared plenty of food. Kamau's wife wondered why Mumbi was cooking so much food and porridge. 'Do you have visitors? Or do you have people coming to help on the farm?' Kamau's wife asked.

'Help with the farm?' Mumbi – disgusted by the question – repeated. 'When was the last day that I heard people helping each other in gardening?' You talk as if you don't know that we are all at the forced communal work during the day, and in curfew during the night. Do you know there are times I feel you ask questions like a child? If I cook too much food, it is my food, and for my children, so that they can have enough to eat when I am busy. Don't forget I am not as lucky as you are to have a husband to perform some duties while you cook. I am the man and I am the woman in this house.'

'You are the woman and you are the man?' Kamau's wife repeated. She went back to her hut annoyed with Mumbi. 'What could have caused Mumbi to talk to me like that?' Kamau's wife wondered. Her unfriendly talk could be caused by nothing else but being interested in my husband. No wonder my husband too has lately been unfriendly to me.

Mumbi watched closely to make sure that no one saw her passing the food into the old lady's hut for the freedom fighters to eat.

The next day, Kamau requested his hidden guests to change and look like ordinary people. Their long, twisted hair was cut, their beards were shaved, their animal-skin jackets were changed for normal trousers, shirts and old overcoats, while their animal-skin sandals were replaced by old worn-out boots. Some were found in Mumbi's husband's box, while others were found by Kamau himself.

The forest fighters decided not to waste any more time before they started on their mission. A dangerous mission too, but whatever the outcome, it was to be undertaken. They must attack the homeguard post and capture or kill the homeguard Kirangi, uncle of that new DO at Kinangop.

'That man, that savage, the traitor. I shall be satisfied with nothing less than to see his head kept aside of his other flesh,' General Gaitangi seriously and furiously told Kamau.

At the thought of this, Kamau was shaken. He imagined a human head severed from its body. This made him fill with fear as if his blood was overflowing his brain. The way General Gaitangi behaved, Kamau was not sure if he could not turn on him, too. The way he opened his eyes, his lips made Kamau's palms run with sweat.

'Don't stand there like a statue,' General Gaitangi shouted at Kamau. 'If you think you have doubts, let us know, then we can fix you before we go for your friend, Kirangi.'

Kamau, seeing that it was no joke, and already involved in it, gathered up his courage. Shaky, frightened and stammering, he answered, 'I am at your service, my general. Whatever you order me to do, I an ready to fulfil. The soil is ours.'

'I order you all to rest. Then after midnight we must go and survey the situation. The ambush at Mukoigo homeguard should not take us more than two days, three days at the most to plan. You know, the longer we stay, the easier it is for us to be noticed.'

After midnight the forest fighters were ordered by General Gaitangi to start their work. Kamau was to lead since he knew the post's layout. More than once he had been dragged inside the camp to be interrogated by the *gakonia* people. Kamau was to show the freedom fighters the possible ways to escape, and the danger corners to avoid.

'On the east side, don't dare pass, that is where the main road is and, in case of alarm, that side is dominated by their good chaps who regard Mau Maus as savages. And they would also definitely follow that road on the north side. That can be dangerous, too, for you. There is that big river, with terrible rocks and cliffs, and in case you miss the crossing, it will be difficult. You can easily hurt yourself or fall from the cliff. That river is very wild and can sweep you off. This now leaves just the west and the south sides as escape routes.' Kamau explained to the forest fighters that the homeguard camp was well fenced with barbed wire, really difficult to penetrate. These homeguards of Mukoigo were well-guarded. There is a big, deep trench surrounding the camp. The trench was so wide that jumping across was impossible. Its depth was frightening, if one fell in it, coming out would be a problem. A real danger. Kamau made sure that General Gaitangi and his forest fighters understood all the points and possible dangers before they ambushed the camp.

The night was dark and cloudy, moonlight was nowhere to be seen, only the stars were to be seen, and then only briefly, as clouds passed blocking out even their feeble light. The night was still, chilly and the coldness was starting to be felt although it was yet too soon for the bitter early morning cold. This was good for the forest fighters. Led by Kamau, they walked slowly and quietly, very well-armed in case of any attack.

Kamau led them to the northern side. 'Do you see that river there?' he whispered. 'Even if chased, make sure you don't follow that side, you can injure yourself on the cliffs and on those rocks. That road there is the one I mentioned, in case of problems that is the best, and it can take you directly to the forest.' Kamau pointed to all possible dangers. 'Do you see that corner there? That is where the entrance is. By the entrance there are two armed guards. They have whistles and alarm devices. You should hear their alarms, they are so loud when they sound they awake everyone and in a fright, too. Over there at the other corner and not far from the gate is a watch tower. They have flashlights which they direct here and there, very dangerous too. As far as I know they are all busy during the early hours of the evening and soon after midnight, but later you can hardly hear or see them. They fall asleep.'

On the following day, General Gaitangi arranged the points of attack. Though now a Mau Mau General, Gaitangi had once fought in the British Army. He had been fighting in Burma, and he knew all the tricks of how to attack: the armoury must by surrounded first, the gate and tower guards should be fixed immediately. The day of attack was a real fight, the target was to capture homeguard Kirangi, and his nephew, the new DO. Dead or alive, they had to be captured, their heads were wanted. General Gaitangi imagined himself leading Kirangi, his hands tied behind with a goat's rope. He bit his lower lip, his breath was faster than before. All his features grew in anger, his big eyes looked even bigger, his whole body was shaking. General Gaitangi groaned, 'I have to capture Kirangi, dead or alive. I would like to see his head sent to his mother or to his wife inside half a gourd. That would teach them and others a lesson about the damage their son has done to the sons of this land.'

The attack on the Mukoigo homeguard post went on as planned. It went like lightning, and before long, Kamau saw two homeguards lying dead. The homeguard post was burnt down. Kamau, untrained, did not know the techniques of fighting, and before long he was shot dead by the DO, the same DO whom they were hunting. The fire and shouts roused everyone, women shouted as the homeguards' huts burnt. For the guerrillas there was no choice but to escape as soon as they could. As they ran away, the whole of Mukoigo ridge was filled with shouts. Women shouted, children screamed, whistles blew, and those at the post sounded the alarms.

The homeguard radioed for help: This is Mukoigo post – Over – Trouble at Mukoigo Post – Over – Post burned – Over – Several dead – Over – Can you hear me? – Over . . . .

Within a short time, several Landrovers sped toward the fight at Mukoigo. The 999 car came with its siren wailing, all the nearby police and guards came running to the Mukoigo post.

By now General Gaitangi and his men had run away, back to the forest. The damage they had caused was not yet known. Whether Kirangi was dead or alive, or the DO of Mukoigo, no one could tell.

How many of their people were killed, still remained a mystery to the General. Anyway, those trained knew how to escape, and where to find others in the forest. For those who were dead, may God bless their souls.

Walking by the river, the forest fighters managed to get to the edge of the forest early in the morning. Thirsty and tired, they hid in a cave by the riverside. Then General Gaitangi put on his small transistor radio: 'Special announcement. Special announcement. Last night a gang of terrorists attacked Mukoigo post killing five homeguards. Among the dead was the homeguard leader Mr Kirangi, while the DO Mukoigo managed to shoot two terrorists dead, and injure one badly. Investigations are continuing. Full bulletin at 1 pm.'

At hearing this, General Gaitangi knew they were in danger, but was happy to learn that their mission to kill Kirangi was fulfilled.

The homeguards, police and all the loyalists were called in to start hunting for the 'gangsters.' They searched all possible hiding places; the helicopters flew low over the whole area, but no trace of the freedom fighters could be found.

With Kamau dead in the attack, Mumbi knew they were in trouble. Later, some of the homeguards recognized Kamau's body and this made them wonder whether that family knew of the terrorists' hideouts. When the guards went to Mumbi's home, she cheated them that Kamau had been called by another man after midnight, and while waiting to see him he heard shouts, screams, whistling, and later saw fire at the Mukoigo homeguard post. He did not even know to whom to report at such a dangerous hour of the night. 'The next thing we heard is that he is dead. I am sure the terrorists killed him. Kamau was such a loyalist.' Mumbi, her mother-in-law and Kamau's family were given a special guard. The family was tears and all sadness since their only hope and the last of their men had died. Mumbi's mother-in-law cried bitterly. She even tried on several occasions to commit suicide by hanging herself.

After a few days no one had disclosed who had hidden the Mau Mau savages and, of course, Mumbi and Kamau's family were the last to be suspected. People stayed indoors, curfew was enforced once again, and made even worse. Now no one was allowed outside their houses from 5 pm to 7 am. Both villagers and homeguards looked frightened all the time.

It was on Thursday afternoon when a patrol helicopter toured

Mukoigo village. It flew low and went round and round. Its wild noise sent children scurrying in, some hiding under the grain stores, others in the bush, or wherever they could. Screaming and frightened children clung to their mothers; mothers panicked.

'Special announcement. Special announcement,' the man in the plane shouted over his loudspeaker. 'Those with ears, let them hear. All of you of Mukoigo village, you are given two days, repeat. Fail to tell us and the action we shall take against you all will never be forgotten. Two days to disclose. Never say I did not warn you.' The helicopter went round and round spinning and announcing; the more it spun, the more people were frightened.

Who hid them please? Many in desperation asked. Please, please whoever knows, please, go and disclose. If not, none of our seeds will be left alive. Please one more day, whoever knows, our village will be wiped out. Kamau is dead, his brother disappeared, and these Mau Mau will finish us all, call everybody to go and disclose.

In the evening, a homeguard who was very kind and humane came back to his village; he was called Hiukia. One of his old friends told him, 'Hiukia, you are the only mature leader, not in the forest and not a known homeguard. Listen to me, I am only a homeguard to save my life, but inside me, in my heart, and in my blood, I am with our fighters fully, and I assure you not to fear me. Listen Hiukia, last night we had a meeting, a very secret meeting, and a decision was reached that tomorrow all the homes except those of known loyalists will be set on fire. The leader who will say which homes to burn, and which not to burn, is with that former DO from Kinangop. Also Kirangi's brother will be advising. You know Hiukia, some of these homeguards are savages, particularly now that they are angry. They will terrorise us all, even if for personal hatred. This time they will really have revenge. My friend, go and whisper to all the people to run away and not to sleep in their houses. Who knows which houses will be set on fire. You can never tell! Never tell!' he emphasised.

The news of the plans for house burning quickly went round. People packed whatever they could, wore as many clothes as they could, and at night they all crossed the river. Running away at night was very dangerous, the road was narrow and dark, and overloaded with important possessions and frightened children. The biggest problem was crossing the river; it was wide and wild and there was no proper bridge. The only bridge there was a set of three poles. The path was dark and the whole place was still. The only noises were of the frogs along the river bank. The insects flew here and there, flashing their lights. Frightened villagers followed each other like goats, wondering of their next destination. Crossing the river to them was a matter of life or death. Mumbi, her mother-in-law, children, and Kamau's wife and family followed too. All crossed the river for safety.

At Gituamba village, the people were kind. Chief Githuku was very popular; in fact the more violent homeguards were not very sure of his loyalty. He never used to allow curfew in his place, and very few people, if any, were victimised. Therefore, people from Mukoigo were all hidden in different homes. Early in the morning the people who had fled from Mukoigo looked across to see their village. True, very true, Hiukia knew, several Landrovers were seen driving to Mukoigo Ridge. The brown dust cloud blew over. Mukoigo villagers all sat on the other hills to watch the scene. Mumbi knowing she caused all these troubles, pretended not to know much; all gazed to see the fate of their homes.

Over there burning wildly is Kiingi's house, Kimani's house, over there seems to have been passed. Mwangi's too could be recognised burning; the flames went over the bananas. Over there, Mumbi's home was passed, they were said to be good people. The same home where Mau Maus had hidden, and the hut where the plan for attacking Mukoigo post was settled was left as it was. Mumbi smiled, but on remembering Kamau's fate, tears ran down her cheeks.

On and on, flames rose from these homes of people, singled out as would-be Mau Mau leaders. The whole village seemed to be in flames; the smoke went high. Goats burned, property burned, many people were left homeless. Yet those most closely connected were left safe, and guarded by the loyalists. If only they knew the fate of helping Mau Maus. Let the top secret remain a secret, known only by Mumbi and her mother-in-law.

Always with such pain, with such suffering, did the food for the fighters in the forest have safe delivery, and the soil remained ours.

The Squatters' Tragedy

Introduction

Squatters were labourers who worked and lived on the White Highlands estates. Such estates were big tracts of land, often thousands of acres, owned by white European farmers. Squatters were housed in small, mud and grass-huts built far from their masters' enormous residences, residences that were bounded by beautiful well-trimmed fences and a long drive-way shaded by the purple flowered Jacaranda trees. This beautiful world of over-grown bougainvillea, nicely mown thick evergreen Kikuyu grass, and magnificent trees stood out starkly against the squatters' hovels.

Squatters' salaries were very low, although they were permitted to cultivate small gardens for vegetables. Occasionally they would be allowed to keep a few goats and chickens.

As a squatter, you and sometimes your wife worked for the master; children from the squatter families also joined the labour-force when they were old enough, or they had to move off the estates. Some big farms with considerate masters had schools for the squatters' children. Generally the children learned only the rudiments of reading and writing. There was nothing much expected of those poorly run schools; very few students had a chance for higher education.

During emergency time, and after several farms were attacked by Mau Maus, some white settlers decided to get rid of all those labourers belonging to groups most involved in Mau Mau. Without warning, colonial officials in army trucks would swoop down on the squatter villages. Squatters were piled into the lorries without opportunity to gather up any possessions or food. All were trucked away not knowing about their other family members unless they had been rounded up together.

You were rounded up whether food was on the fire cooking, whether your goats were out in the field, wherever you were found; you were shoved into transport without any questions. You left your maize, beans and vegetables in the garden, your goats in the field, your chickens unattended; you left your laboriously − collected belongings, your clothes, blankets, your pots and pans, and maybe even your food for lunch still boiling in an earthenware pot.

Later those collected would be dumped in a relocation camp and interrogated about where they came from, even though some had never known another home other than the white settlers' estates. They did not know where their grandparents came from, perhaps all they had heard mentioned was a district, a district they had never before visited.

And here they are dumped with forgotten relatives, a place they had never before seen, facing a village of strangers, they were left there to find who was in their clan. They were dumped among the strangers, none of whom could not afford to help these newcomers.

*   *   *

It was early on Friday morning when Nyokabi woke up, tired, gloomy, and in a bad mood. She stood outside her hut half asleep, raised both her arms as she yawned loudly and deeply. The yawn seemed to take away some of her tiredness, bringing an early morning freshness to her body.

The morning was cold and calm and the greenness of neighbouring Karati Forest Station clearly showed how fertile the Kenya White Highlands could be. In such a fertile forest even *mugio* and *mukeu* plants grow as big as *mugumucano* trees. Whoever thought *mugio* could be so big that only an axe could cut it.

Nyokabi stood outside her house for a while in her serious mood, thinking, her left hand resting on her hip while her right hand was touching her chin. What is this life for? she wondered. What can this life offer me? Day by day working like a donkey, morning till night, always busy? Here comes another day, a day yet like all the others! Nyokabi looked to the east, she then turned and gazed to the west, she turned to the north, and finally to the south. It was all beautiful, beautiful with Major Greying's pyrethrum flowers. Turning to the north, to the south, to the east or the west, nothing but thousands of acres, nothing else but the whiteness of pyrethrum covered by early morning up-country dew. Occasional sparkles emanated from its whiteness when the early morning sun, escaping from the Karati forest, caught them.

Over there, up that hill and across acres of pyrethrum flowers stood a settler's house, his double-storey stone and wood house was partly covered by hibiscus plants. What ever they did to God to give them all these good things, no one knows! And me, here I am a mother of several children with a labourer husband in a round hut! What a life!

Nyokabi had another look on all sides of Major Greying's pyrethrum farm. The flowers were indeed ready for picking. Yes, ready for harvest. This was the time, time to get some casual labour, the time to earn some extra shillings, time to buy a new *kanga* and to clothe my family. Nyokabi gained a flicker of hope. My elder daughter, Wanjiru, is now big enough; with some help, she can pick flowers. Even for my second child, I'll cheat the headman with their ages so that they may be allowed to do some casual labour. I can say my daughter was born during cassava famine, my son soon after it, they are indeed ready for casual work. Mother, father and the children will all have to labour at Major Greying's pyrethrum farm.

The only drawback with this casual labour is that it comes once, then next time there is nothing to do, and with this *bwana kiko*, so cunning with labourers! I know he may invite other labourers from neighbouring farms to come and finish the harvest, quickly forgetting or without caring about us, the squatters, on his farm who need to earn some extra money.

At the thought of this, Nyokabi started to break some dry leaves and some twigs which were stuck on the verandah of her hut. She re-entered the hut, and lit the fire to make morning porridge for her family before they left for work.

In general, life at Major Greying's farm was not all that bad, compared with life of squatters on other farms. They recalled some of their friends who were squatters at Mr Vendorwep's farm. This *kaburu* was a very bad Boer, so bad that he said a relative coming to visit you would be a trespasser, to be taken to court or to have dogs set on him and in some extreme cases even shot. Anybody not working on the farm was not allowed to stay on it.

This mad *kaburu* went as far as ordering your own grown-up children either to work for him or leave the farm. And as rich as he was, he never had a school for the children of the squatters as was common with the other farmers. One labourer, however, who could read and write was allowed to gather squatters' children together in an unused farm garage full of dust and debris. Here is where this young man who claimed he could read and write taught them how to write numbers and to read a few words. Some people said that he could not read well himself. He was called on to help read the Kikuyu *Muiguithanis* Newspaper which had a lot of politics, and he found some difficulties in reading it well. He wrote letters for others, but complaints came back that they were badly written and difficult to understand. This teacher the *kaburu* employed was just a lazy man who was trying to escape hard work.

'I, for one' said Nyokabi, 'would rather have my children to help me in the house than waste time with such a hopeless teacher. After all we were born to labour. Let my children labour, but if only this talk of getting our land back from Europeans could come true. But how will this ever happen? A black man to earn as much money as Major Greying? I doubt it very much, but in our Mau Mau oath, they make us believe we can. Let us wait and see!'

After the porridge was ready, Nyokabi's husband shouted at her for his porridge. He called in an angry voice, 'Am I being offered this porridge or shall I leave it? You women, if you ever think?'

'Let me cool it a bit so that you can sip it quickly,' Nyokabi answered as she poured it from one calabash to the other.

'You think time is standing still waiting for you to make it cool?' Kariuki scolded his wife in a disgusted voice.

Nyokabi said, 'How many Nyokabis do you think there are? Nyokabi to chop the wood, Nyokabi to light the fire, the same Nyokabi to hurry and cool the porridge! Take your porridge, it is ready for you.'

In anger, he refused the porridge, instead he took his hoe and *panga* and started to go out of the house as Nyokabi stood still with the half calabash full of smoking hot millet porridge ignored by her husband.

Kariuki walked a few steps, then turned his angry face to his wife like a rhino disturbed, and while pointing at her he said, 'One of these days you will explain to me where you have learned the language in which you answer your husband. I have noticed your behaviour these days. Go ahead and we shall see who is the head of the family.' Kariuki walked off in a temper for a day's work, Nyokabi stood still looking at him until he disappeared from her sight.

'Whoever made men,' she said as she poured the rejected porridge back into its container. 'There he goes to do hard work with nothing in his stomach.'

During this time the forest officer in the Karati forest was looking for labourers to help in planting young trees on the other side of the forest. This forest officer preferred to have women working for him. He said they were better and quicker for planting and he was so good to women that he would just say, when you plant so many plants you can get a full day's pay, and if you work quickly it is just a matter of two, three hours and you are through and have a day's pay.

Another good thing about this forest officer at Karati forest was that, together with your daily payments, you are allowed to cut dry wood for yourself, and you can carry as much wood as you can. The only strict thing was that each women was only allowed to take just one load of dry firewood. Sometimes women could hardly walk, sometimes a woman's load needed two to lift it onto her back, and she carried it like a donkey.

They would use a sisal or leather strap, passed across the forehead leaving a permanent valley on their heads. Their overworked legs would crack like falling trees, the veins showing all over. Then too, the neck veins would stand out pulsating and looking ready to burst. On the arms the veins were twisted like a knarled tree trunk, all round these rough hands labouring to survive.

Sometimes, when Europeans pass these women, they take out their cameras to photograph the groups following each other, all over-loaded with firewood from Karati forest. They look astonished at what a Kikuyu woman can do. If only they knew! This was the only time when Kikuyu could walk in Karati forest and collect firewood without being arrested. One carries as much as possible for the cold season was soon coming.

Before Nyokabi left for the planting, she decided to put some beans on the fire for her children. The oldest girl was good and could serve the other children. She was able to fetch water and take care of the young ones. Nyokabi prepared some fresh maize and beans, put them into an earthenware pot to boil, then chopped enough firewood for her daughter to add to the fire, put aside some more porridge for the young ones, and finally left for Karati forest.

The headman of the Forest Station supervised the women as they worked as some were careless in their planting, hurrying to finish and collect their firewood. Unlike her usual self Nyokabi, on this day, was miserable and gloomy. She was not feeling happy. Other women kept on asking what was wrong, but she did not know. All day long she was in a dreaming mood. 'Maybe it was the way my husband behaved this morning,' she thought. 'But I should be used to him by now. After all this was not the first time he behaved like this. Let me pull myself together.' Then all of a sudden she would helplessly relapse into the same mood.

'I wonder what is wrong? Is somebody close to me sick, or is somebody I know in trouble?' Nyokabi's hands were weak, her mind disturbed. She had been like this since she woke up early that morning. Nyokabi picked just a few dry twigs for her firewood and left for Major Greying's farm where she lived. One woman laughed at her, 'You stupid woman, why don't you carry more firewood? You are cheating yourself! You are allowed as much as you can carry.' Nyokabi paid no attention to her but tied her few pieces of wood. She asked the headman to accompany her for she was frightened of the dark forest, but did not want to wait for the other women to walk home together in a group.

Arriving at the squatters' village of Major Greying's farm, she was surprised not to see her children playing outside her hut. Where could they be playing? Nyokabi wondered as she walked a little further entering the village. 'It was so quiet, as quiet as a deserted village. Where could they be playing? Where are the children? Where are the mothers?' Nyokabi asked as her heart started to beat fast. She at once dropped down her load of firewood and ran quickly towards her hut.

'Wanjiru! Wanjiru!' she called out. 'Mwangi! Uuuuuuuuu! 'Where are my children? And where is everybody? Where? Where? My God! Where are they? Where? Uuuuuuuuu!' Nyokabi cried loudly, and with all these cries no one answered.

The whole village was empty, only a lonely stray dog moved

among the huts. Nyokabi, crying and frightened, entered her hut in fear. After all, whatever ate my children, let it eat me too! The house however was as she had left it. There was no sign of blood or struggle, nothing disturbed. The food she left boiling on the stove for the children was burnt, the fire completely out, cups and pots and left-over morning porridge were as she had left them. The only intruders were flies resting on the food. Her goats were as she left them in the morning, but without leaves for food. It was all dead, the atmosphere frighteningly dead! Nyokabi cried as she looked around helplessly. The dog barked, the goats cried, and the unconcerned hens scratched the ground here and there in search of food for their chicks. And poor Nyokabi watched helplessly without knowing where the family was.

'Uuuuuu,' Nyokabi cried once again. 'Uuuuuuuu, come and kill me too,' she continued. 'Don't leave me! Leave me for what?' She shouted loudly, 'Come quickly, do to me what you did to my family? Come and tell me before I hang myself with this rope! Let me die knowing what happened to my children! Wanjiru, Wanjiru, my daughter! Uuuuuu.... Kill me.'

A short time lapsed, then Nyokabi began shouting again. 'Mwangi! Njeri! Kamau! Wairimu! and Kariuki my husband! Uuuuuuuu . . . Kill me! Tell me where they are before I kill myself!' Not a sound. No response from anywhere.

By now Arap Chemuor, the Kalenjin, who was a watchman on the farm, heard Nyokabi's cries in a distance. He was coming under cover to see who was still left on Major Greying's farm, and whether Mau Mau terrorists had come to fight. Chemuor saw it was just Nyokabi who was tying a rope on a low tree outside her hut in an obvious attempt to commit suicide. Around her neck the cord went and she let herself slip. Chemuor ran to her quickly and cut the rope. He comforted Nyokabi, and gave her some water to drink.

When Nyokabi could speak, she asked that Chemuor spear her. 'I want to die. If not, go away and let me hang myself. I beg you to spear me. For what and why should I live? Tell me Chemuor, tell me quickly, where are my children? I sense something terrible has happened.'

Nyokabi threw Chemuor unaware to the ground. 'Tell me, otherwise I'll chop you with my axe, and then hang myself! Quickly, tell me where are they?'

'Listen, sit down and listen!'

'Are they dead?' Nyokabi asked desperately.

'No, they are not dead.'

Nyokabi burst into tears again, hugged Arap Chemuor and shouted, 'Tell me what happened.'

'You see, Nyokabi, that next door *kaburu* is very bad! He thinks all Kikuyus are bad and kill people. He says you are all Mau Maus. He came and told *bwana kiko* that Kikuyu squatters are administering an oath ceremony on this farm. He even said that they want to murder all white settlers and that they are responsible for burning those stores the other day. Now, you know! I think even the DO there is *kaburu* and even those young boys, sons of these settlers, hate Africans, Kikuyus in particular.'

'Don't give me a long story!' interrupted Nyokabi, 'tell me where my family is! Tell me quickly or leave me to die.'

'So the whites sent several lorries with barbed wire. They went over to where people were working, asking all Kikuyus to go in. They moved from section to section and later moved into the squatters' village and moved all the children and women. Kikuyus were all to be repatriated to where they came from, back to their villages where they could be kept together under guard.'

Nyokabi listened carefully and quietly. 'And did they allow some people to take their belongings?' she asked.

'Belongings?' Arap Chemuor repeated. 'Nyokabi, we all cried. We have never in all our lives seen anything like this! These Kikuyus were pushed on lorries like goats, their children packed in another lorry. Maybe when they get them in camps, the children will be able to find their parents.'

'Their parents!' Nyokabi repeated. 'Some of them are sitting here in a deserted village! Oh! my children! Oh! poor blood of mine! Did they take anything for them to eat?'

'Nyokabi, taking food, when and where? You should have seen these cruel homeguards pushing them around, throwing them on the back of the lorries as if they had no blood in their veins. One woman tried to grab a calabash of porridge to carry for her children. You should have seen that Headman Calandi knock it out of her hand. The calabash broke. The porridge spilled leaving the children's dry lips with nothing to wet them. Food was left burning on the fires, goats left tied as they were by their owners this morning. The only thing those homeguards had time for was to inspect people's huts and take all the money they could get hold of. Some even stole blankets and other belongings. The children were not able to take anything, not even their sweaters or shirts, some were running around almost naked. They were loaded on trucks without compassion. They cried from shock until they became tearless. The barbed wire lorries then drove off to the unknown villages of their forgotten ancestors.'

Arap Chemuor was a very kind man and he told Nyokabi to dress up like a Kalenjin woman so as not to be noticed. 'You can stay with us. Leave your pierced ears like those of Kalenjins. No one will recognize you. Live with my wives in our village.'

All this time slow tears trickled down Nyokabi's cheeks. Arap Chemuor's offer to help went unheard. Her mind was with her hungry children. She imagined how dry her children's lips were, and how cold they might be. Oh God of Mount Kenya, help us that my children meet their father in the camp! Let him comfort them! In case they die, let them be together. At the thought of this Nyokabi walked boldly to Major Greying's house. The dog tied outside barked wildly at Nyokabi.

'Come and kill me too!' she shouted as she passed through the bougainvillea arch by the gate. 'Come with your guns! Bring your pistols! Kill me quickly or take me where Mau Maus are!'

His children who were outside the house ran inside and locked themselves in, thinking that Nyokabi was mad. His frightened wife looked through the curtains of her upstairs room in fear. She recognized Nyokabi. Through the window and in her poor Swahili, she asked, 'What do you want?'

'My children *memsahib*,' Nyokabi answered. 'My family Take me where they are now.'

Major Greying had just finished supervising the work on the farm, but for him today there was an extra curiosity: wanting to see how the squatters' village looked without all those Kikuyu Mau Maus in it. He finally arrived just as his wife addressed Nyokabi. He sat on his horse dressed in corduroy trousers, gum-boots on his long feet, and on his head he had a cork hat protecting him from the fierce sun. On his hip, a pistol rested, all set to shoot any Kikuyu Mau Maus.

'*Bwana kiko*,' Nyokabi turned to him as he passed through the bougainvillea arch, 'come and kill me! I am waiting for you. Draw your pistol and gun me down! I am a mother of all those Mau Mau children you sent away during my absence. Kill me quickly or send me where they are.'

At this time Arap Chemuor, who had been following Nyokabi entered Major Greying's farm to help explain how Nyokabi was left behind. Major Greying listened, then went to the radiophone and called the DO: *This is 19Y20 calling. Who is that? 19Y20 – Major Greying's Farm. He is on patrol again. He is busy making sure that not a single Mau Mau is left behind. All Kikuyus have to go. . . Good, very good,* Major Greying went on. *That is why I am ringing too. Do you have any of these barbed wire lorries there?. . . . Yes, there is one van left. Wait until I come . . . There is one mad Kikuyu woman forgotten at my farm. She looks pregnant too, and I would not like to breed any more of these Kikuyu seeds on my farm. . .* The officer at the other end laughed loudly then he said, *True, I don't blame you Major Greying. I can send a homeguard in a Landrover. I don't think she can over-power my homeguards. . . . She might,* Major Greying answered. *She looks half mad, and quite strong too. Don't worry. . . . We shall inspect her first.*

In a few minutes, the Landrover arrived at the farm and Nyokabi looking angry and disgusted entered it without asking where she was being taken. She did not talk to anybody. When asked where she was when the others left, she spat in the face of the homeguard who gave her a bad look, laughed mockingly, then said, 'My dear, you know what you are asking for. You shall soon see if you cannot behave yourself.'

Once again Nyokabi spat on his face as a sign of contempt. The homeguard slapped her in the face very hard. She then screamed at them. 'Kill me! I don't want to live! Shoot me, you have your guns! Don't waste time!'

They later pulled the Landrover by the roadside, pushed her into the bushes and poor Nyokabi had to struggle in vain with four men. They attacked and raped her as if it was the only thing they wanted in the world. And Nyokabi who wanted to die did not care but made them know that what they took was through sheer bestiality and nothing she would give to the likes of them. Nyokabi was overpowered, bruised, battered and raped. She was then thrown back into the Landrover unconscious and the journey continued.

On arriving at the homeguards' camp they all came to laugh at her and spat on her face. Her broken self now had not the strength to make even a flicker of protest. Eventually, she too was transferred to the camp where all the others were.

At the camp they were fed maize porridge, badly prepared and with no sugar. They slept in the open air of the barbed wire camp. In rain, sun, dew, heat or cold they were now part of unadorned nature. Several were called into offices to be interrogated about the part they took in the Mau Mau movement. In some cases they thought it best to make up stories, just pretend to be Mau Maus and surrender. They tried to satisfy noisy interrogators with what they wanted to hear. Then they would be better treated, and some of these were sent to their own home districts. Those stubborn ones were sent to detention camps and were mistreated in various ways; some eventually disappeared, many became fatally ill.

Nyokabi was regarded as a Mau Mau gang leader. They said she was left behind because she had gone to take food to the Mau Mau terrorists in the forest. Although she tried to accept these lies, and surrender so that she could be allowed to go with her family, the homeguards regarded her as one of the most dangerous women. 'She fights like an injured lioness,' one homeguard said. And so, she was kept in detention.

As for the good ones, they were called one by one and asked to give their original home location. Kariuki, Nyokabi's husband, like many others said they did not know. His grandfather said that they had come from chief Karuri's area, but he did not know which village, and his grandfather was now dead.

'Do you know whether your family had a garden in the village?'

'My grandfather sold it to come to the settler's farm. We all moved away, and we know no one in these areas. And even if we go there, we now have nothing.'

They, Kariuki and the children, were finally transfered to Murang'a District and shown the way to the chief Karuri's, who in any case had died a long time ago. They were now all put in another camp waiting for their ancestors to be traced.

Here we are, Kariuki said to himself, no brothers, no clan, no food, no shelter, with six children, their mouths dry and hungry. Where do we find them food? I have no idea.

Like Kariuki, others had the same problem: they did not know where exactly they came from, they knew talk of chiefs Kibathe, Waiyakis, Wambagus. This said only where they came from, but who would take care of them, no one seemed to know. Knowing your ancient chief does not indicate your origin. What clan? Where are the ancestors' land? Where are the huts? Homeguards stood there watching these people without homes as if they were not even alive.

In Kariuki's camp a woman called Njoki pinched her friend, Njeri and whispered to her, 'Njeri, we cannot sit here and watch our children die.'

'What do we do?' Njeri asked as her baby continued sucking the milkless breasts. 'You are a very stubborn woman, where do you think we can go. My husband has been already arrested. What do I do with these hungry children?'

'They are hungry, Njeri, you too are hungry, so are my children and I. Let us try our luck. Njeri, they have been telling us repeatedly not to leave the camp, but I am not going to watch children die. If they die, they will die while I am doing something. Let us go'

'Go where?' Njeri asked.

'I do not know, but just follow me.' At this moment Njeri and Njoki were seen strapping their babies on their backs. Njeri was in tears, while Njoki was showing a bitter face.

'Where are you going?' Kariuki asked.

'Where are we,' Njoki answered. 'We are going to climb any hills or mountains. We shall walk through any valley, where we go no longer matters. I cannot watch my children die here in the camp, like mice in deserted homes. Since we came in this camp, we have already had the deaths of two children, not to mention those of old people. Kariuki I shall die on the move. Njeri, let us go,' Njoki called as she walked through homeguard gates. She turned to Njeri and said, 'This is a poor area, it is near the forest, people are harassed by the homeguards. They are working in communal labour all day so that they have no time to look after their gardens, and Farms have now turned into bushland, but as we came along I noticed the lower part was better. We passed millet growing, we saw maize in the gardens and people looked brighter, Let us go there, maybe those are the areas where there is less trouble. They might be needing some help on their farms, labourers to help in their gardens.'

'Yooo' Njeri answered. 'I don't even care for payment, if only they can give me food and shelter for my children. Let us try our luck.'

Led by their children and with nothing with them, they walked. After a few miles they met a woman who asked them where they were going. They said they did not know and explained their story. This woman gave them a Mau Mau sign which made them know they were in good hands, but she told them that they were now near the end of the division and that they could be arrested if they went further without any pass. 'So don't go beyond there, I advise you.'

'But we have to go,' Njoki explained. 'We must try our luck.'

'Then if you have to go, avoid walking on main roads. They are more dangerous without a pass, you better go down the river. Then walking along the river, and if by an chance anybody asks you who you are – pretend you live around here.'

Njeri and Njoki followed the advice and by good luck they reached a farm where people were working, they asked them if they could help and those people were very happy. Njoki took her child from her back, dug a little hole on the ground to support it from falling down, spread a few leaves for her child to sit on, and she was ready to join the others.

Njeri also tried to do the same, but as Njeri untied her baby, the baby seemed to have unusual sleep. 'Kamau, Kamau, what is wrong with you?' Njeri shook Kamau vigorously but Kamau would not turn, he was lifeless. 'Kamau wake up.' Kamau would not turn. Njoki and another woman came to help Kamau, but Kamau was already dead. Njoki cried and Njeri cried bitterly for her son. 'Your father is detained, Kamau! Kamau,' she called, 'Kamau the only son I have, died tied on my back.' She cried so much that the farming work was stopped and they had to comfort the mother and bury Kamau.

Later Njeri was employed by the owner of that farm as a labourer. She first started earning just a meal, but by showing what a hard worker she was, they promised her 25 shillings a month and this way she lived. Njoki too managed to get an old woman to give her a place to stay. Every morning she would work on coffee farms, and got casual employment. She kept the lonely old woman company. Whatever she got was shared by all. The old lady helped to look after Njoki's children.

Njoki's example was followed by many, young women, and men managed to join forest fighters. Kariuki and his young children followed. They had nowhere to stay. It seemed easier for women and the youths who could become freedom fighters. 'What a life for a lonely man with young children? With their mother locked in for an unknown period, surrounded by these unkind homeguards. There is no future. I know they will rape her, rape a wife of a helpless husband who cannot fight back. And with all these children, which relatives can accommodate us if there are any left? Who will feed us all? I wish we were left in the detention camps, at least we would have food.

'Here, we are forced to stay homeless, my hut standing deserted far away, my children hungry when potatoes, maize and beans are feeding mice at Major Greying's farm. We are cold and naked. My clothes, blankets and belongings added to the homeguards' plunder. I have only one left, with the children! I am as empty as I came from my mother's womb. And my poor wife!'

The Interrogation Camp

Introduction

Any written work on the state of the emergency in Kenya could not be complete without a discussion of the interrogation experience where people were mercilessly tortured, roughly handled and inhumanly treated. It was during interrogation that innocent people were mistakenly or intentionally accused, sometimes because of personal differences, hatred or jealousy. Some malicious people would hide things like bullets or medicine or other unauthorised items under your chairs, in your house or in your garden and later report that you are a supporter of Mau Mau, saying that you collect guns and bullets for them or that you send medicine to the forest fighters. I knew of one nurse at Kenyatta National Hospital who had stolen penicillin hidden in her flat and later was reported as one of the drug transporters for the forest fighters. And when she confidently opened her flat for officials to search for the medicine, she was shocked to see a case of penicillin hidden in her house that she had never seen before. I knew this nurse well; she was so hurt that she committed suicide before she underwent the interrogation.

While interrogation was a common exercise during freedom fighting, there were some particular interrogations that will never be forgotten. The one known as *Operation Anvil* is remembered by the people of Nairobi even to this day. I had *Operation Anvil* in mind when I wrote this chapter. It was common to wake up in the morning to find all the village surrounded by police, army people, homeguards, and other loyalists. Then all the grownups would be lined up and taken to an area enclosed with barbed wire. There they would be very roughly, rudely and nastily handled; they would be abused and kicked around. Then they would be asked to sit not flat on the ground but with their legs bent, in a position that is very painful. They could sit there in the hot sun for hours and hours, well guarded, as the authorities called them one by one to enter the tent for a thorough investigation. Those who entered the tent would find a person who had covered his head with a *gakonia*, a bag of rough cloth with just two holes left for him to see through. The officials would ask many questions about your activity in Mau Mau, sometimes accusing you of things you did not even know, such as whether you feed or hid Mau Maus. In some cases you would be punished if somebody in your family was in the forest or being detained. If you did not satisfy the interrogation, they would even punish you and torture you so that you would speak. They could burn your fingers or force you to sit on hot things. Bottles were pushed into women's private parts. Some men were roughly handled and castrated. In this condition, you said whatever you thought would make your interrogators happy, whether it was true or not. The most important thing was just to get away.

After the interrogation, the authorities will give you one of the cards, either red, grey or white. If the *Gakonia* man shouted red, you know you are in for a serious trouble – this means you are a bad conspirator, a Mau Mau, and you will definitely be placed in a detention camp. Grey means that they are not sure so you can either have a house arrest or some simple punishments. If you had a white card that means you are clean and you can be left free. In some cases very serious criminals may be given a white card and left free. In some cases, particularly where personalities and personal jealousies were involved, a very innocent person can be given a red card and said to have committed a serious offence. In this chapter you can see an innocent person given a red card, just because the interrogator's family had a land dispute with his clan and practised malice.

To make the interrogation effective and easy to manage, all Kikuyu, Meru and Embu peoples were forced to leave their scattered homes on their farms and to build villages close together so that it was very easy to check them.

*   *   *

Thursday morning began bright enough. Njambi felt it as she started her day's work: preparing her children to go off to Morrison Primary School at Bahati location in Nairobi. This particular morning she set out porridge for them. She thought of warming some left-over sweet potatoes to add to the breakfast. She roused her children and sent them outside to the communal water tap to wash up before they left for school while she readied their food.

Njambi took a piece of soap and a pumice stone and ordered them to scrape their feet properly. 'Scrape your feet well!' Njambi shouted at her son Kimani. 'And take care of your brother's too. I don't want you sent back home again by that new headmaster for your untidy feet.' Njambi grumbled as she went back inside. It is as if the headmaster doesn't know how dirty children can be, and with these poor children who walk bare-foot and in the dirty location; when it rains it's full of mud, and when it is sunny, it's full of dust. 'Poor Kimani' Njambi thought as she went to help him to wash his legs properly. 'When did you get this other jigger in your toe? You should have told me as soon as you felt your toe itching. Kimani! Have you watched your uncle walk? His feet are crooked and his toes, deformed. When he walks his feet are sideways. So you have already noticed.' Njambi called her big daughter Gathoni to bring her a safety pin so that she could remove the jigger from her son's toe. 'Look how big it is, Kimani! After all you have Githu's blood. This Githu's family must be having tasty blood for jiggers. That is why your father and his family have their toes deformed. Jiggers' blood is not in my family!' Njambi shouted to her son who almost was in tears because of pain, 'Wait until I finish, it is nearly out. There it is, a really big one. That surely is not from my son's toe. Wash your toe with salted water or it will get sore.'

'Go now and put on your school uniform and get ready to run off to school,' Njambi said to Kimani. 'Kimani! Come home straight from school. Your brother's trousers are really ripped. Let him have your trousers this afternoon after your morning classes and you wear your old rags. I just cannot afford to buy you an extra pair of trousers.' Kimani did not like the idea and complained to his mother that his trousers were too big for his younger brother. 'Don't worry! I can fit them with a safety pin. Just do what you're told and leave the rest to me, but take care they are not too dirty.'

All this time Gathoni was busy feeding porridge to the young baby. She envied those who went to school. She wished she too could be in that blue tunic uniform for girls, but she was the elder, and the only girl. Her mother tried explaining that they didn't have enough money and, anyway a girl's education was not necessary since she'd get married and be supported by her husband. But with the boys, life is difficult without schooling. Even with enough money, Gathoni would be needed at home, learning to be a mother – taking care of the youngsters and cooking food for them and her father. That need was more important than just going to school as far as Njambi was concerned. Njambi had to start her daily work as soon as the children had gone to school. Njambi who was not employed had been longing for employment as a sweeper with the City Council.

It was difficult for her to feed five children in Nairobi. Like many other Kikuyu women, she could never be idle. She used to walk to empty unbuilt plots and plant more vegetable gardens. She would plant maize, beans, sweet potatoes and cassava. Sometimes she was lucky to have good crops that contributed to her family's food supply. The best among all her gardens was along the Nairobi River. There she had arrow-roots, cow-peas and sugar-canes. The only trouble with Nairobi gardens is that the plot is not yours, and the owner can decide to put up a building just when your crops are near ready, and there is nothing you can do. Other things Njambi used to do included going at 4 am to the wholesale vegetable market to buy some vegetables and sell them. But that business was a big risk because she might be arrested for not having a peddlar's licence. She had tried selling vegetables from door to door, but this too was a tiring job, and the Asian women bargain you to almost nothing. They never look to one's condition. Their interest was only to get things cheap.

Njambi never forgot the time she walked all day carrying a heavy load of vegetables to Ngara Road, Parklands, Pangani, and to Eastleigh in a scorching sun. Her bare feet got sore, she was hungry and thirsty, so she decided to sit and eat one of her pineapples. When she got home she was disappointed to learn that she had a deficit of five shillings all because she refreshed herself. Since that time Njambi swore she'd never again carry a basket of vegetables to trade in the locations.

Njambi started today by showing Gathoni how to cook maize and beans. When leaving she put some sweet potatoes in her small basket to eat at lunch time while visiting her garden in the Industrial Area. She heard a knock.

'Who is that?' Njambi asked.

'We are the visiting Health Officers, health visitors, Mama, we have come to visit you.'

'Visit me?' Njambi asked in disgust.

'Yes Mama, open the door.' Njambi opened the door. 'Is that your child? Yes. Why don't you bring him to the clinic? Bring him maybe tomorrow to us so we may weigh him and also give him a check-up. We also give advice on what sorts of food your child needs to make him grow strong and healthy.'

'OK. Thank you for visiting me.' Njambi answered.

They left for next door. Njambi murmured to herself: Telling me how to take care of my child! Are they giving me the same old story, give the child milk, fruit and eggs, or they are giving us free food to give to the children. I have not even got maize flour, leave alone milk. I hate the whole lot, tell them to go and make a queue for weighing babies. Heavy or light – it is my baby. 'Gathoni! take care of the baby and feed your brothers when they come from school.'

'Mama! Mama!' Njambi heard a call as she was starting out.' 'Where are you going?'

'I am going to the garden. What can I do for you?' Njambi asked.

'Wait a minute, Mama,' the two uniformed women called. 'We are from Bahati Community Centre, and we are going round telling all mothers like you about our clubs. You are invited, come to our centre and learn how to read and write, and also learn how to cook.'

'Cook what?' Njambi asked.

'Cakes and other things,' one woman said to Njambi.

'Like those eaten by the Europeans, the ones they cook with milk mixed with eggs?' Njambi's voice had a bitter, quiet edge.

'Yes, and you can also learn how to make clothes of your own and also for the children.' The visitors moved on to yet another house.

Njambi told herself, let me go to the garden that gives me beans to cook for my children because I can't afford eggs for the cakes. And even if they teach me I don't have a house to decorate with embroidery and no tables to put those cloths on. She left the community workers and walked away briskly to her garden. 'Don't they bother people!' Njambi thought as she was walking, but after thinking on what they said, she decided to send her daughter to learn and know how to read and write, and maybe how to stitch clothes. After all, poor Gathoni ought to be in school. If by good luck she married a man who can read, she may need to write him letters whose contents would be a secret between herself and her husband. But if you are illiterate and somebody comes to write it for you, the letter is no longer a secret. Also the idea of learning how to make dresses is a good one. One can even sew for other people and make money.

Njambi had a busy day in her garden, she dug some arrow-roots, picked fresh beans and some maize – although it was not ready – but at least the children would enjoy eating it. That day Njambi went home loaded. She walked home carrying beans ready for cooking. That day they had good supper enjoying eating the arrow-roots and roasted maize.

By now Githii, Njambi's husband, had come home from work. He was a labourer at a coffeehouse. He used to walk early in the morning to his place of work on White House Road. He always returned late and was tired when he reached home. He always came straight home. After all where could an old Kikuyu man like himself go without a watch to tell him the time. There was the danger of curfew catching you without being aware. In any case, where could one go, and go and mix with whom? To mix with those unnoticed terrorists meant being spied upon. After a few drinks, one could never be too sure that one's tongue was still listening to one's head. One could be in trouble.

Githii never forgot when one evening soon after pay day, he had decided to go to a local bar to enjoy a drink for a few minutes. There he met a friend who offered him a beer and some roasted meat. The bar was noisy and everyone was trying to drink in a hurry to beat the 9 pm curfew time. At Bahati Location people were said to be behaving well. At about 8 pm, the crowd was happy and the bar noisy. People were ordering one drink after another. Some sent people to the nearby butcher to hurry him along with roasting their meat. Men who were accompanied by their wives, sat in pairs inside the quiet rooms separated by dirty curtains.

Sitting in one of the corners, sipping his last beer and chewing some of the left-overs of roasted goat ribs, Githii was busy discussing life. Sitting, enjoying himself with his friends, he noticed two young men wearing coats, hats and dark glasses entered the bar. They walked past most of the customers and hurried up to the end of the bar. They took the high stools by the counter. There they ordered some drinks, but the bar-man said it was rather late. 'We must close before 9 pm.'

'We'll drink up quickly,' one of the young men said while when the other suggested forgetting the drinks, the young men scanned the crowded barroom. One of them stood up and began hurriedly to inspect people in every cubicle of the bar. He pulled down the screens covering the cubicles one by one, gazing at each customer. Both men moved on into the next room. When they reached Githii, he asked them 'What's the matter, young men? Have you lost a comrade or what?' They answered 'Yes,' as they moved into the other cubicle. Githii and his friend Kanja gave each other suspicious looks and they decided to clear their bills and leave.

Just as Githii and his friend approached the door, they heard three shots. People started screaming and running off a way in all directions. Kiiru, the bar-man hid behind the counter while others jumped through the windows. Police and all the homeguards came rushing to Gaita Bar. Any man seen running away was stopped and arrested. Those who refused to stop were shot at by the police or homeguards. Poor people, some did not even know why the others were running, they had not been in the bar at all. Many had not even heard the shots, nor were they concerned with what had happened. Others were running away, so they too had to run away and seek refuge in their rooms as no-one knew what was going on. Githii managed to get into his room before he could be arrested. He entered his room in a hurry and jumped straight into bed and put out the lights. Njambi insisted that her husband say what was happening, and so, with a whispering voice, he explained. Poor Githii did not even eat his supper. Since that day he swore not to go out of his house after work, that he would never move about.

'The only place where I shall be seen is my house. The only place I will step in with my feet will be my house.'

On that same Thursday, in the evening, as the family was enjoying fresh food brought in by Njambi from her garden, Kimani the big son started to tell a story of what he saw during the day. 'Mama,' Kimani started, 'today there were many *askari*s walking around Bahati. Even some Europeans were about on horses. They passed near our school. They went up and down near the river, just near our garden where we have sugar-cane.'

'Me too, I saw them,' the young boy added. 'When I was playing near the Public Works, they passed and they took the direction towards Burma market.'

'Be quiet,' Njambi told her children. 'You always see them. What is new in seeing *askari*s at Bahati? A place selected for Kikuyus, Merus and Embu only. The Mau Mau they label us, Mau Maus to carry passbooks, Mau Maus to be arrested, Mau Maus to be disturbed. Eat and don't remind me of the troubles.'

'No mummy,' Kimani insisted 'I have never seen so many before. Ask the other children, we all went to watch them.'

'Yes it is true, Mama.'

Githii looked sadly at Njambi and said, 'This is trouble time. Let us hear what they have seen. Gathoni, tell us what you saw.'

'When I was washing clothes at the communal tap, I saw some children standing by the fence looking excitedly toward the Nairobi Nanyuki Railway line. I thought the train was passing, but it was not time for the train. I also saw a group of people running away, so I too took the baby to go and see. I saw some *askari*s in different uniforms, some walking, others on horses and there were some with dogs. I even saw the head and the chief.'

'What did they do?' Githii asked.

'Nothing, they were very friendly. We waved at them and they waved back. We shouted *'jambo'* and they answered *'jambo'* and they then left! They were not in a hurry, Daddy. They waved to us as we followed the horses. And they went round the whole of Bahati location.'

'I think this sounds like the usual round. Nothing serious has happened,' Githii commented as he pulled an enamel basin of water near his bed to wash his feet before bed.

'Nothing serious, let us hope.' Njambi took the story lightly but with some reservation. She said all day she had not been happy. She had funny feelings that were very unusual for her, the sort of feelings she has when something serious was going to happen.

'Go to bed.' Githii told everybody, complaining to his wife that she liked to frighten children at bed time, and they would have nightmares because of her. Whatever it is to come let it come. We were born once and we shall die once.

On Friday, Githii woke as usual at about 6 am to get to his work at Coffee House on White House Road. He woke up his wife to give him a cup of tea. Njambi knowing how charcoal burners take time before the fire is lit, had a thermos flask where she kept her husband's tea. As she poured tea for Githii, he went outside to wash his face at the tap overlooking the Nanyuki Railway Line. The Line divided the unfenced Government Quarters and St. Stephen Church from Bahati location. It ran parallel to Donholm road toward Shauri Yako Estate.

As Githii was busy rinsing the soap from his face he heard the location whistle blow. *'Funga safari!'* the voice continued . . . *'Pheeee, all grown-ups, funga safari!'* Still with soap bubbles on his face, and water dashing full force from the communal water tap, he felt a tap on his shoulder. With a shock, he stood and turned. He looked back. There stood an *askari* with a furious look on his face. Without a word, he looked to all sides to find the whole of the Nanyuki Railway Line was lined by *askari*s all facing Bahati location. At once Githii knew he was in trouble, and with so many *askari*s around, there was no use thinking of escaping.

'Funga safari,' the *askari* repeated. Githii knowing the emergency problem said nothing but tried to rinse the soap still on his face. The *askari* struck him hard with a whip. 'Are you deaf that you did not hear what I said? *Funga safari,'* the *askari* shouted.

'Please I did not hear,' Githii pleaded. At this time his wife Njambi heard the talk and opened the door quickly.

'Githii, Githii, what did you do? *Askari*, what has he done?' Njambi looked from the *askari* to her frightened husband. 'Leave him please, *askari* leave him, where are you taking him? Tell me *askari*, we are not Mau Maus, where are you taking him, *askari*?'

'He is going to join your leaders. There they will get him a big European farm and a European house, then you will be able to employ me as your servant,' the *askari* said.

'Please *askari*,' Njambi continued as she was pushing back her excited children showing them signs to hide under the beds. Githii did not utter a word. By now, he saw all his neighbours following each other quickly and quietly, their wives and children left to gaze through the windows, not knowing whether they would ever see their men again. No questions and no words of good-bye. All the adult men were herded along the edge of Bahati location, leaving behind weeping wives and weeping children and going to unknown destinations. They all quietly followed each other, the fate of their *safari* unknown. Through the gates all grown-up males passed the nasty looking *askari*s who observed them closely as they passed like sheep heading for a slaughter house. Each following the next. Women wept, but the answer to the fate of their husbands no one knew.

They were moved to Kamukunji where they were lined up in one 'pipe line', as the *askari*s' leader called it. They stood outside the barbed wire camp surrounded by the army, police, the homeguards and all the loyalists. Many, particularly the young men, didn't believe in dying like sheep, and were looking for a chance to escape. Their minds raced over the chances to run away. They passed through a line of *askari*s who searched their pockets, their trousers, under their arms, inside their shoes, and even in their mouths.

The screening team was harsh. They were rude and passed nasty comments. They screened you ruthlessly, turning you from side to side like a cook frying fish. They were pushing and pulling people here and there, and some shirts were torn. You pass them without unbuttoning your clothes and they lose your buttons. They were giving slaps to those who showed the slightest resistance. Then they would throw people to the next *askari* as you threw a ball. The screening was to check for weapons, for any sign that one was a Mau Mau. It was ruthless. To the *askari*s, it was a chance to make money. Any found in your pockets, the screeners put in their pockets.

Men were driven into the Kamukunji screening camp from all the surrounding locations. They were mainly Merus, Kikuyus, and Embus, and they were collected together for the first screening team. When they arrived, the guards and *askari*s stood surrounding them, alert for trouble. The crowd was still waiting to hear their fate. All sat still.

In the middle of the Kamukunji barbed wire camp, the men sat cross-legged motionless. The mid-day sun beat at their faces, sweating hungry faces. Many were with nothing, some were without good clothes, some without shoes or hats.

Githii was tempted to whisper to his friend Kanja, who was sitting next to him. He gave Kanja a kick to make him pay attention. 'Kanja, do you think they are going to shoot us? I suspect they will, maybe they will burn us all.'

Kagwa sitting close to them said, 'Did you know of the bombs that were used during the German War? I heard they may throw them at us.'

Githii also gave another explanation. 'I also heard that there is an injection they want to give all us Kikuyu men so that we can never produce children again.' Such whispering voices finally reached an *askari*'s ears. He walked quietly to where Githii was sitting. Githii did not notice the *askari* coming. His friend Kanja had, but couldn't warn Githii soon enough. While Githii continued his talk he was badly whipped across his face and on his back. As the *askari* raised the whip again, Kanja grabbed hold, and all those nearby stood alert, ready to protect their friend. Githii shouted to everybody to be quiet and sit down. The *askari* went wild, other *askari*s joined in, but no one was fighting so the disorder was quickly over and the camp became silent again.

Now the DC and other administrators, all well armed, came inside the camp. Mr Scott, the DC, wearing his khaki uniform and a pistol suspended around his waist, and a stick protruding out the side of his khaki jumper coat, addressed them in Swahili, 'I can observe your ugly bitter faces, your minds are full of bitterness, your evil expressions are well displayed on your unwashed faces.' Then he called to one of his *askari*s to shoot in the air. The DC returned to the frightened crowd, 'Shoot your guns if you have any. Come and shoot now! Go on and shoot! Those with ears let them hear, and those with eyes let them see. If any one dares once again to create any disturbances, I shall not talk to you with words, but with that gun you have just heard. Try to make any movement, or some other problems, and you will soon see action.'

The DC went back to his Landrover. No one dared to speak again, apart from the eyes that filled with expression. At the far side the squatting, thirsty, sweating and hungry Kikuyu, Embu and Meru noticed the faces of the two young men who had shot a loyalist in the Gaita bar. These two looked as if ready to act, but others warned them off. Too much trouble would come and they had no weapons. What could empty hands do? They all must wait.

By now several police lorries were standing by the camp's gate. Those lorries looked more like cages for animals. The doors of the caged lorries had big iron locks.

'In one line' chief Karia shouted to them. 'Quick, in one line. Be ready for the *safari* at once.' At last Githii felt happy as he stretched his already suffering legs. What a comfort to be able to turn from the fearful burning sun of the afternoon. If only they knew their future, he thought.

At the camp's gate stood the chief of the area, all the sub-chiefs, and leaders of the homeguards. Githii and others were by now all standing in a line circling completely the camp's border. Chiefs and men stood facing each other, a narrow path between them. Each of the homeguards and chiefs had several cards put on a small portable table near the gate. A clerk was seated there with three stacks of cards. Each lot had a different colour. One was red, the second, green, and the third, grey. The guards, the loyalists, and the administrators also had cards in different colours. The men were asked to pass through the middle, each one to take a card.

Looking along the line of homeguards, Githii saw an acquaintance from his childhood, Muraya; they got circumcised at the same time and the same place. They were not friends because their families had had a land dispute, and also Muraya wanted to marry Githii's sister, but Githii had refused the dowry because he had known Muraya's bad character. Muraya had married another woman who unfortunately had not born him a son. Long without a job, Muraya had joined the homeguards.

When Githii saw Muraya, he lost all his hope. They were now going through the gate. One man got a white card. Kanja, Githii's best friend, followed next and was given a grey card. It was now Githii's turn to get a card, and when he entered he was given a black card. Before he could move along, Muraya came up and ripped the black one from Githii's hand and gave him a red one instead.

Githii did not know colours. Githii was still standing with his red card, the terrorist had a green card and his friend Kanja with a grey card. Gaita, the owner of the Gaita bar, had a black card. The second terrorist also had a red card.

As they moved, they passed the cages of the police lorries. When the distribution of the cards was finished, those with green and white cards were told to go back to their homes. Some clapped and laughed as they ran home as though they were mad, others were interested to know where they are taking those left behind. '*Safari!*' the chief shouted to those who were leaving for home. Those who were left were all transported in lorries to unknown destinations.

All the lorries were filled with the hungry, dirty, worried and miserable men with the unlucky coloured cards and were driven away to another barbed wire camp. There the men met others who had been subjected to screening teams like the one at Kamukunji. The people were coming from all over. Some were from Githii's home, and others were his work-mates. At the same place he met his friend Njue who worked as a cook at Muthaiga Club. He also met Ndubi, a hospital dresser from the King George V Hospital; Wahome, a clerk at the Railway was also there.

There they had another screening. No talking was permitted. All who were there had either a grey or a red card. They were served badly cooked porridge with no sugar; the flour was not good, but there was no time to notice the badness in the porridge.

Early on Saturday morning the whistle was blown. 'Get into the line,' the Headman called. 'All of you line up.' Githii had not slept that night, bitterness clouding any rest. He remembered he had left his family without money for food.

Stretching a sore and hungry body, he noticed one police lorry coming in with people cowled in sisal bags. The bags had holes, one was for the nose, two for the eyes, and the fourth for the mouth. These people were interrogators. Maybe friends or workmates. They had their heads covered to protect their identities. They came to ask questions: 'Have you taken an oath?' 'How many oaths have you taken?' 'Who administered the oath to you, and who else was there?' 'Do you know who feeds Mau Maus?'

Githii, like many Kikuyus that had taken only one Mau Mau oath, was just a quiet man that people did not bother. After all he would not make a good terrorist. He looked like a man who could easily give in, if that would save his soul, and who wanted to waste time with such people. He was harmless, not a talkative man, a stay-at-home type. He would not make a good Mau Mau, not even make a good loyalist. Nevertheless the screening team gave him a red card, and with a scar on his face, he was even labelled a terrorist, number one.

As Githii passed the gunny-bagged men, one asked him where he got the scar on his face from. 'At the camp.' Githii answered. 'I see, you are the big terrorist who created disturbances at Kamukunji camp? OK, go ahead, we shall show you.' Without facing any more questions, Githii was directed to another group.

When the interviews were done, some were released to go home, but Githii and others were put in to yet another camp.

Later the interrogations continued. This time it was really bad because they were beaten up. Their bodies were pierced with safety pins, and for Githii, he was really punished, since he did not know much about Mau Mau, he could only answer 'I don't know' to their questions. The interrogators thought him to be the most secretive and the deepest Mau Mau supporter. Githii was taken to a small room where he was badly beaten to force him to tell them about Mau Mau.

On the side of the room there was a piece of heavy wire mesh. The charcoal burner was on and Githii thought somebody was preparing to roast meat on it. The wire on the hot charcoal burner was red hot.

Twa! the homeguard slapped Githii. 'Come and tell us all you know about Mau Mau. How many times have you taken the oath?'

'Only once, sir!'

'Who gave it to you?'

'I did not know their names, they dragged me from Gaita bar.'

Twa! another slap on his face. 'You must tell us if you want to live.' Githii recognised Muraya's voice and he knew, with Muraya there, nothing good would come out. Definitely Muraya will do everything to put him into trouble. Githii was pulled closer to one of them. They pulled his trousers down and forced him to sit on the hot wire. 'If you prove to be cheeky with us, you will get more of this.' Githii screamed as his naked buttocks touched the red hot wire. Other detainees wanted to break in to rescue him. The young man who took part in killing the loyalist at Gaita Bar lost control. He wanted to go and rescue Githii. Others held him tight, but when he was noticed by the *askari*s, he too was sent to sit on the burning wire.

At last Githii no longer able to stand the hot wire, decided to tell lies. He made a very good imaginative confession just to make things easier for himself. With scars on his face and burns on his buttocks, he wondered what was wrong with him.

From there the detainees were transferred yet again. One camp had the letters 'GDO' on the board, the other had 'DDO'. Many people did not understand what these letters meant. The GDO camp had the most detainees with red and black cards. GDO meant the Governor's Detention Order, while DDO was District Detention Order. Innocent Githii with his scars all over his body found himself in the murderers' group along with business people, politicians, and even religious leaders. Later they were scattered to different detention camps. Some went to Lamu, some to Mandera and others to Senya.

Githii was sent to Senya detention camp with the younger murderer. Those detained under DDO had a chance of being released soon. Githii cried, he did not know the fate of his family, he did not know what to expect next.

Vanishing Camp

Introduction

In this chapter, I describe the suffering people endured while in the detention camps. Many Kenyan writers have written about these camps from personal experience. These camps were poorly run; the food was inadequate and treatment of the prisoners brutish. Women detainees were isolated in these camps far from any other people. They were not allowed to have visits and any words they uttered were taped; all the letters they wrote were censored.

Food in these camps was very bad. The diet was maize-flour and potatoes, made with water from polluted ponds infested with malarial mosquitoes. Malnutrition meant that such diseases as pellagra, vomiting and diarrhoea were the sicknesses of the day.

The story shows how attempts to improve the detainees' health also brought them the chance to communicate with the outside. The camp officials bring in a health care worker from one of the 'loyal' Kenyan ethnic groups. But he too sympathises with his fellow Africans. His wife is from Central Province and had taken a Mau Mau oath. Both work to keep the detainees in touch with the outside. They smuggle letters, while he also arranges for detainees to be sent to the hospital where she is a nurse when they require 'special care.' The story gives a clear picture of a woman's concern to help the freedom fighters. Most women contributed in many unrecognisable ways. Without the women freedom fighters, the struggle could

160

not have managed. The wife's clever plan saved the detainees, and, by smuggling complaints to the overseas authority, she helped improve camp conditions. The story also shows how a Taita from the Coast – a member of a 'loyal' ethnic group – aided the detainees.

I myself am a Kikuyu and the wife of a Maasai medical doctor. During Mau Mau, he was very much trusted and allowed to enter the detention camps. I had the pleasure of passing letters for the detainees. My husband helped get some detainees hospitalised, enabling them to talk to other people and pass messages.

*   *   *

For many years now, Nyaruai has been living and working at Msambweni General Hospital in the Coast Province along with her husband, Mwacharo. Nyaruai was an assistant midwife and Mwacharo, a medical assistant. She had her training as a midwife at Tumutumu Missionary Hospital; her first work was at the Nyeri General Hospital. This was the principal hospital for the whole of the Central Province. Working at Nyeri Hospital had been exciting and challenging for Nyaruai.

Central Province was densely populated; it was home for the Kikuyu, Embu and Meru – the farmers, the business people, the people who became forest fighters. Nyeri town was home for Dedan Kimathi, General Mathenge and General China, and for many more Mau Mau forest fighters. The thick green Aberdare Mountains and its forest met the district on the west, while the slopes of Mount Kenya and its forest approached the town from the north. Nyeri town was ever green; the hills and villages around were green. This was beauty. Nyaruai's home was not far from the town; she had been pleased to serve her own people.

Not for everyone was the town and province so beautiful; for Europeans, transfer to Central Province headquarters at Nyeri was unpopular. Nyeri was the most troublesome and dangerous of places. British officers left their families elsewhere for safety. Beautiful, but most dangerous town of famous Mau Mau fighters, transfer to Nyeri seemed a transfer to death's den.

While Nyaruai worked at Nyeri Hospital she met and fell in love with Mwacharo who also worked at the hospital. Mwacharo was a

Taita from Wundanyi in Taita Taveta District of Coast Province. They soon married. Later, Nyaruai and her husband were transferred to Msambweni General Hospital in Kwale District, Coast Province. For Nyaruai, it was quite a change from the cold weather of the mountains to the hot humid weather of the coast; from viewing snow-covered Mount Kenya in morning light to seeing the Indian Ocean surrounded by the coconut palm and mango trees; from the district of Christians to that of Muslims, with women wearing black veils; from the place of bitterness to that of unconcerned community, just the calm slow moving, relaxed life of the Coastal peoples. For some time Nyaruai wondered whether she was still in Kenya. The only Kenya she knew was that of Central Province: the land of farmers, Christians, and the land of political bitterness surrounded by freedom fighters. 'What a peaceful life at the Coast,' Nyaruai felt. She was happy to be the wife of Mwacharo and happy to be at the Coast, free from the worry and bitterness of Nyeri.

Nyaruai found the work at Msambweni Hospital interesting. Even more, she enjoyed listening to people talk of things other than killings, arrests and detentions. Here she did not have to face the police and military lorries bringing in the injured or police patrolling the hospital wards, watching. She felt years had passed since feeling so comfortable and happy.

She soon learned from other women how to cook the coastal dishes, using fish, coconuts and other ingredients new to her. Nyaruai also learned to speak good Swahili, and her husband's Taita language. Soon no one would suspect she was anything but a Coast woman.

During her time in Coast Province, Nyaruai watched Mitaaboni and Uaso Camps fill with Kikuyu detainees. Soon they were crammed beyond their limits. Good sanitation was impossible and the people were too many to feed properly. Anyhow, the young sons of European farmers who were battling the forest fighters or administering the camps thought, 'After all why make our enemies healthy? Feeding them well, giving them better facilities, what for? So they can go back to the forests and plan for our murders?'

It was not long before an epidemic broke out in Mitaaboni Detention Camp. The skin of many detainees became covered with blisters and sores particularly on those parts constantly exposed to the hot sun of the coast. They grew weak, their tongues and the corners of their mouths became swollen and sore; they suffered through days of diarrhoea and vomiting. The detainees lost energy and hope. Their minds became confused and full of depression. They lay waiting for their fate – death – hopeless, emaciated, diseased, distraught, in the middle of a jungle surrounded by animals hungry, waiting to feast on their flesh.

The camp chief, nasty as he seemed, grew concerned as the disease spread. The thought of being attacked in the world press worried him even more; he would not like to see his name appear in history books as a man who oversaw a death camp. The chief, Mr Cooper, became suspicious that some white might have poisoned the detainees. He did not think himself cruel by choice, he felt he was a kind person, one who would never condone sordid acts against the detainees. He had never trusted the Boer, Mr Jacobs, who had wondered why the British were so lenient and, on several occasions, had suggested mass killings to end the fighting. Mr Cooper seriously suspected Jacobs of trying to murder the detainees. He had no proof, but kept pushing Jacobs for information about the epidemic.

By now the situation was pathetic. The whole camp was wrapped in the shadows of dying detainees. The diarrhoea, the vomiting, the skin diseases, sore tongues and mouths, and mental anguish of the detainees were frightening. This could not go on, Mr Cooper hated himself for being head of the camp. With great urgency he turned to his superiors for aid. He reported the camp's condition to the Coast Province Commissioner.

'Shall I send reinforcements to safeguard your people?' enquired the Provincial Commissioner.

'Oh no, some in the camp cannot even stand without support. They are a dying lot. The only people you must bring with you are medical staff.'

The Coast Province Commissioner, the District Commissioner, the Police Commissioner and the Provincial Medical Officer flew at once to Mitaaboni camp. They were shocked and bitterly protested Mr Cooper's failure to inform them earlier. Mr Cooper expressed his suspicion of Mr Jacobs, and Jacobs was at once removed from the camp and sent on leave.

Now the whole matter was left in the hands of the Medical Officer. Dr Taylor, the Coast Medical Officer, had no special interest in Kenya politics. He was a British doctor in the Colonial

Service. He had never thought of settling anywhere other than in his English home. After all, his past experiences in Africa were not encouraging: his wife was attacked by malaria in Nigeria, the heat in the Sudan was unbearable, and now yet another heat on the Kenya Coast, and the situation complicated by talk everywhere of emergency and the bitter experience of Mau Mau fighting. After his long leave Dr Taylor thought he would ask the Colonial Office either to send him to Australia, New Zealand or somewhere in the Carribean. Otherwise he planned to resign from the Colonial Service.

For Dr Taylor, what he faced in the detention camp was nothing different from any epidemic disease anywhere else in the world, and he would treat the detainees as a doctor would treat the sick, not as a doctor treating his enemies. Dr Taylor was almost in tears as he viewed the camp. 'I have been in the medical field for over 25 years, and I have never seen anything like this.' At once, he began the work of examining a few detainees, giving orders for their specimens to be collected and sent to him at the Coast General Hospital. He imposed restrictions on the movement of personnel in and out of the camp, even on those who seemed immune to the disease. None of the workers serving the dying showed any signs of infection. Why the difference? Knowing the symptoms wasn't enough to give Dr Taylor his answer. The question of 'Why only the detainees, not the wardens?' kept returning to his mind. He began to review what he knew of the living conditions and food in the camps. His medical books discussed a vitamin deficiency-related disease for rice eaters, another for maize eaters. Reading on, he found that a lack of B1 caused the beriberi found among rice eaters ... At once, Dr Taylor felt certain he had his answer. He put an urgent radio call through to Mr Cooper at the detention camp.

'Dr Taylor, Mombasa ... over,' 'can you hear me? ... over.'

'Yes Dr Taylor, Mr Cooper camp number one ... over.'

'Mr Cooper ... want weekly menu for detainees ... over ... Can you hear me? ...over'...

'Yes ...' Dr Taylor waited, ready with pen and paper.

'Breakfast ... Maize porridge ... over.'

'Taken with what? over'...

'Nothing, only one spoon of sugar, over ... Monday ... Tuesday ... over. The same all week over ...

'All Week?'

'Yes, over . . . For lunch? . . .

'Mr Cooper, yes? over . . . Lunch . . .

'Dr Taylor can you hear me?'

'Yes . . . Ugali . . . over,

'What is ugali . . . Mr Cooper?

Ugali, posho meal – dough –

posho, what is that? . . . over . . .

A maize meal, cooked with water, African corn bread . . . over . . .

Prepared with what? . . .

I don't know, it is just that Dr Taylor . . . Wait a minute . . . Let me ask
. . .' Mr Cooper came back after whispering to one of the officers,
asking how *ugali* is made:

Dr Taylor, can you hear me? . . .

Yes, go on . . .

This is just white maize flour mixed with water, no salt, no oil, no
onion, no spices . . . over

Served with what? . . .

Sometimes with potato soup or tea . . .

Potato soup? . . . Just that . . . Oh my God! . . . Tea time? . . .

Porridge made from maize meal and water . . .

Any milk? . . .

Oh how do you expect detainees to be fed on milk? . . . Just maize meal
porridge. . .

Go on, shouted Dr Taylor from Mombasa And supper? . . .

Same as lunch time . . . But Dr Taylor, can you hear me? . . . When a
season is good we occasionally give them some beans, but with the
drought now, beans are hard to get and when found, too expensive,
over . . .

Thank you for your information, Dr Taylor shouted sourly as he
banged the receiver down. Mr Cooper was annoyed with Dr
Taylor's behaviour and left the radio complaining that Dr Taylor
didn't know what he was doing.

'This is how all the new arrivals act; if only they knew what they
were dealing with – that the same man he is feeling sorry for can turn
around to slaughter him. Dr Taylor is a fool indeed,' Mr Cooper
murmured as he sat down back at his desk.

At Mombasa Hospital Dr Taylor had a feeling that he knew the
answer to the camp's problems. That epidemic disease which only
attacks the detainees but not the wardens, if it is not poison, then it
must come from the bad conditions and the poor diet.

By now news had leaked out that the camp was vanishing with sickness, detainees had already died. Some politicians passed the information to their overseas sympathisers and the newspapers began writing about the vanishing camp. Their articles caused quite a stir; even the Colonial Office decided to send a delegation to enquire into the epidemic's causes.

By then, Dr Taylor had sent some of his senior medical staff to rescue the dying detainees. The treatment started on the spot. Dr Taylor ordered changes in the camp diet. He required the detainees to be provided with vitamin pills, powdered milk, meat, vegetables and even fruits. This angered the authorities, but improved the situation in the camp. Before long, the disease started to disappear, though leaving the detainees very weak. Dr Taylor recommended that one of his staff be attached to the camp; nothing less would satisfy his concern for the detainees' health. The selection of the hospital assistant was a careful one. It couldn't be forgotten that these were political detainees, bitter Mau Maus, who had taken the oath and some had done unmentionable things before they were detained.

Mr Cooper did not like the idea of a stranger coming into the camp; while treating detainees, such a man might easily cause political trouble. We must make sure that no trouble-makers get in contact with the detainees.

Dr Taylor was sensitive to the repercussions of defeating the epidemic. Not only the camp superintendent's job might be jeopardised, but his own high post as well. After thinking for a while, he decided to put Mwacharo as a visiting medical assistant in charge of the detainees' health.

Mwacharo was a quiet, religious man, whose polite and considerate manners earned him respect from high authority. After all, he did not belong to any of the Mau Mau groups and with his innocent looks, there could not be a better and safer person to be mixing with Mau Mau terrorists. Soon Mwacharo's name was recommended as a Health Visitor to the detention camp. The top administrators, the police headquarters, and those in charge of the detention camps were informed about the decision to select Mwacharo for the camp.

Mwacharo was called by Dr Taylor into his office at Mombasa and informed that of all hospital assistants at Coast Province, he was now to be promoted to a higher grade, and not only that, but the Government had recognised his good behaviour, and he was the only one to be trusted as a visiting health officer at the detention camp. Dr Taylor shook Mwacharo's hand with joy and excitement added, 'Good luck, Mr Mwacharo. I know you can manage the camp.'

Mwacharo did not quite show excitement on his face, in fact, he looked disturbed, his mouth left open as if he had thoughts to say but no words to express them. The way his eyes blinked was a clear sign of his nervousness and uneasiness; he was dissatisfied with the transfer, but was not in a position to tell his boss straight away. For what can a man like Mwacharo do but obey? By now Dr Taylor had clearly assessed Mwacharo's feelings, realised that he would rather not go, but Dr Taylor had no alternative but to send him on to the camp.

'Do you have any small photographs?' Dr Taylor asked Mwacharo.

'No Sir, I have never owned a passport, Sir,' Mwacharo answered.

'If you don't, you had better go to a photographer; you will need four copies. Bring them here with you, they are needed for your entrance pass to the camps, no one is allowed to enter without an identification pass. One will be left with the camp superintendent, the other with the administration and another with the police, and you will have to keep one with you all the time. Please make sure you have them all before Saturday, and ready to start working on Monday. OK?'

Mwacharo with his disappointed face turned from Dr Taylor's office door to leave for his unwelcome promotion, and its most difficult task. As he left Dr Taylor called again, 'Mr Mwacharo.'

'Yes, Dr Taylor,' Mwacharo answered.

'Oh, one more thing, Mr Mwacharo. Occasionally the British Council organises three month study courses for government workers, and now I am very happy to tell you that I would like to suggest your name for such a course. Headquarters in Nairobi has asked all Provincial Medical Officers to forward names of suitable candidates to be selected for a three month Health Visitors Course.

'Great Britain next summer. This would give you a chance to see how a health department operates, and to attend a health course with many others from all the colonies. Kenya is entitled to send three, and I am sure one will be from the Coast Province. Take these forms, study them carefully, then fill them in properly. You must return them no later than next week, this will give me a chance to send them back to Nairobi before the closing date.'

The thought of going to England forced a smile to Mwacharo's face, and as a matter of politeness, he thanked Dr Taylor for thinking to recommend him. Mwacharo left Dr Taylor's office, called at the photographer's studio for his photograph, then went back to his house at Msambweni General Hospital.

By now Nyaruai was getting rather concerned about the association of her husband with Dr Taylor. There are many qualified doctors who would do the job properly, why him and not the others? This thought left Nyaruai even more puzzled.

Mwacharo explained to his wife his discussion with Dr Taylor, the new assignment as a health visitor to the camp, the need for the four photos for his passes, the proposed British Council Scholarship; all exciting and promising chances.

'Are you not excited?' he asked his wife who had said nothing.

'Excited?' Nyaruai asked in disgust.

'Are you not proud of my promotion?'

Nyaruai behaved in a manner unexpected of a wife. Wrapping a *kanga* round her waist, she walked back to her kitchen without answering. She sat down on a low stool, and using a charcoal burner continued to knead and roll her *chapati*s. Mwacharo stood for a while, then followed her in the kitchen.

'Are you going to talk to me or not?' Mwacharo asked as he stood leaning on the kitchen door. Nyaruai continued kneading her *chapati* adding oil to a frying pan, and uttered no word. 'Are yo Mwacharo asked once again after keeping quiet for a whi' He stared at his badly behaved wife, this was very unusual for N yaruai, and wondered whether this was the same Nyaruai he knew.

Looking at Mwacharo, the bitter Nyaruai, still holding her rolling pan, her hands full of *chapati* flour said, 'I am Nyaruai, the daughter of a Mau Mau, and a sister of Mau Maus, even the children I shall bear, they too will be labelled as Mau Maus, why don't you send me back where Mau Maus live, they are my people and whoever I produce will also be a son or daughter of Mau Maus.

'You and your white friends, whether or not you are planning to eliminate my people, you expect me to come embracing you with kisses. I can see you have now become a loyalist, no wonder you have been named for a trip to England.'

'What is wrong with you, Nyaruai? Why do you talk to me like this? You know very well my feelings towards your people, and you should be the last person to call me a loyalist.'

'Yes, I should be the last one. But Mwacharo as much as I know you, and as much as I trust you, your association with Dr Taylor leaves many people wondering. You are not the only trained hospital assistant, and in any case there are several qualified doctors working under Dr Taylor, then why have you been selected from the many?'

'Why do you then not discuss this matter with me?' demanded her husband. 'Do I look like one to betray another African for the sake of colonialists? And besides, I am worked like a donkey in these dangerous detention camps just so my masters through my sweat will get their promotion and medals. What do I get from it? I come back to my *makuti* house with my plate of *ugali*. Look here Nyaruai, shall I go tomorrow and resign from my job? I am ready to go back and sit digging in my garden if you wish. Alright give me a writing pad, I shall straight away write a letter of resignation. That will assure you that your Taita husband is not going to betray your brothers. Nyaruai, you surprise me with your comments. I thought by now you knew me well,' Mwacharo said as he pulled out drawer after drawer looking for his writing pad.

Nyaruai sensed that she'd been too harsh and unfair with her comments, tears ran down her cheeks, as she listened to her husband searching the drawers for paper on which to write his resignation. She hated herself for her words.

Mwacharo imagined how he was going to face life without work, but his writing pad was nowhere to be seen. After all, he thought, I can write this letter tomorrow when I go to collect my camp entrance pass, then I can hand in my letter. Mwacharo went to bed without eating, nor did he say good-night to his wife Nyaruai who was still confused and in tears. She was left sitting on her kitchen stool unable to continue cooking her *chapati*. She put them aside, and she too went to the bedroom to sleep without any supper; she was too upset to take any.

Lying in bed, Mwacharo began to feel that he should not have been quick to agree to work at that dangerous detention camp. There was the danger of being accused by both sides. If I am too good to the detainees, I can easily be associated with them, and may be put into a detention camp myself – or in prison for that matter. If I am unfriendly, then the freedom fighters may hate me, and God knows what they might plan to do to me. Anyway, who knows God's plans. Maybe it is God's wish that I pass through those fearful gates and enter that camp surrounded by its frightening barbed wires. It must really be God's will that I was selected among the many. Why me? Why me indeed?'

Nyaruai, realising her mistakes, had decided to apologise to her husband for her nasty words, and she begged him not to resign. 'After all who knows what such an unexpected assignment can turn out to be. Maybe you can be of help to my people, you at least can help your in-laws.'

'Yes,' answered Mwacharo. 'Look here, Nyaruai, I believe that some things are Godsent. Here I am, but that Dr Taylor does not know my relations with the Kikuyu Mau Maus, neither does he know that I speak their language. I can see that my not being a Kikuyu made them think I can be trusted. What fools they are; let us leave it as it is. I am sure I shall be of a great help to your people.'

After they talked long into the night the misunderstanding was cleared up, and a few days later Mwacharo was appointed as Health Officer in charge of the camp.

This camp was one for hardcore Mau Maus; it was a camp for suspected terrorist organisers. They were criminals and savages in the colonialists' eyes, and were regarded as heroes among the freedom fighters. Facing this ambiguity, Mwacharo packed some clothes, and left for the Provincial Medical Headquarters. He collected his camp entrance pass, a letter of introduction to the camp superintendent, and a big box filled with medicine and other medical equipment for the camp. A government Landrover arrived ready to transport Mwacharo to the camp. Nyaruai unfortunately was unable to see her husband off as she was on duty; in any case she did not want to stir up any interest in her background and tribe.

The journey to the camp was interesting. In the front seat sat the driver, with Mwacharo in the middle and a well-armed policeman by Mwacharo's side. In the back seat were three other policemen, all armed to the teeth. On both sides of the Landrover hung four jerry-cans filled with water and firmly held in place. In the far back of the Landrover was Mwacharo's suitcase, a basket, and his big medicine trunk, and sitting on it were two funny-looking men wearing torn hats. Their eyes did not look like those of Coast men, and their Swahili accent was evidence of an up-country person.

At the start of the journey they passed many villagers and watched the naked children waving to them, shouting '*jambo*'. And they saw women carrying water and babies, busy with their daily chores, and tending their farms. Slowly the country scenery changed, with fewer children, fewer huts, and later no human being was anywhere to be seen. Before long the Landrover was completely within the jungle. This part of the trip had no human life at all and the only life Mwacharo noticed were the flying birds, and small wild animals crossing their path every now and then.

Later the Landrover left the main murram road, turned to the right and drove into deeper jungle. The road was very dusty and bumpy. An expecting mother in a vehicle on such a road would definitely have a baby before time. The Landrover made a big cloud of dust as it passed. All were covered with dust; the hair, eyelids, clothes were nothing but dust. The driver did not seem to worry about it; he, in fact, was laughing and making jokes which did not amuse the others. They were too uncomfortable and too set on holding themselves together to enjoy the jokes. He even started to hum Kamba songs; these Kambas seem to be singing all the time. Later the passengers caught glimpses of giraffes, zebras, wildebeests and many other wild animals. Here and there, elephant droppings were scattered, several big trees were knocked over and fresh elephant droppings meant that elephants were around. By now the road was really getting from bad to worse. It was narrow with many potholes. Later a big fallen tree halted the Landrover's progress. The funny looking up-country men jumped off the Landrover, brought out two axes, cut the tree into bits and removed it from the road. Then the journey continued.

'There must be elephants around,' one of the up-country men said.

'There are always elephants,' the other one answered. Later the Landrover driver crested a very steep hill. Mwacharo's eyes were alert, he was not sure of what to expect next – an animal attack, an accident or what. 'I hope they have enough petrol and spare parts,' he thought. 'Otherwise we would definitely have to suffer much.'

At the steep hill's bottom, the Landrover passed some green grass and later came to a very dirty stream. There was no bridge. The driver told everyone to get out to reduce the weight. The passengers crossed by foot. The river here was not very deep; the driver knew the place to make the easiest crossing. Mwacharo and the others crossed the river first, then turned to watch the driver show off his skill in driving. Then the Landrover flashed through the dirty water and crossed it. After the crossing they all decided to rest a bit. Mwacharo had some tea and bread; no one else had carried any food. They all shared Mwacharo's. Surely it was not enough, and Mr Mwacharo wondered why they never thought of bringing something to eat. 'Suppose the car breaks down?' The water in the jerry-cans was for drinking; it was so cold as if from the fridge. The river water was dirty and a possible breeding place for bilharzia. Opposite the river and partly hidden by the bush, Mwacharo noticed a thing big like a rock, but too brown to be one. Still wondering about the smooth brown rock, he was shocked when he noticed a small tail wiggling. Surely it could not be a brown rock, he whispered to the driver. In a few seconds, the tail wiggled again.

'Do you know Mr Mwacharo, that could be nothing else but an elephant, we better clear off from here. A lonely elephant can be very dangerous, most of the lonely elephants are males, chased away by others after fighting for a female, and they can be very furious and dangerous. Look Mr Mwacharo, that thing lying flat by the side of the river, it looks like a crocodile, my goodness, a real jungle and dangerous.'

'Shall we shoot it?' one of the passengers asked.

'No don't, the blast of the gun will wake up all the other sleeping animals; they would start running every which way. This can make driving very difficult for us, as animals know no road.'

Leaving the river, the Landrover continued on to the camp. As the weather became cooler, more and more wild animals were to be seen. The driver told Mwacharo that this is the time the animals start eating; when it is hot they go to sleep under the shade and shelter of the rocks and caves. It was a real jungle. Driving was impossible, sometimes the road was blocked by herds of zebras, wildebeests and the slow moving, graceful giraffes. Dusty elephants were noticed here and there, so were the birds. Worst of all was the ugly sight of rhinos, they were frightening and stupid looking as they tried to attack the Landrover. Mwacharo felt sorry to have accepted the offer. He wondered how he was going to survive, and wished that his wife should never know the kind of place it was.

Arriving at the camp, Mwacharo saw a well-cleared camp right inside the jungle. The place was very well kept, and had that air of the colonialist. The barbed wire coiled all around the camp, and yet more wire, closer in, hemmed the camp barracks.

At the entrance a very high tower stood with windows on all sides. In it, the heads of helmeted officials could be seen, there were three Africans and one white. As soon as the Landrover approached the camp the white man followed it through his binoculars, the others stood erect with their guns pointing at the Landrover. It was all very frightening for Mwacharo who had never visited a Mau Mau detention camp before.

The gate was well guarded. The Landrover driver approached the gate with confidence, screeching the brakes with pride and authority. The other armed officers jumped out and saluted, shook hands with the guards, and making some sort of comrade jokes, exaggerating their feelings of being home. They later waved to Mwacharo, then disappeared.

The driver explained who Mwacharo was. He displayed his new pass with the photograph, then one of them took it to show it to the senior officer. Before Mwacharo was allowed in, the senior officer came by the gate and asked several questions. The senior officer then showed Mwacharo to his new home, a room in one of the little square houses made of corrugated iron sheets. The roof, the walls, and even the doors were all made of these shiny corrugated iron sheets, the floor was made of slabs joined together. After entering the house, Mwacharo unpacked all his luggage, made his bed and arranged his room.

Another officer at the camp introduced himself to Mwacharo and invited him to his room, one identical to Mwacharo's. He gave Mwacharo some *ugali* served with a little game meat. The meat was very tasty. He explained to Mwacharo life at the camp, the difficulties of communication and food supplies, the danger of detainees, and also the danger of the colonialists if they ever suspected him of associating with Mau Maus.

The following day Mwacharo began his work by checking on the health of the detainees. The next morning Mwacharo reported to Mr Cooper, where he spent a lot of time hearing the *do's* and *dont's* of camp life . . . Cooper explained to Mwacharo what type of people the detainees were: murderers, savages, cunning and most dangerous, and that they at the camp keep a very close watch on each officer, as some cannot be trusted. We have trusted you Mr Mwacharo, and that is why your name was selected. Don't forget this is a camp for Mau Maus hardcore. Don't let us down. Mwacharo was later shown around the camp and introduced to all the camp officers.

Later in the morning, Mwacharo saw for the first time the camp's insides. The buildings were long barracks made of shiny corrugated iron sheets, scattered here and there, some tents were also erected by the corners of the camp. The women's section was further east, with barbed wire dividing it from the male camp, and with a separate well-guarded entrance.

Entering the camp, he noticed detainees scattered all over the compound, some lying down on the bare ground, basking in the morning sun of mother Africa, others sat leaning on the barrack walls. The depression of bitterness was visible and the sick were many, explaining in some measure the sadness Mwacharo read on the detainees' faces.

The officer taking Mwacharo around the camp shouted with authority, 'You always say that the Government of Her Majesty the Queen has poisoned you. You say we give you medicine to kill you all. When we give you injections to prevent you from sickness, you say it is a dose to make you barren and impotent, now here is a highly qualified hospital assistant employed full time to take care of your health. He is not a homeguard, he is not a policeman who you wish you could chance to kill. This is Mr Mwacharo, a Taita by tribe, who is not interested in your silly politics, but in your health, your sickness and suffering.' Mwacharo greeted them in Swahili, but they did not bother to answer. Some moved from where they were sitting and leaned on other barracks at a distance from where Mwacharo was introduced, others gave a bad look, and the whole attitude was really frightening, especially the angry yet vacant stares from the pellagra victims.

He re-examined the detainees and started treating those who were sick and ordering a proper diet for those who had not yet been affected. The queue was long for those needing medical tests; one by one the ragged sick, the miserable detainees entered the examination room as several police officers stood guard in case of attack on Mwacharo. 'Next one,' Mwacharo would shout after finishing with each patient. Entering through the door Mwacharo was shocked to see his best friend and school-mate from Alliance High School, Mungai. Mwacharo just managed to recognise Mungai who had grown a beard. His well-built body had nothing more left to it than a skeleton covered with yellowed skin, his former beautiful eyes looked extra big, his knee bones sticking out like drum sticks, with no flesh to cover them. Mwacharo was shocked by Mungai; then slowly he closed the door and embraced him. They both cried, as they remembered their school-days.

'I did not even say good-bye to my wife and children. When I went to buy things for my wife who was expecting a baby, I met that DO Mr Mwanja. We never liked each other since our childhood; he insisted that I was giving Mau Mau oaths, and recommended that I should be locked in. What my wife produced, I have no idea,' came Mungai's sad story.

The examination of Mungai took longer than was usual. The police guarding the line became suspicious and knocked on the examination room to interrupt and asked 'Have you not yet finished that one?'

'Leave me alone,' Mwacharo answered, 'do your work and leave me to mine.' Then, turning to Mungai, 'Anything I can do please let me know.' Then to the door and the guards behind: 'Next one.' Mwacharo went on and on until all the detainees were attended to.

Shortly after Mwacharo was stationed at the camp the situation improved, the food became better, and the good food plus the vitamin tablets cured the pellagra and other vitamin deficiency diseases which had been wasting the detainees.

Mwacharo became very popular with the detainees, and of course Mungai had whispered a good word about him to the others.

'And do you know I hate to tell you, Mwacharo, it is better that I was married young, at least I managed to father three children, the first two were boys, but the third – I don't know what it is.' Mungai holding Mwacharo's hand and almost in tears continued, 'But that is all I shall ever produce in all my life. I hope they will be safe.'

'You never know,' Mr Mwacharo sympathetically answered, 'Maybe they will one day let you out, then you can once again be reunited with your wife and your family.'

At this point Mungai burst into bitter tears, 'With my wife again? For what? Look at me, Mwacharo! – They have already castrated me. During the interrogation they would not believe me if I told them the truth that I knew nothing about Mau Mau. I have never taken any oath, but they thought if they tortured me like this I would disclose Mau Mau secrets. I wish I knew, I would have taken all the oaths there were. I would have been the most brutal Mau Mau ever.'

After Mwacharo had finished his daily check on the detainees' health, talking to many of them, he went back to his small lonely room for rest. As he lay down on his bed, he bitterly renounced colonialism. Do colonialists really know that some of the so-called hardcore Mau Maus never took the oath? Do they know that some of them are even unaware of what Mau Mau is, though they are inside this well guarded detention camp? In here they sit frustrated, miserable and sick, cut off from their families and the rest of the world, with no ideas as to when they will come out. Why should they suffer? What crime have they committed? And who am I to be getting special treatment from the colonialists, walking around with special passes to treat my fellow Africans, who are suffering by the hands of the homeguards and these colonialists. Mwacharo, all the men you see here are not men, they are just women. I wish I could get through these gates, I would fight any white man I would meet.

*   *   *

Night duties were very unwelcome to the nurses and midwives at Msambweni Hospital; the thought of working when others were sleeping, and sleeping when they were working was never regarded as an easy task. Any suggestion to transfer a nurse from night work was very warmly welcomed, but who was prepared to be working when others sleep! None indeed until, all of a sudden, Nyaruai, who was known to hate night duties, was heard inquiring for someone to change duties with her. This was not a problem as many midwives were keen to be relieved of these hard night duties. Nyaruai continuously worked these hard night duties. Lack of sleep and several times going without food made her look thin and old. For Nyaruai, she had an aim for these continuous night duties. The aim was to have those few days off offered to those working at night so that she could go to visit her husband at the detention camp.

Already Nyaruai had written to her husband saying that she wanted to visit him at the camp. Mwacharo looking at the condition of the camp, and fearing that the authorities might find that his wife was a Kikuyu and her people were Mau Maus, did not welcome the idea. It could add more trouble than happiness. In any case, Nyaruai decided to give a surprise visit to her husband.

Nyaruai plaited her hair in Coast style, borrowed a *buibui* from a Muslim friend, then left for Mombasa Provincial Police Headquarters. There she introduced herself saying she was the wife of Mwacharo, and had a very urgent family matter that she must discuss with her husband. She wondered if they could give her permission and also a lift in one of their Landrovers to visit her husband at the detention camp.

'Can you tell us the exact problem you have that you must see your husband?'

Nyaruai said, 'A family matter, rather personal Sir.'

'What is your name?'

'Amina is my name,' replied Nyaruai.

'How come your husband is a Taita? Most Taitas are Christians and you are a Muslim.'

'Yes, my husband is a Christian, and I am a Muslim; love does not know tribe or religious boundaries.

'Where is your original home?' asked the policeman.

'I am from Kwale District, just near Msambweni Hospital. The land of Muslims.'

The police looked at her innocent face then said, 'The place is not worthy of a woman's visit, but there is a Landrover transporting a few things to the camp this afternoon and coming back tomorrow. Be here at exactly 1 pm, then you can get a free lift. Here you are, have this pass, and if anybody asks you who gave you permission, say Chief Inspector, Mombasa Station, also take this note to the Commander in charge of the camp to avoid further interrogation as you go in.'

At exactly 1 pm, the police Landrover left for the camp, carrying the usual crowd and camp supplies. Well-guarded and with drinking water in jerry-cans hanging on both sides, the Landrover followed the usual road; dry, dusty, rough and with wild animals, the like of which she had never seen before. The journey was slow and long, and had several stops, either they were waiting for animals to move from the road, or removing fallen trees. And it was not before 6.30 pm, that they finally arrived at the camp. Nyaruai travelling as Amina, was left at the gate of the camp with the officer on duty. The driver and others who came with her disappeared inside the camp. The officer on duty asked who she wanted to see; Nyaruai gave him the note she was given at Mombasa, and the entrance pass.

'Are you Mr Mwacharo's wife?' inquired the officer.

'Yes, I am,' Nyaruai answered.

'I thought Mwacharo was a Christian.'

'You are right, but I am not a Christian,' she lied.

The officer in charge sent one *askari* to go and call Mwacharo, and tell him his wife was at the gate.

'My wife?' Mwacharo asked again.

'Yes, your wife Amina, she is wearing a black Muslim veil, very shy and a real Muslim. She does not uncover her face in the presence of men. Aren't you lucky? We all wanted to see her beautiful face, but I understand her beauty is reserved only for you.'

'Are you sure she is asking for me?' Mwacharo further asked.

'Yes, just you,' the other replied.

'OK I am coming.' Walking through the door Mwacharo wondered, my wife, Amina? A Muslim? Who the hell can she be? Altogether though, he decided to keep his confusion secret to himself, until he had finally found out who the lady really was. When Mwacharo was approaching the gates, Nyaruai was very alert, she at once uncovered her face, and her husband recognised who this Amina was. He welcomed her warmly and was happy to be together again.

'Why did you wear this black veil?' Mwacharo asked his wife.

'I had to. I did not want people to recognise my features. Some can tell which tribe I belong to, and this can lead to watching you carefully.' she explained. She, then, narrated to her husband how she planned to come and how she worked extra night duties to get a few days off. 'I was always worried about you, and I decided to come.'

For the few days Nyaruai spent with her husband, she stayed most of the time indoors. The only times she went out were to collect water from the communal bore-hole or charcoal for cooking.

One day Nyaruai walked by the camp barbed wire, trying to look for her husband who forgot to give her money for the charcoal. Mwacharo was in his clinic attending to several patients. The clinic was near the side of the barbed wire. Nyaruai was trying to call somebody by the side to pass the message to her husband. She was not allowed to enter the camp.

As she gazed through the wire, she saw Wahome, her former boyfriend and school-mate, and who came from her village. He was sitting on the ground unconcerned and waiting his turn for treatment.

Nyaruai's heart beat faster. She forgot what had brought her to the camp fence. Tears ran down as she looked closely at her former lover, sitting there motionless, lonely, with torn clothes, being roasted by the hot sun.

'Sir,' Nyaruai called Wahome with tears filling her eyes; Wahome turned his head, but did not answer, wondering what a woman was doing by the fence of the camp.

'Sir! Please, who are you?' asked Nyaruai.

'Don't put me into trouble,' Wahome replied indignantly.

'Come closer to the fence,' Nyaruai invited Wahome. 'Wahome, it is me Nyaruai,' she finally revealed in desperation!

'Who?' Wahome repeated, as in a dream.

'Nyaruai. Mercy, Nyaruai, the daughter of Simon Wachira from Karatina. Did you forget me?' Nyaruai asked as she opened her black veil to show her face.

Wahome's heart started beating fast. 'What are you doing here?'

'I have come to visit my husband. The Hospital Assistant, Mwacharo.'

Wahome stood with his back against the fence, facing the other side, but continued to talk to the black-veiled Nyaruai. He told her the problems in the camp and how they were preparing to send a letter to the Colonial Office in London and the Queen of England, but they had no one to post it for them as all the letters were censored. 'Can you help?' Wahome asked.

'Yes, I too have taken a Mau Mau oath, even my husband knows, but I have never been an active Mau Mau because of my work. I will be happy to be of any assistance to you, my people. Anything you like, I am ready and willing to help, I am ready.' Nyaruai heard a watchman shouting to her, then she turned her head.

'What are you doing there by the fence? Women in this camp are supposed to stay in their quarters, so go back at once.'

'Please come, I wanted to get some money for charcoal from my husband, Mwacharo,' she replied innocently. 'I have nothing in the house and none of these detainees would ever turn their heads to talk to me, so could you please tell my husband that I have no money to buy charcoal to cook lunch.'

'OK. Just go back home, I will tell him. These detainees you see here are very dangerous men and you should keep yourself as far away from them as possible.' The *askari* asked Mwacharo for the money and took it to Nyaruai for the charcoal.

When later Mwacharo came home he was annoyed with Nyaruai for trying to follow him inside the camp. 'I am already worried somebody may disclose that you belong to the dreaded tribe of Mau Mau, and now you come by the camp. No woman has never tried to come near there. And don't put me into trouble. Nyaruai you are a little daring!'

'Don't get angry with me,' Nyaruai answered. 'I was brought up to believe that I was born once, and I shall die once. Do you know Mwacharo, I think forgetting to give me the charcoal money was a Godsend.'

'Why?' Mwacharo asked in a surprised tone.

'Praise the God Almighty,' Nyaruai added.

'What did you do? Please tell me.'

'When you were busy treating the detainees, I came to collect money for the charcoal. I saw one of my old best friends, Mr Wahome.'

'That boyfriend of yours you always used to talk about.' Mwacharo was furious.

'Boyfriend? Oh no, not Wahome my former boyfriend, that one still works in Nairobi Post Office,' she lied. 'Wahome is a common name at Nyeri, very few homes you may pass without hearing the name of Wahome. It is a very common name. This is Wahome, my school colleague from my village, and among other things a cousin.'

'A cousin? We have heard of cousins before,' said Mwacharo.

'What do you mean?' Nyaruai asked.

'Just that, continue with your story.'

'Now, I had a short quick chat with Wahome. They are in great problems, and as we decided, I feel if there is anything we can contribute to the African fighters, let us do it now. This is our chance.'

'How can we help? I am helpless; the only help I can give is to see to their health, otherwise I cannot do anything.'

'Let us use the excuse of health; first call Wahome for further examination, talk to him, he has an important letter he would like to draft and see posted overseas for help. He wants to send a copy to the Queen of England, and one to the Colonial Office. They are also in great need to contact some outstanding lawyers in Nairobi.'

'But this will put me into great trouble.' Mwacharo commented.

'Yes, I know,' Nyaruai continued 'and I would hate to see you inside these wires. Do this Mwacharo, recommend some of these leaders for hospitalisation; say there is a good doctor at my hospital and that they need a special check-up. Say you suspect they may have tuberculosis or even leprosy, and they need isolation. At the other end leave everything to me.' A few days later Mwacharo's wife left the camp in the police Landrover returning to the Hospital.

As a pretext to follow up his wife's plan, Mwacharo decided to once again have a thorough medical check-up of the detainees. He later recommended some detainees for hospitalisation; they seemed to be suffering from some serious infectious disease, which could cause a lot of trouble, and this time not only to detainees, but to all.

Mr Cooper did not approve of this. He told Mwacharo, 'I am employed by her Majesty's Government to make sure that her Union Jack flies high and is not torn down by these detainees. I cannot see how very dangerous Mau Mau terrorists can be admitted into a general hospital with other patients. You never know what they can plan next or what harm they can do to the other patients. I have to protect my Union Jack.'

'That is your duty, Mr Cooper,' Mwacharo continued. 'The Queen's Union Jacks have to fly high and high, that is why you are here. It is your duty to see that the flag will not be torn into pieces. I am employed to make people's lives fly high and longer. These are detainees, Mau Mau savages.

'Yes, Mau Mau savages, but also human beings, this is the reason why our Majesty's Government pays my salary, to look after their health.'

Mr Cooper did not say anything. After a short silence, he walked briskly out of the office to his house next door. Mwacharo watched him through the window, walking away. Cooper really looked haggard and tired, indeed he looked a pitiful sight. His skin was rough and peeling from the hot sun, but the covered parts which would be seen through the neck and under the arms retained their normal colour. He really looked disturbed and worried.

Is that flag so important; is human life of less importance than the Union Jack? wondered Mwacharo. If the colonialists think so, then I think I am making a mistake not to help my people to have our own flag, slightly torn, flying outside the camp where masses stay helplessly frustrated. The flag is tearing just as their colonial power is falling to pieces. Mwacharo felt all this as he shook his head with surprise and bewilderment. Mwacharo stood for a moment thinking deeply upon which steps to take. He felt deeply of where he belonged; he looked at his hands, yet I am a black man, black African and a Kenyan. Then what kind of blackman I am if I cannot help my people? Do I expect to be one of the whites or to be recognised by them – for what? I am a real Kenyan, a black Kenyan.

I am going proudly to remain so. What other sons of the land are going through, I must go through, though in another way.

After he had made up his mind, Mwacharo decided to call Dr Taylor. He reported the need of some detainees for hospitalisation. After all these detainees are human beings, and as human beings, they must be treated properly in a hospital. Dr Taylor who in any case was more interested in his profession than in the politics of the country agreed with Mwacharo's suggestions, though he knew very well he would face very strong opposition from the administration official, the police, the PC, the homeguards. In any case, he thought Msambweni Hospital was isolated enough, cut off from any dangerous communication. The staff members were just those from the local area.

On the following day Mwacharo ordered health checks of the entire camp. Many were declared healthy, but some were recommended for outside hospitalisation. Mungai was called in, he has a thorough and very long check-up, was then declared a tuberculosis victim.

The selection of the hospital for such dangerous Mau Maus was carefully considered. The place must be safe, easy to guard with limited communication. And after much serious thought, there could be no better place in the whole province than Msambweni Hospital. Msambweni is far from the Mau Maus, far from the forest, and far from their people. Escape would be difficult. Msambweni Hospital was selected.

On the day following the decision, the ambulance arrived to transport the sick detainees who were accompanied by Mwacharo. Mwacharo called on his friend Omondi and briefed him on the detainees problems. Some of them really were ill as described in the report. 'We had to help them. They need to be out of the barbed wire camp. Their minds are dead and confused. Look at your hands Mr Omondi, look at mine too. We are both black, and blacks we are going to remain. Whether we are innocent or not, we are listed with these same people, if blacks are to be eliminated, you too and your family will be eliminated by these white people.'

Omondi felt strongly nationalistic; for some time he had been wondering what he would do to contribute to the struggle of the freedom fighters, but he had not seen a way.

'Mr Mwacharo,' replied Mr Omondi, 'Leave them with me. I shall be at their service. I shall be at the service of my people, my fellow Africans. Feel confident with me here and you will hear the news, the results will be heard far and near.'

Mwacharo after seeing his wife, left and went back to the camp in the same ambulance.

Omondi called some nurses, he pointed to Mr Mungai, 'That man is a serious victim of tuberculosis, his tuberculosis is chronic, keep him far from the others. Put him over there in that isolated hut to avoid infecting others. That Wambua, look at him, he really looks a mental case. His mind is confused. He looks as if he can cause damage. Keep him alone too. That Wahome there, we suspect him of suffering from leprosy. Place him in an isolated corner. His belongings should not be mixed with others. He is very sick.' On and on went the admission instructions.

It was not long before the hospital was turned into a freedom fighters compound. The sick detainees started preaching their aims and objectives. The soil is theirs, it is high time they ruled themselves. Look at the discrimination; see your standard of living. Compare yours and that of your white masters. Compare your salaries, compare how you are housed and how they are housed. Listen to the stories of how these colonialists are killing and making our fellow Africans suffer. We need all of you. You must join the freedom fighters, support them morally and physically, contribute all you can. The sick detainees continued with their preaching until many people were convinced. The sick detainees decided to start operating the oath ceremony so as to be sure of their loyalty. Nyaruai agreed that they could use her room for oath operations, and the hospital became a Mau Mau sanctuary. The letters and reports were prepared and with the help of Nyaruai and Omondi, much good news was achieved. Letters reached the Colonial Office in England. Others were sent to overseas political supporters and sympathisers. Reports were well prepared and circulated to the world newspapers. The relatives of the detainees were smuggled to the hospital and the bad condition of the detention camps became known to the whole world.

The colonial officers were puzzled on these continuous reports. The Government wondered on how a very well checked camp managed to leak news. The Colonial Office with pressure from the outside was forced to order a Commission of Enquiry on the condition of the camps. Many officers suspected of carelessness were sacked, thus the camps' conditions improved, and many detainees were released. The sick continued to be treated. The news continued to flow, but from where the damaging news was yet coming remained a mystery.

Hero's Welcome

Introduction

Most Kenyans who obtained university education overseas were financed by their community. It is also a fact that it was the women who initiated, planned and organized the raising of funds for those clever and promising young men – and later women. Communities found that they could make future leaders this way. Parents might be very poor and unrecognized in their society, but if they had a clever child, their poverty would not prevent a son from being sent abroad by the community for further education.

Before students would leave, the people in the community would make a very big farewell party. Some leaders would be invited to speak and during such speeches elders would advise their young men on how not to let them down: 'We are sending you to this white man's country to bring us back the wealth of knowledge. Your knowledge is awaited here by your people, you must come back and not get lost there.' Women would remind the students that they went alone, should come back alone, that is, they should not get married there.

In such a farewell party, people would present the young man with an elder's *lobe*, special leather cloth worn by the leaders of the community, saying 'Wear this, this is a leader's *lobe* to remind you of these crowds. Look my son, look at all this crowd, they are all waiting for you to come and lead them. So have this leader's *lobe* to remind you that your people are very proud of you, so don't let them down.' Then another leader would present him with a spear and a shield saying, 'My son, carry this spear, it is to remind you that you are to come back and protect us and this shield is for your protection, protect yourself from all the evils in the white man's land, and bring it back, you shall need it to protect us.'

Such a ceremonial occasion made a young student sense the responsibility to his or her people. As for the colonialists, the ceremony was a threat: this young man or woman will come back knowing too much about them and it will not be as easy to rule them as before.

To send off such a young man or woman, everybody hired trucks to take them to the airport or to the Mombasa Port. Everyone there again would remind the young man or woman on how to behave and say that they are all waiting for his or her services.

The return of a graduate was a big affair. Very big crowds would meet the student. Traditional foods and drinks would be readied, they would make porridge to drink in gourds and not in the European cups. Alcohol was made of honey and sugar-cane and served in cow horns, not in European glasses. And all night the returning hero would be telling of the white man's life. To hear that even a white woman could cook or wash dishes was unbelievable or to hear that a white man can travel in a crowded bus or work in a garden was exciting.

For the parents, the clan and the community, this ceremony and first days back were exciting. For the colonialists, particularly during the Emergency, a ceremony needed special watching. Homeguards and loyalists were both jealous and frightened of a return of such an educated person, and it is this kind of fear and suspicion that led the innocent young man in this account into trouble. All the excitement of the hero's welcome ended in harassment, confusion and detention.

*   *   *

Only one month now separated my son Joseph Kamau from his home-coming and from me, Wanjiru remembered. With this happy feeling, Mama Wanjiru clasped both her hands together, set them against her chin, shut her eyes, looked heavenward and, with deep feelings, began her prayers. 'Oh God of heaven, Oh I beg your pardon – I should not have prayed that one.' Wanjiru changed her mind quickly, she at once unfolded her hands. These were the words with which that European missionary always began her prayers, that woman who had so much abused Wanjiru and her husband when they decided to send Joseph overseas for further studies. She had called Wanjiru and her husband politicians, unchristian, and Mau Maus for wanting further education for their son. This European just wanted them to be teachers, even before they had enough education. That jealous European gave Wanjiru and her husband too much trouble; she was cheeky and used to make nasty comments abour their son overseas. Wanjiru's bitterness even made her drop her Christian name, Elizabeth, just because this teacher's daughter's name was Elizabeth. At the thought of this, Wanjiru decided not to pray to the God of that European teacher. Instead she put her open hands close together, and side by side, as if ready to receive millet porridge. She then turned her face from the skies and looked to the northern side to face Mount Kenya. Despite the missionary's harassing word, God took care of my son when he left and I am sure he will take care of him when he comes back.

Still holding her hands open and close together, she went on to pray to the God of her ancestors who dwells not in heaven, but at Mount Kenya: 'Thathaiai nangai. Thaai.' Still looking serious and thoughtful, Wanjiru spit in her hands, smeared the spit on her face, stood still for awhile and then walked outside of her hut.

She called out to her daughter: 'Njoki, Njoki. Eeeee.'

'Yuu. . .uuu!' Njoki answered.

'I hope you are not waiting for me to remind you that we need more water fetched from the river. Go for water quickly. Take the big barrel, it is not all that heavy. Take the gourd too, extra water is always useful. Please run. And you, Mwaura, playing there, I hope you know where the goats are browsing. Don't you dare leave them to wander around people's gardens when the plants are so young. You know they can spoil them. I hate quarrelling with neighbours, I have had enough of it.'

Wanjiru, carrying her winnowing basket, walked to the grain store still giving orders to Mwaura whose mind seemed to have been taken by *giuthi*. She went on to the store climbed up the stairs to the store's door and entered. She took some pigeon peas from a big old cooking clay pot and put them in her winnowing tray. She went back outside and sat in the shade of the grain store, picking through the peas, discarding any small sticks or stones.

While winnowing, she remained thoughtful. She would think and stop for a moment, then remember that she was supposed to be cleaning the pigeon peas, and begin again. She would shake the tray rhythmically – one, two, three – then bounce the peas up and blow off some of the dirt. Wanjiru's mind would then go back to the son who had been away in England for such a long time. Joseph, my son, my second son, the son I named after my beloved father, Kamau. Oh my son. The son I have not seen for many years. I wonder how he looks now. I wonder whether he is now fat. Oh no, he cannot be. The last time I heard from him he was complaining of wanting to eat home meals, he was fed up with potatoes and bread. He asked me to send him some beans, and cornflour, or maybe he was just homesick. He's probably well-dressed just like the white man. My only fear is that he may be tempted to bring me a white daughter-in-law, and suppose he does, what will I do? Nothing. But I would not know how to cook for her, she could not eat my beans. Europeans get sick at their stomach when they eat beans. She could not enjoy my special millet porridge. I would not know how to talk to her either, and where can I keep her? I only wish he comes back alone. and suppose he had left our seeds behind, that would be terrible, the blood of Mbuguas to be left in a foreign country? Oh, that is even worse. At the thought of this, Wanjiru spat on the ground saying let such imaginations never come true, let such feelings be lost like that spit in the soil.

Now the preparations must start for my son's big welcoming home. He is the first boy from our area to go for further studies overseas. Other women envied me, but truly, I really don't deserve it, all this was done by my community. I had no idea that a black boy from a poor family could be selected for such an honour. After all, we are nobody, we are poor, my husband is nothing but a poor peasant farmer with just a small piece of land. I am nothing, my ancestors are just ordinary people. The only thing that my son has is brain; my Joseph could pass exams well. How he used to pass his exams is just God's miracle. We never had enough light for him to study at night like rich boys with their whole houses well lit. The small tin lamp was all the light we could afford. And where to study? In a crowded dirty hut, goats and sheep making noise inside the house. When not in school, rich children had time to do their homework; my son's spare time was given to work for others, digging their gardens, helping teachers in their houses so that he could help pay for his school fees and uniform. Early in the morning my son would run to school without any breakfast. Maybe just some cold sweet potatoes left from dinner the night before. Maybe even a piece which the rats had already shared. Cold as it was, Joseph would serve it to himself as a wonderful breakfast. Then, with a schoolbag hanging from his shoulders, barefoot, and in his khaki uniform, my son was ready for a day's work at school. In such poor conditions, he would pass his exams very well, better than those from rich families, and that bright brain of his, and his good manners were recognized by the women's group and without me expecting anyone to select him, it was him they picked to send to England for further studies. A selected one who would be their future leader.

Wanjiru recalled the sense of disbelief she felt, when her son told her how much money he would need to get to England. He had to have clothes and some pocket money to keep him going. These people worked so hard to send her son there, yet the money was so much. The mention of 10 000 shillings almost made Wanjiru faint. She wondered how ten thousand shillings would look. she had never seen 1000 shillings, leave alone 10 000 shillings. Such an amount was really frightening to Wanjiru. And how to raise it remained a mystery, and so she had suggested they all forget about it. But to Mama Rebecca, the leader of the women's group, that was nothing. She called together all the people of the village and explained the need to educate their son overseas. For the fight we are fighting we need to educate Joseph overseas. For the fight we are fighting we need to prepare one who will take the whites' places when they leave. Rebecca, the women's leader, was a very good organizer. It was not long before she had good ideas on how to raise the money. One day by holding a dance, another day something else, she would even hold tea parties to raise money. Rebecca appealed to the people to contribute to such a good cause. Education for our children, education for future leaders, let us from Kabuku village see one of our own as a doctor, operating in that theatre, in the big hospital. Let us see one of our sons sitting in that big DC's office. Oh Rebecca's voice! Rebecca's approach would make big things look small.

On the other side of all these studies, Joseph's sister started to feel big. As Joseph was expected soon, I shall be sister to a big man. I shall be associated with the learned ones, a sister to a man who has been overseas. Girls will envy me, boys will fear me, even the one who will marry me will have to treat me with care. They have to know who I am, a sister of the learned Kamau.

With the days of Kamau's homecoming nearing, Wanjiru and her husband as yet, had no plans on how to receive him back. After all they were not responsible for their son's overseas education, they would never have dreamt of a poor peasant's son being aided by the community to go and study with the white people. Going abroad was no more than a miacle, an unexpected dream. Kamau's parents decided to inform that dynamic Rebecca. Maybe she would have some ideas on planning the welcoming programme.

On the following day, Kamau's mother called on Rebecca.

'I have come to inform you of your son's progress. Let me call him your son, for besides me producing Kamau, the credit for his achievement goes to you,' Wanjiru proudly and confidently started, her hands busy unwrapping a newly arrived, framed photograph. 'Look! That is him your son, Kamau. He got it. They call it, I do not know, B or something like that, Bs. I don't know what they call it.'

Oh! Oh!' Rebecca was very excited. 'These are degree gowns for the very learned.'

At hearing this, Rebecca's daughter rushed to have a look at the photograph. Very smart. The writing underneath says B. A. COMMERCE. There it is.

'Now Mama Rebecca, it is you who had made him get all this. He has got it like Europeans. He has not only that, but he is now arriving on the 2nd of July. Arriving by a Europlane at the Nairobi Airport.' Wanjiru looked closely at Rebecca. Rebecca pulled her dress by the neck, she spat on her chest, then said, 'Let him be. Let God be praised.'

'Now Mama Rebecca,' Kamau's mother continued 'you know very well I have no ideas on how to go about with such things. I have no idea. I hate to disturb you, but who else do I know? And who else has the right?

'Rebecca, you sent Kamau off to England and I leave it to you to welcome him back. I am helpless. The son is your's. The community's son.'

'July 2nd? All right, let me think, let me talk to my women's group, then I shall let you know what we decide

'Thank you, Rebecca. And hang Kamau's photograph on the wall in your house. Let your visitors see the fruits of your hard work.'

'Thank you,' Rebecca said. 'It is my wish to see more children educated.'

Later Rebecca called her women's group together. Facing the other women, Rebecca began, 'It is four years now since all of us women decided that it was high time to see one of our sons getting a degree. We said our sons from this location must be called Sir, when the time is ripe for calling black people Sir. Now ladies through your own effort one of our sons has a university degree. It has now entered this small village, a son of a peasant. Kamau, the son of our son.' She then proudly unwrapped Kamau's photograph to show it to the crowd of women.

'Alulululu,' the women's chanting was started. . 'Alulululu,' the second, third, fourth and fifth times. Kikuyu women have to say 'Alulululu' five times the traditional chanting only offered for the brave boys, never for girls.

'Look,' Rebecca repeated, 'B.A., B.A. in this village. Now ladies, it is you who raised money to send him off to Europe. And it is our duty to welcome him home like a hero.

'We must plan a welcoming for Kamau, our son. We must prepare an African cloth for him, to be presented to him and be worn by him as soon as he approaches the airport gate. We must give him a shield and a spear, let him arrive home knowing that he has a spear to fight for our country and the shield to protect it. At the airport, we shall give him a welcome not by drinking beer, but by offering him a calabash of sour millet porridge. Let those white people be shocked by the loudest chanting of Alulululu.

'We shall meet him in thousands as we sent him off. At home the party will be the biggest all have ever seen. The goats will be slaughtered, the pigeon peas, the black beans, the millet porridge, all ceremonial dishes will have to be prepared to welcome the hero. The son of the soil come back from the white people's country.'

After deciding on the need for the welcoming party, responsibilities were divided. Who will look after the party, who will raise the funds. It was not long before the money was raised, they needed money for the party, to buy presents, to hire lorries to take them to the airport. And under Rebecca's guidance, everything was well planned.

On the 2nd of July, the women of Gachage village were ready to give a big welcome to the village hero. The excitement built even more than expected. Some villagers had never been to the airport before, others had never even seen an aeroplane. What an outing! Leaving the hoes, travelling by lorries to Nairobi Airport. Even more exciting to welcome a son of the village with a degree, coming back from a white man's country.

By 8 am, the airport was surrounded by the people of Gachage village waiting to meet their hero, whose plane was expected to touch down at the airport by 11 am. The crowd was too big, noisy and very disorderly. The airport authorities kindly asked them if they could go home and come back later as their passenger would not arrive before 11 am.

At hearing this, Rebecca was angry, 'Leave us alone, we have now learned where the airport is, our son has travelled inside the aeroplane, and many more will.' The airport official left, shrugging his shoulders with dismay.

By 9.30 am, a soft voice from the airport information desk was heard announcing on the microphone: 'Attention please. BOAC Flight No. BA 257 from London and sheduled to arrive at Eastleigh Airport at 11 am, this morning has been delayed at Khartoum Airport due to minor technical problems. Expected arrival time at Eastleigh Airport is now 3 pm.'

'Sh-sh-sh,' One of the teachers in the crowd and who understood the English language asked people to keep quiet as he listened to the announcement. The crowd listened carefully, Kamau's mother's heart started to beat wondering whether something bad had happened. Rebecca stood by the teacher waiting to hear the announced news.

'What did they say?' Rebecca asked.

'Nothing much,' the teacher answered.

'Any crash?'

'Oh no! Please, don't mention such things. But the plane has been delayed at Khartoum, Sudan. That is Africa. Kamau is in Africa just next door, he will arrive this afternoon at 3 pm that is late, what shall we do?'

Rebecca called the group of women together and announced what had happened, 'We better go home then come back later.'

'Oh no, we shall not leave this airport without Kamau. We came to meet him and we shall go home with him.'

'It is a long time to wait,' the teacher said. 'And it is a very long time we carry a baby, for nine good months,' another woman answered.

'OK., then we wait.'

The villagers from Gachage turned Eastleigh Airport into a market place; noisy, hungry, tired villagers, waiting to give their hero a wonderful welcome, crowded the place. Luckily some had brought with them ripe bananas, tea, and other kinds of food; others bought tea at the airport. They walked up and down in the airport terminal while the hired trucks remained parked. After all there was much to see: the planes, the travellers and the atmosphere, all different and a good change too from the village life.

By afternoon everybody became alert and excited. With every aeroplane that arrived, no matter where it came from, they all gazed expecting to see the black face of their son arrive. At last a voice, announced the exciting news: 'BOAC Flight No. BA 257 arriving from London, has arrived at Nairobi Eastleigh Airport. Will the passengers travelling on to Nyasaland and Capetown proceed to the passenger lounge.'

'He is here,' the teacher reported to the villagers.

'He is here,' the excited crowd whispered to each other. Kamau's sister was overjoyed, wringing her hands as she jumped and laughed with excitement.

Wanjiru, Kamau's mother did nothing. She said nothing, but kept calm wondering if it is true that it was Kamau, her son, who brought all these crowds to the airport. She wondered if Kamau would fulfill his promises to this expecting crowd who all day waited, hungry for his arrival. Who is he in any case and who am I to be his mother?

Soon after the plane had touched down, people started to come out one by one, all whites, as the big crowd watched and waited for Kamau.

'Maybe he is not there, maybe he hasn't come,' the mother said. Rebecca was too shaken to keep a close watch.

'Alulululu,' Rebecca chanted in relief and expectation. Alulululu was done, the five chantings for the brave hero.

Kamau was shocked by the welcome, tears welled in his eyes. Tears mixed with a smile, why all these people? What do I have to offer them? Kamau felt as he came off the plane. It took a long time to go through customs and immigration. The customs officials went so far as to read his books' titles as if it was illegal to buy books. At long last he was let through the gates. Alulululu. The chanting was repeated once again as women commented on how well he looked.

Rebecca was seen organising the next efforts: 'You, Mungai, you are responsible for dressing him in the African cloth. Macharia, give him the spear and the shield, and I and his mother will feed him with the sour porridge.'

Soon Kamau appeared by the airport door. There was more

chanting, more singing, more excitement. There was Rebecca ready with the calabash of porridge, the mother was ordered to feed him. Mungai placed the skin cloth on him, saying, 'You are one of us. Welcome home.' And Macharia gave him spear saying, 'This is to fight for our land, and here is a shield to protect us and our land from our enemies.' 'Alulululu,' the women went on singing as they rushed back to their trucks.

Just before they left, the village teacher called them all back saying, 'It is all right, we are happy that Kamau is back with us, but we must thank God who brought him back to us safely.' Prayers were said just outside the airport gate. Other passengers gazed, they looked around wondering, some laughed as others took pictures.

'Who is he?' one tourist asked a villager.

'A clever man from UK, clever just like you.' The white tourist did not see anything so important.

The trip to Gachage Village was exciting. The women sang, the chanting was repeated several times. Kamau, overcome by the welcome, sat quietly in the front of an old hired Ford, his mother, father and sister, and Mama Rebecca all squeezed in with him.

The country had completey changed. Now the village houses were bunched close together. The homes Kamau used to see were no longer there. Instead, there were groups of villages tightly backed together and bound by a fence.

'Why all these villages?' Kamau asked.

'Get home first, then we shall talk,' Rebecca answered. 'It is emergency time.'

At last Kamau arrived home. To his surprise, their old home had been demolished, and he was taken instead to a little village hut. 'What happened to our home? Our beautiful home, surrounded by our gardens, the trees, the fences and our cowpeas. What happened? Where is the home I always dreamt of?'

'Sh sh sh, Kamau don't talk too much. Some of these people you see here are spies.'

'Spies, spying for what?'

'What?' Rebecca repeated. 'Many things, Kamau. A clever young boy like you, they have to watch you, so be careful.'

'Yes, but where is our home?'

'Your home? Everybody's home was demolished. The authorities said they could not control the Mau Maus if we lived scattered on farms as we once did. So we were forced to live in a group. The villages were fenced and no one stays in another village without a permit. Nor can one sleep in one's sister's or brother's house. Even you, you Kamau, the son of Irungu, you cannot sleep in your father's house without reporting to the authorities. We have already reported your arrival, and now we must confirm that you are here.'

'Me Kamau? To report that I am in my father's house, and in my own country? Why?'

'Yes, you have to, otherwise you can get into trouble.'

'What kind of life is this? When did this happen and how did you all get money and time to build the villages?'

'Kamau, a problem is the best teacher, and because of problems people began to work together, we help each other in ways you cannot yet understand.'

'Believe it or not, when the whistle was blown – and so much of our talk is now done by government whistles – it was blown all over the village. Then the announcement came that we have been given three weeks to erect huts in the village, and demolish all our old houses no matter how good or expensive they were. Some people did not have trees to build with, nor even a cent to buy building materials, and no time to build, with people either fighting as Mau Mau or homeguards, or busy doing communal work. And God is love, Kamau, God is there; in three weeks all the huts were there.

'Do you remember Mr Kiambi's house, that beautiful house everyone used to admire? It was demolished. His hut is just a few yards from your mothers.' Mama Rebecca looked at Kamau, sadness brimming in her eyes.

'Kiambi in a hut?'

'Oh yes, Kiambi lives in a small hut, rich or not, he is a Kikuyu.'

'And who compensates them for their houses?'

'Kamau, you just keep quiet. You are safe when your mouth is shut.' Mama Rebecca and Kamau moved on toward his hew home.

At Kamau's house there were even more people waiting, some had prepared food for the party, there was plenty of food, tea and goat meat. Kamau was given a special place to sit. As the guest of honour, he sat at the high table. It was wonderful to be home again and enjoy this home food.

Later Rebecca introduced Kamau to the crowd. She praised him for his achievements, and for bringing the degree 'which we sent him to bring.' and also he did a wonderful thing, that is Kamau decided to come and get a home wife, he did not bring a wife from overseas. Alululululu, was repeated five times.

After the speech, Kamau stood up to reply. He said how happy he was to be back home, and thanks to those who made him go abroad, especially Mama Rebecca. 'I was very touched for the skin you presented me when I arrived, and I can assure you the spear in my hand and the shield will protect my people. My fathers and mothers, brothers and sisters, I promise you that now I have opened the door for Gachage youth to go overseas. I now have many contacts and I know the place very well, and it is my duty to see many more boys and girls go overseas and get degrees like me.'

'Alululululu,' the chanting continued.

Bang! Bang! Bang! The teacher banged the table. 'As you know, there is curfew. We ask you all to try and finish the food, run home before curfew time. We do not want to end our happy day with problems. Kamau is back with us and we shall have more time to talk to him. Neither do we want our guest to get into trouble when he has just arrived.' In a very short time all the people at the party dispersed in fear of being caught by the curfew. Curfew was now at 7 pm.

'Where are they going?' Kamau asked.

'As you have heard me say, it is curfew time.'

'So early? Why do they have curfew?'

'This is emergency time, and some of the villagers here have been accused of being Mau Mau or oath operators. In fact, it was not an oath operation. It was Kariuki's daughter whose dowry was being paid. As you know, the fat ram must be slaughtered for the clan to give the daughter away, I do not know who reported that it was an oath operation.

'Now Kariuki, his son-in-law, his brother, and many relatives were all arrested. They tried to explain the reason why the ram was being slaughtered but no one would listen.' 'Yes, just a *ngurario* ceremony, and the authorities will not listen to the facts of why the goats were slaughtered. Now they are all in detention camp.'

'Which Kariuki is that?'

'Kariuki, you must know him, Kamau. Or are you forgetting your people?'

'It is a long time.'

'Do you remember that Kariuki who used to sell bananas to Nairobi? He was a business man. Kariuki Njuguna, that tall brown looking man?'

'Oh yes, now I remember him. Is paying of dowry also prohibted?'

'Not paying dowry as such, but a *ngurario* ceremony needs a goat or a ram to slaughter. But the stupid homeguards, every time they see blood they think you are operating a Mau Mau oath. Mind you, they know the truth, that no one is so stupid so as to operate such a hunted oath in a crowded village, but if they dislike you, they can easily put you into trouble. In a way, this was Kariuki's fault. I told him that he should not have any slaughtering ceremony without a permit from the DO. Our DO here is a good man, he doesn't like troublemakers. He has no interest around here.'

'Where is he from?' Kamau asked.

'I am not sure, but he looks like Nyanza people. He is a tall, strong and dark young man, maybe he is Luo or Luhya; he even looks fed-up with these homeguards troublemakers. He knows that you are here, and when we approached him, he very quickly, and without problems, gave us a permit to slaughter this goat for you, and also allowed all those people coming to meet you to get off from communal forced labour. But these homeguards are really bad. If they have a personal grudge, they hunt for you, and of course they will get you.'

'No wonder my people's faces look miserable. They look old and ragged; they are thin, their clothes torn. The houses I used to know, the beautiful fenced gardens, the trees of the home, and the well-made gates to protect the herds are no longer here. I read about Mau Mau, exaggerated stories, you people sound like savages overseas. I even sometimes feared to say I was Kikuyu, some children might have run away thinking I eat people. But no one, none at all gives us a story of how it is to be a Kikuyu. The forced communal work is shown in films, they call it a spirit of self-help. People clap and enjoy seeing the achievements. The colonial days seem to be numbered. And for those who will survive, the time will come.'

Kamau's quiet father interrupted at this point, 'It is time to sleep, Kamau. This is all we have. We are in a village now, not like home, where I used to have a room for young men. We will all share the single room for tonight. Kiambi's son has a spare hut for young men, but this is curfew time. Too late to go get permission.'

'But Kiambi's place is just over there?'

'Yes, across there. Don't you know what curfew means? You are not allowed to get out of your room, not even on your verandah? Yes, curfew means to stay indoors.'

'Yes, but you don't have facilities inside these huts. What about going to the outside toilets? My goodness, God Almighty, what is all this?'

'Kamau,' Wanjiru interrupted,' I repeat once again. Shut up and go to sleep. Sleep in that bed over there. Tomorrow we can make other arrangements. And thank God that we at least have seen you, and you have seen us, but who knows if the so-called obedient self-help workers have had even a bite for the whole day? Who knows where the babies are when women are busy digging? Who knows that such hard work forces some women to produce still-born babies? Do those clapping hands for the hard workers see the whip scars caused by *askaris*? Thank God even their torn clothes still cover the scars. If only they are told of the curfew, and those good work? Never mind, God is life.

'Joseph, Joseph. Joseph, Rebecca warned you to shut your mouth. If you have any sense, shut up. Behave like a fool for fools live better than the clever. These days it does not pay to know too much. And as for you, rest assured, you will be watched.'

'Watched for what?' Kamau asked.

'You who have come from their country. The white man's country, you with education like their's. You who know how they live, and with all these jealous people around, my son, you are too young to know and too innocent to realize what we are going through. You have degrees from books, I have a degree in life. Me, as your mother, my sincere advice is just shut up, and cool down what is burning inside you.'

On the following day, the village chief was seen waiting at the DO's office. The DO arrived later and greeted the chief who was dressed up in a khaki uniform, with a crop under his left arm and his helmet in his left hand. The DO welcomed the chief.

'Bwana DO, I have important matters to discuss with you,' the chief started as he closed the office door, his eyes blinking nervously.

'What is up this time chief?' the DO asked.

'Sir, you are my boss, and a clever man too, but I am older. You are from Nyanza, I am from this village. Listen, this young man Kamau who came back from the white man's place is going to create problems. I did not trust him, so I ordered some people to go and listen to his talk. Last night he was discussing very dangerous things. He did not sleep, he was complaining about everything we do; and that fat woman Rebecca, was the one stirring up all the trouble. I have always warned you of that woman Rebecca, but you seem to overlook her. You underestimate her. You think she is not a dangerous woman. Other women have been detained and even imprisoned, but the head of the problem is left loose to go on producing problems. Why Rebecca is left loose, Bwana DO, I cannot understand. Now don't say I never warned you. I have done my duty, I have reported to you this troublemaker Rebecca.'

'Look here chief, I am a Christian, educated at Maseno, a missionary school and at University College, Makerere. I am now an administrator and I have my own policy. My policy is that I never act on hearsay, show me a genuine case, lay it out, point by point on my table, then I will act according to the law of this country. I have found this area the most interesting division in the whole of my administrative career. Anyway chief, your report has been noted.' Chief Kimakia left the DO's office very disappointed and fed up.

As soon as Chief Kimakia left, Mr Onyango made a radio call to the DO at the District headquarters:

This is Gachage Division calling . . . Over' . . .

'What?' . . .

'Mr Onyango, DOI Gachage Division'. . .

'Yes, can I help you?'. . .

'Yes . . . Give me DOI Mr Wilson.' After a while Mr Wilson came on.

This is Mr Onyango. DOI Gachage Division . . .

Yes Mr Onyango, any Problems? . . .

Not really, but Mr Wilson, are you in the office this afternoon? I would like to talk to you . . .

OK Mr Onyango, come at 2.30 pm I shall wait for you.

At exactly 2.30 pm Mr Onyango was at DO Wilson's office.

'Now Mr Wilson, I mentioned to you that my father is ailing, he is very sick, and I am his elder son. According to our Luo custom, I should be at his bedside to take care of him. As you know communications here are very poor, and it's too dangerous to ask my family to keep on coming here. Sir, I would like to request you to recommend me for an urgent leave and later for a transfer nearer my home. When my father is better, then I can come back here.'

'Do you like working in this emergency place?' Mr Wilson asked.

'Oh yes, I don't mind, but there are problems disturbing me. Mr Wilson, I am an administrator and I enjoy challenging work. But just now my mind is disturbed with a sick father. I only hope he does not die and leave me a curse for not taking care of him during his last days on earth.'

'OK,' Mr Wilson said, 'I shall recommend you. I'm sure the DC will not object. Any more problems?'

'Not exactly, but chief Kimakia seems disturbed by a young man who has been studying overseas and who has just come back with a degree. I don't see a cause for alarm.'

'Where was he studying?'

'Britain, somewhere in Britain, I do not know exactly where or even what he studied.'

'Why is the chief worried?'

'Chief Kimakia is always worried. I sometimes think he likes meeting the DO and that is why he creates these fictions to bring to me. In any case, this student had a very big welcome from the villagers. They asked me for a permit to go and meet him at the airport, and for a welcoming party. They were orderly, with no problems, so I don't understand why the chief is so excited about it. I had my people watch their movements closely, and they said everything was alright.

'Mr. Wilson, please never listen to chief Kimakia, his imagination is too active. He pretends to be very busy and according to my observations, he can exaggerate any situation or create his own stories.'

'Look here Mr. Onyango, never underestimate any situation, take note of every report you receive. This is emergency time. Try to get more information and keep a close eye on this young man. I shall also inform the police about this man. He is worth watching. Mr Onyango, I shall recommend your leave for a 30 days.

Mr Wilson did not take the matter lightly. He informed the District Commissioner, the police; even the Provincial Commissioner learned of Mr Kamau's arrival and the big welcome. A cable was sent to the Kenya Students Office in London requesting a full report on Mr Joseph Kamau's education and activities while in

London. The student office was prompt with their reply, and a file on Joseph Kamau was opened.

Before long, Mr Kamau was looking for a suitable employment. He wrote to all the big companies in Nairobi, and also to the Government; he wrote to the oil companies, East African Tobacco, East Africa High Commissioners and many Government departments and statutory boards, but all in vain. Kamau was becoming restless as many letters came back with polite regrets. He started to wonder if it was really right for him to have come back. Many people warned me not to come back just yet, but love of my people made me ignore their warnings. And now here I am, with no proper accommodation, no employment, just surrounded by homeguards, police, and miserable women looking to me for help. Help from a helpless person.

One morning chief Kimakia was heard knocking at the door of Mr Mbugua, Kamau's father's hut.

'Yes, chief,' Mr Mbugua answered. 'What can I do for you?'

'Nothing bad, Mr Mbugua. I have an important letter for your son.'

'A letter? From where?'

'From our DOI Mr Wilson.'

'Who is that?'

'The big District Officer number 1 from the District Commissioner's office.'

'What do they want from my son?'

'Nothing much I wouldn't think. Maybe to employ him. Don't you know these white people respect those who have been in their country. Why don't you give him the letter to read?'

'Kamau! Kamau! Come here. There is a letter for you from the District Commissioner's office.'

'From the District Commissioner? He does not know me. What does he want?' Kamau came out of the house, took the letter and read it while the chief was still standing there. The letter had just three lines on government stationery, signed with an unreadable but impressive signature. The letter read:

Dear Mr Joseph Kamau,

Welcome to Kenya.
I shall be grateful if you can kindly call at this office on Monday 16th August at 9.30 am.

No more, no less. That was the entire letter. Kamau did not comment on the letter. His father was worried. The excited chief Kimakia waited impatiently to hear what the letter said.

'Kamau folded the letter, placed it back in the envelope and said to the chief, 'Thank you very much' He withdrew without any discussion, leaving the chief very disappointed, and still eager to know the letter's contents.

Kamau's father followed him into the hut. 'Any luck with a job?'

'Any luck?' Kamau repeated.

'What is the letter about?'

'I don't know Kamau answered as he opened the letter and showed it to his illiterate father. 'That's all Dad. That I should go to the DO's office on Monday at 9.30 am. Why he wants to see me, I just don't know. How he came to know me. I cannot figure out.'

'Kamau,' Mbugua said, 'that chief Kimakia is the worst troublemaker I have ever known. He gossips like a woman. He is ever at the District Officer's office, doing nothing but cooking up trouble for others. He is most likely the one who introduced your name to the DO. It is not just once that he has made some nasty remark about me, saying that I am getting big headed because I have a son overseas. I never answered. Do you know that son of his, Njoroge, he never studied, he became a thief. This very minute, he is serving a sentence in prison. His two daughters are problems also; Mary became a prostitute. The other, Joyce, has four children at home without a husband, each child has a different father. I can assure you, he is very jealous of you. But let us wait and see.'

At exactly 9.30 am on Monday morning, Kamau was standing outside the District Officer's door. A very efficient elderly European lady kindly offered Kamau a seat as she informed Mr Wilson that Kamau had arrived. 'Mr Wilson will be with you in a minute,' the secretary told him.

Mr Wilson was not long. Soon Kamau was following the secretary into the DO's office. Mr Wilson, dressed in a Khaki jumper coat and khaki shorts, welcomed him warmly into his office and back to Kenya. Kamau felt at ease and settled into a comfortable chair opposite a rather large office desk.

Mr Wilson's office was quite pleasant. The room was big, though housed in a rather oldish wooden building. It had wall-to-wall maroon carpeting, two easy chairs, the rather unimpressive sort supplied by the Public Works Department, a coffee table, all quite a contrast when compared with the impressive executive desk. The

Queen of England's photograph hung on the wall.

Mr Wilson instructed his secretary to prepare some coffee for them. 'How did you like England?'

'Very much,' Kamau answered, 'But there is nothing like home.'

'I guess not' Mr Wilson said. 'What were you studying?'

'I was studying Commerce. I got my B.A. and I wanted to continue for my Masters, but I decided to come back home.'

'For how long were you there?' Wilson asked.

'Oh, nearly four years.

'Then you must have made a lot of friends and I am sure you know a lot of my people.'

'Make friends. Oh no not in Britain. It is very difficult to make friends with your people. They are too conservative, they are always reading or pretending to be reading, so unconcerned with your existence. Anyway, I made a lot of friends with foreigners like me.

All this time Mr Wilson wore a frozen smile, which made his middle-aged wrinkles show up more clearly. His eyes were sharp, displaying both intelligence and suspicion. 'You should have joined the British Council to meet and make more friends.'

'I did, and that is how I came to meet people from other countries.'

'You must have found a good hobby to occupy you? Oh yes, I learned that you have been very busy with student demonstrations. Students, whites or blacks, enjoy demonstrations. Sometimes they are rather funny. Mr Kamau, such things are full of fun. Demonstrating at Trafalgar Square, attending political meetings addressed by big colonial politicians held at some very impressive places like Westminister Hall or in the open air of Hyde Park Corner.'

'Oh yes, they are funny,' Kamau agreed.

'And also very instructive for future leaders,' Mr Wilson commented. Kamau did not answer.

Mr Wilson's face changed, his friendly smile drifted away. His expression, as he filled his pipe with tobacco and started to light it, was of a man deep in thought. 'Now Mr. Kamau, what are your future plans?'

'I do not know. I am looking around to see what I can do.'

'You don't need to look around,' Mr Wilson said with a touch of irony, 'I understand it was your people who collected money for you to go overseas, and when you returned, everybody came to welcome their hero.'

At this point, Kamau interrupted, 'Mr Wilson, it is you who called

me to come to this office may I know what you invited me here for?'
Wilson's face turned red. Kamau could see problems coming. But I
am going to tell this man my mind. He cannot harass me like this; I
want to lead a very quiet life, and I wish only to get some employment.

'I invited you here for this kind of talk.'

'Which kind of talk? You seem to know all about me, how I went
to Britain and my activities there,' Anger flooded across Kamau's
face, anger and frustration.

'Yes, Mr Kamau, even how you were welcomed,' Mr Wilson
added. 'You already have a spear to fight with, a shield to protect
your people, and the leader's cloth. All these with your degrees, you
are really equipped for the leadership.'

'Mr Wilson, is that all you called me here for?'

'Oh no, I have not said half of what I have to say. Maybe some
other time, or perhaps, I should leave that matter for a better
person,' Mr Wilson said as he walked to his telephone.

'Miss Newton,' Mr Wilson called his secretary, 'ask Mr Douglas,
the District Superintendent of Police to come in here for a minute.'
Superintendent Douglas must have been just next door as it did not
take him a long time to come.

'Mr Douglas,' Mr Wilson said, 'This is Joseph Kamau, the highly
learned man who has just come back from studying in Britain where
he obtained some degrees. I am sure if you take him to your office,
he has alot to tell you. He has a degree, he knows the whole of
Britain, Hyde Park Corner, Trafalgar Square demonstrations, and
surely as learned as he is, he can teach us a lot. He is the man who
had that very big welcome, with spear and shield presented to him.
The leader-to-be, welcome the big man.'

'OK Mr Wilson,' Mr Douglas said, as he led the way to his office.
From there, Kamau was pushed to a camp with many Mau Mau
detainees for serious interrogation. The welcomed now is here in a
cell.

At home, Kamau's family waited impatiently to see their son, but
all in vain. Kamau's mother sat quietly by her fire unable to speak,
unable to eat and even unable to perform her daily duties.

Just before curfew time, Mama Rebecca decided to pass by
Kamau's mother to say hello. 'Mama Wanjiru,' Mama Rebecca
called 'Why are you so quiet? Are you sick?' Mama Wanjiru did not
say anything. 'I am sorry to find you so upset, anyway I just thought

I should see how your young man is settling in.' At the mention of the young man, tears began to rush down Kamau's mother's face. What is the matter, Mama Wanjiru? Why are you so sad? And where is he, our Kamau?'

'I don't know, Mama Rebecca. You see that chief came here and brought Kamau a letter. It said the DO wanted to talk to him. Since then he has not been back.'

'What?'

'Yes Mama Rebecca, and there is no hope of his coming back as the last bus has just arrived. Surely he cannot walk all the way home, and don't forget this is curfew time.'

'I know. I can guess,' Rebecca said in confidence. 'That chief Kimakia, he is very jealous of your son. Mama Wanjiru, he never liked hearing about your son. I never bothered to tell you, didn't want to worry you. I know if he had a chance, he would really hurt your son. That would please him. That is why I advised Kamau to keep his mouth shut.'

The following day, the whole of Gachage village knew that Kamau was locked up for further interrogation, while some people were happy, many were very disappointed and prayed that the matter would be solved soon. Many were the faces that were unhappy and bitter. The bitterness grew like the rain forest; Chief Kimakia kept a close eye. During forced communal labour women were noticed crowding together and whispering to each other, avoiding the loyalist group. Every movement was recorded.

At about 3 am the rain started drizzling as was usual for this time of year. The whole village was asleep. Ngong, Ngong, Ngong, several doors were being knocked at. Ngong, Ngong, Ngong. The sounds of knocking were from several directions and in many huts.

'Who is that?' Kamau's mother asked.

'Open the door. . . .'

'I am asking who is that?' Kamau's father shouted.

'You are the man. Open the door, we are the Government.'

'What are you up to at this time of the night?'

Ngong, Ngong, Ngong. 'Open the door at once, before we break this door of yours.'

'Let me open,' Kamau's father yelled. He opened the door just to be stormed by a group of homeguards, police, and that stupid chief Kimakia all dressed in raincoats.

'Get out of the hut. All of you at once,' the head of the

homeguards ordered. Kamau's father and mother and the children, some only partly dressed, were pushed outside into the rain. Children cried, Mama Wanjiru said nothing. Father was very bitter, but had nothing to say.

'How are you, father of the hero?' Chief Kimakia greeted Kamau's father. Kamau's father did not answer. 'Are you so proud that no longer greet ordinary people?'

Chief, what brought you to my house at this time of the night? And why not just let us alone? Isn't my son enough?'

In reply to this Chief Kimakia slapped Kamau's father hard in the face. 'Leave him alone,' a homeguard shouted at Chief Kimakia. 'The old man has done nothing wrong and he is one of the less troublesome around here. Let us do the duty which brought us here.' The police and homeguards entered Kamau's father's hut, they forced Kamau's luggage open and looked at each and everything in it. Using their rather powerful torches, they were busy flashing here and there in Kamau's father's house. Some were busy checking on whether he had any prohibited literature or some unauthorised papers.

'Nothing bad,' Captain Mutisya shouted. 'Nothing at all. Chief Kimakia, next time make sure you have a genuine problem before you come to harass people at this time of the night.'

'This Chief Kimakia, I don't understand him,' Constable Kipkwany whispered to another police officer. 'Let us go, no case for alarm. This Chief Kimakia is the same man who at one time led a group of homeguards who raped women in the presence of their husbands and sons. And now there he is again harassing everybody for nothing. I am sick and tired of him.'

The following morning, Captain Mutisya went to report back to the office that there was nothing bad found at Gachage Village. All Kamau's luggage was checked and the only books and papers found were on business school subjects, nothing more. People were all fast asleep, even that Mama Rebecca had nothing, nothing at all. At hearing of this Superintendent Douglas called Mr Wilson.

'Anything?'

'No, nothing at all. The man is clean.'

'But what is wrong with that Chief Kimakia, he seems to give false reports all the time. Not long ago, he reported that a women's group was singing Mau Mau songs. There was nothing to that. He also reported that Mr Kariuki was operating an oath ceremony with the goat. The true story is that it was nothing but a dowry ceremony. I am going to sack him from his job. Ask Captain Mutisya to go and get that Mr Kamau.

Captain Mutisya found Kamau. 'You can go home now.'

Kamau who by now had decided to go on hunger strike and not to speak to anybody did not answer. 'Mr Kamau, Mr Kamau, did you hear what I said?' Captain Mutisya called again.

'What?' asked Kamau.

'That you are now a free man.'

'Free from what?'

'From the authorities. Go home Mr Kamau, it was all a mistake.'

Kamau did not answer. He did not even say thank you, he did not smile. He just walked out of the usually locked gates, but now open and went back to his family.

After all this trouble, Kamau sent for Mama Rebecca and said, 'Mama Rebecca, I now must take that Mau Mau oath. It is a shame that I never took one. I must be a real Mau Mau.'

Glossary of Swahili and Kikuyu words

(s) Swahili   (k) Kikuyu

Askari (s)   Soldier, policeman, guard.

Askari kanga (s)   Untrained policeman, attached to administrators or official chiefs. During colonial times, their uniform was a colourful calico known as *kanga*.

Ayah (s)   Domestic, nanny, maid.

Baraza (s)   Public audience, meeting or reception.

Buibui (s)   Black veil enveloping the whole person used by Muslim women to cover their bodies and face.

Bwana (s)   Master, owner, possessor, man of dignity.

Bwana Kiko (s)   Man with a pipe.

Chapati (s)   A local flat bread made of wheat flour.

Funga safari (s)   A command meaning get going, get started.

Gakonia (k)   A bag made of coarse cloth which homeguards used to cover their faces while interrogating people.

Gikoni (k)   Husk, skin.

Githeri (k)   Traditional food, maize cooked with beans, peas, or cowpeas, served plain without its usual complements.

Gitiro (k)   A Kikuyu woman's dance.

Giuthi (k)   Children's games, any other games; a wooden pestle.

Iregi (k)   A past age group; the oldest Kikuyu age group.

Irio (k)   Food; good crops; a Kikuyu dish made of maize, beans, peas and cowpeas mashed with green vegetables and bananas or potatoes.

Itara (k)   Platform built high over a fire place in a hut, used for keeping and drying firewood.

Jambo (s)   'How are you?' 'Hello' 'What's new?'; matter, affair.

Jembe (s)   Hoe, a flat, pear-shaped piece of hammered iron.

Kaburu (s)   A term for South African Whites, occasionally used as a negative term for whites in Kenya.

Kanga (s)   A piece of calico of bright colours worn by women. Also used as wrappers around the waist and on the head.

208

Komerera (k)   Lie low, lie down, to go into hiding.

Lobe (k)   A special leather cloth, worn by community elders.

Maigoya (k)   Shrub (*coleus barbato*).

Makuti (s)   Coconut leaves used for thatching houses.

Memsahib (s)   Mistress of the house.

Mirugia Aka (k)   Aka means women. Term refers to a time of day, around 5 pm, when women are busy picking fodders and preparing meals before dark.

Mugio (k)   A shrub; the bark is used to provide stuffing for bags and material for ropes.

Mugumucano (k)   Large timber tree.

Mukeu (k)   A shrub, used to make baskets and ropes.

Mzee (s)   An old person, a parent, a respected elder or an ancestor.

Mzungu (s)   A European, a white person.

Ndururu (s) & (k)   A five cent coin. An age-group when the coin was introduced.

Ngurario (k)   A Kikuyu marriage ceremony where a fat ram is slaughtered as a sign of marriage acceptance.

Nguri (k)   A piece of metal used for plucking beard. Kikuyu men did not shave, but plucked their beards.

Nyori (k)   Ornaments worn by Kikuyus on pierced ear holes.

Panga (s)   A flattened sword.

Posho (s)   Daily supply of food, clothing, maintenance, given to workers on a plantation.

Rungu (s)   Club, war club, mace.

Safari (s)   Trip, journey, travel.

Shamba (s)   A piece of ground, a small or large farm; a plantation; a plot of cultivated land.

Shuka (s)   A piece of calico about two yards long used for clothing.

Simi (s)   A sword.

Thathaiai Ngai Thaai (k)   A Kikuyu traditional prayer meaning praise God, Praise Him, Peace; equivalent to *Amen.*

Ugali (s)   Stiff porridge commonly made from maize, millet or cassava flour mixed with water.

Wapande (s)   A response to an order. When called by an askari or big man for an order, one is supposed to salute and answer *'Wapande!'*